VOLUME 4
ISSUE 1
SPRING 2000

WOMEN/FEMMES

sites

the journal of 20th-century/ contemporary french studies

revue d'études françaises

D1434773

GB

GORDON AND BREACH

VOLUME 4 • ISSUE 1
SPRING 2000

WOMEN/FEMMES

**the journal of 20th-century/
contemporary french studies**

revue d'études françaises

Table of Contents

SITES IN WOMEN

FICTION AND POETRY

Introduction

The three previous issues of *Sites* dedicated to fiction and poetry of the 90's contain numerous contributions by women. In the works of these (women) writers and poets, the status, the very identity of women *as* women was not a primary or, at least, an immediately perceivable concern. Could it be that we have gone from an era of "militant feminism" in which the most basic issues regarding women *as* women were being debated, to an era of "serene post-feminism" in which women can now rely on what was acquired by previous generations and could now "take it from there?" The unsettled mood in France these days is far from corroborating such an assumption, leading us to ask: what is new in French feminism at the very end of the 20th century? While the essays in this issue of *Sites* do not attempt to answer such a broad question, they point to several directions which may help establish an assessment of sorts.

It has been almost three decades since "French feminisms" attained star status on US campuses. In a recent essay, Claire Goldberg Moses presents a convincing analysis of what she calls "Made-in-America French Feminism" which, she argues, was in large part a construct of American academics during the 1970's. Because these academics were predominantly professors of French literature and culture already much taken by what was known at the time as "French theory," she states that they played a significant part in the construction of what became known as "French feminisms[i]." Moses argues that the highly abstract and fairly narrow work of celebrated theories such as those of Cixous, Kristeva, and Irigaray did not, in fact, reflect the much broader activities occurring in the French women's movement at the time. She concludes that American writers and critics appropriated (and exoticized) the heavily psychoanalytical approach of a small number of theorists without much regard for the more general French context, where more concrete and less media-dominated efforts were being made to change real legal, medical, and political conditions for women in French society. This is not an inaccurate view. What it tends to ignore, however, is that the novelty and originality of concepts such as "*écriture féminine*" accounted not only for a great deal of intellectual innovation, but were also and often directly connected to specific social and political issues. As Terry Eagleton writes, "Feminist theory provided that precious link between academia and society, as well as between problems of identity and those of political organizations...if it yielded a good deal of intellectual excitement, it also made room for much that a male-dominated high theory had austerely excluded[ii]." There was much that was also difficult, esoteric even, in French feminist theory, but the link to the socio-political, especially

1

in the heady days of the early seventies, was present, even if in a different way from what was happening on the American scene.

After a period of quiescence - some would call it a backlash - during the 80's, new impetus was given to the subject of French women's rights by the *parité*[iii] debates of the 1990's. While these debates have become somewhat dominated by academics and intellectuals on both sides of the issue (Badinter, Ozouf, Halimi, Agacinski, Fraisse, Sineau, Mossuz-Lavau), they have nevertheless become broadly integrated into the fabric of national discourse, making discussions about *parité* very different from the more rarefied theoretical and literary issues of the 1970's. This is partly attributable to the fact that, in 1996, a pro-*parité* manifesto signed by ten prominent women who had held political office both on the Right and on the Left was published in *L'Express* (as opposed, say, to the more controversial, pro-abortion, "Manifesto of the 343" which appeared in the leftist *Nouvel Observateur* in 1971) and was subsequently endorsed by the Jospin government - now a staunch advocate of such constitutional reform. The *parité* debates have yielded heated political maneuvers as well as provocative statements. The consciousness of French women's scandalous under-representation in political structures has even been theorized by thinkers such as Geneviève Fraisse as constitutive of the French democratic system. Parité has been vigorously opposed by Elizabeth Badinter and Mona Ozouf in the name of "l'exception française," i.e. a kind of natural harmony ("*le doux commerce*") between the sexes in Gallic society; and it has been defended by Sylviane Agacinski, who positions herself somewhere between these two approaches, positing the difference between the sexes as "the only universal difference." All of these arguments, however, have been made in the context of historical and political research, confirming the evolution of women's issues away from the psychoanalytic and literary realm to that of the social sciences. But chase away cultural specificity and it returns with a vengeance, for these "new" battles often ring as a continuation of the "old" "essentialist" vs. "materialist" debates of the 70's, only replaced by a newer version of these binary oppositions: namely the "universal" vs. "differentialist" arguments (the latter also known as "*particularisme*.") The attempt to reconcile these two notions account for somewhat elaborate arguments such as the anti-quota position of Agacinski who claims that since sexual duality is the only human "universal" difference, women do not make up a "category," hence closing the door to any other minority claim, a stance which is discredited by the gay movement in France (although the latter is not extremely vocal, also for fear of being "ghettoized" at a time when the concept of universalism dominates). A number of the essays in this issue of *Sites* address various aspects of the *parité* debates and the role of women in politics.

This controversy, which speaks directly to the complex issues which have emerged since the Bicentennial of the French Revolution and have been exacerbated by growing concerns about national identity, immigration, and globalization, situates itself at the heart of larger discussions about French Republicanism. It is, as Eric Fassin writes, the "defining tension within French feminism today[iv]." It also accounts for a number of discussions which, in the US, have long ago been settled; for example in the acrimonious exchanges between feminists and the Académie française about what can only be called a timid attempt to change the French language in order to better reflect women's professional roles in society. While writers such as Benoîte Groult make a case for such changes, the Académie francaise objects to these, conflating its fight for the "purity of the French language" with a virulent anti-feminist stance. Meanwhile, many French women whose daily condition tends to be made easier by a strong welfare state, and whose preoccupations are situated outside of intellectual discourse, continue to work on a number of fronts such as employment, sexual harassment, violence against women and reproductive health.

Complicating this picture has been the increasingly important role played by the joining of anti-feminist and anti-American forces from both the Left and the Right. Whether in debates about feminism or sexuality or ethnicity or race, the anti-American/anti-"PC" discourse has made it extremely difficult for women to make any sort of specific claim without being mocked and labeled as followers of Anita Hill, Monika Lewinski, and the "PC brigades" which allegedly dominate American campuses and courtrooms. This may also explain in part why there are virtually no women's studies programs in French educational institutions. Such upholding of the American counter-model to disqualify any effort at feminist critical thought or action is questioned in no uncertain terms by several of our contributors, including Susan Suleiman, Michèle Sarde, and Eric Fassin. The perennial Franco-American misunderstanding indeed took new forms and became increasingly fierce in the 90's. While some in the US decried the domination of French theory, as exemplified by the Sokal affair, the French Left and Right seldom resisted an opportunity to castigate so-called puritanical Anglo-Saxon peculiarities which allegedly threatened French definitions of Republican citizenship.

On the artistic scene, one of the most interesting developments in women's creative production is in the domain of film. The number of French women who have moved behind the camera is remarkable, and filmmakers such as Claire Denis, Diane Kurys, Coline Serreau, Josiane Balasko, Brigitte Roüan, Anne Fontaine, Sandrine Veysset, and Dominique Ferrera are amply represented in film festivals as well as in popular venues. Brigitte Rollet and Sylvia Reid-Blum discuss some of these works. The fact that some directors see in their own work a more "universalist" approach while others acknowledge a more "specificist" point of view is reflected in the very different views offered to Anne Gillain in answer to questions she asked filmmakers Brigitte Roüan and Françoise Romand. As for literature, the contributions in this issue by Christiane Makward and Odile Cazenave on francophone women writers attest to a search for authenticity in the to and fro between

3

the Hexagon and the post-colonial world as these authors increasingly attempt to build a bridge between these realms. Additional selections by Hélène Cixous, Assia Djebar, and Leslie Kaplan offer only an extremely limited sampling of the poetry and fiction produced by women in French today. (As mentioned above, this production is presented in greater depth in the three previous issues of *Sites* on contemporary writing.)

In the end, there may not be much difference between French and American women in terms of social gains and losses; but the cultural representations and the broader historical contexts continue to reflect large gaps and perhaps unbridgeable divergences between the two societies. What we need are more dialogues based on facts rather than on misrepresentations, and more skillful mediators like those who have contributed to this issue of *Sites*.

Roger Célestin, Isabelle de Courtivron, Eliane DalMolin

Notes

i   Claire Goldberg-Moses, "Made in America: 'French feminism' in Academia" in Feminist Studies 24, no. 2, Summer 1998.

ii   Terry Eagleton. *Literary Theory*. Afterword to the 1996 edition; University of Minnesota Press.

iii   Basically: concrete, legislatively and constitutionally enforced equality in the respective numbers of men and women who run for political office, leading to more "gender-equitable" political representation.

iv   Eric Fassin, "The Purloined Gender: American Feminism in a French Mirror" in *French Historical Studies*, Winter 1999.

Photos

French Actresses

Catherine Deneuve in *Le Temps Retrouvé*

Isabelle Huppert

Isabelle Huppert

la fille
sur le pont

Vanessa Paradis

Vanessa Paradis

Virginie Ledoyen

Romane Bohringer

Juliette Binoche

Jeanne la Pucelle ~ Les Prisons

Sandrine Bonnaire

French Actresses: From <u>Nymphette</u> to Mummy, via the Woman-Woman

Geneviève Sellier

The French actress most often seen on the screen during the final year of the century is also its most senior member: after a decade when she seemed to become an inaccessible icon, Catherine Deneuve is on the comeback trail, after the age of 50. Good news? Yes, of course, since this is making a noticeable difference in the standards of what a desirable woman is. But, in "auteur" films, where she is most often seen, the *actrice* is literally mummified in roles of a tragic or fallen lover (André Téchiné's *Les voleurs*, Raoul Ruiz' *Le temps retrouvé*, Philippe Garrel's *Le vent de la nuit*, Leos Carax' *Pola X*, and even Nicole Garcia's *Place Vendôme*). One must look to the somewhat disdained popular cinema (Gabriel Aghion's *Belle-Maman*) to see her laugh, dance, give off a kind of vitality that makes her desirable in another way...

Other actresses carry on brilliant careers beyond the age of 40: Miou-Miou (Anne Fontaine's *Nettoyage à sec*), Isabelle Huppert (Diane Kurys' *Après l'amour*, Claude Chabrol's *La cérémonie*, Hal Hartley's *Amateur*, Benoît Jaquot's *L'école de la chair*) or Nathalie Baye (Jeanne Labrune's *Si je t'aime... prends garde à toi*, Tonie Marshall's *Venus Beauté Institut*). Women directors who, unlike the first wave in the 70s, manage to get beyond the barrier of the second or third film, certainly have something to do with this. But the recurring theme of passionate love tends to mask the problematic place of older women in a society that is dominated by older men.

In fact, even if women's films do provide a new visibility of female desire, they do not evoke the preference of men endowed with

15

social power for much younger women (a particularly frequent social occurrence in "cultivated" circles). In French cinema of the past 20 years, this "incestuous figure," which allows continued masculine domination even in love relationships is, however, the object of film representations that are equally frequent and complacent, in literary, as well as popular cinema. Vanessa Paradis continues to play blond or brown-haired Lolitas, whether in a light (*Une chance sur deux*) or dramatic vein (*La fille sur le pont*), in films by Patrice Leconte who travels easily between popular and "auteur" cinema.

A more modern variation of the woman-child appeared with Virginie Ledoyen, whose androgynous appearance associates the idea of a body not yet "marked" by femininity and the stormy independence of adolescence (Benoît Jaquot's *La fille seule*, Olivier Ducastel's *Jeanne et le garçon formidable*).

From Romane Bohringer (Martine Dugowson's *Mina Tannenbaum*) to Charlotte Gainsbourg, French cinema offers a new image of the rebellious young woman, of which Sandrine Kimberlain (Laetitia Masson's *En avoir ou pas* and *A vendre*) and Karin Viard (Christian Vincent's *Je ne sais pas ce qu'on me trouve*) would be the latest incarnation. The seduction they practice is not linked to an attractive or provocative physique, but rather to their willful independence, which men perceive as a challenge.

Between these two extremes (the older woman and the woman-child), the woman-woman unfurls her charms in a more conventional fashion, as if the "30 year old woman", who is supposed to incarnate the full blossoming of female beauty, would have to sacrifice all other aspirations. Emmanuelle Béart, in a dramatic vein, crossed through the decade with parts characterized by the most traditional misogyny, from Chabrol's *L'Enfer* to Ruiz' *Le temps retrouvé*, via Sautet's *Nelly et M. Arnaud* and Wagnier's *Une femme française*. Victim of marital jealousy, abandoned wife or sadistically abused secretary, her beauty draws all types of violence towards her, as she unhesitatingly accepts them...

Juliette Binoche, who goes from top-notch literary cinema (Leos Carax's *Les amants du Pont Neuf*, Louis Malle's *Fatale*, Kieslowski's *Bleu*, Chantal Ackerman's *Un divan à New York*) to national (Rappenau's *Le hussard sur le toit*) and international superproductions (Minghella's *The English Patient*), is undoubtedly the only one to have successfully crossed these borders, thanks to a beauty whose saintly purity is most often associated with saviors and ill-fated heroines.

On the other hand, Sandrine Bonnaire, undoubtedly because of a less classic beauty and a face whose features have hardened, has

turned towards a rather austere form of literary cinema: in Chabrol's
La cérémonie and Rivette's *Jeanne la pucelle*, she evolves outside the
realm of desire.

If these three generations of women attest to a certain diversity
of female roles, the dominating male imaginary, even more so in
"auteur" than in popular cinema, continues to give weight to its own
fantasies.

Translated by Dawn M. Cornelio

Interview with Brigitte Roüan:

Anne Gillain

Post coïtum animal triste has been among the most successful films by a woman director recently released in France. Presented in 1997 both at the Cannes Film Festival and the New York Film Festival, it immediately won critical acclaim. The film tells, in the form of a classical and elegant narrative, the provocative story of a middle-aged married woman who embarks on a passionate affair with a younger man. Brigitte Roüan's first full-length feature, *Outremer*, which depicted the life of three sisters in Algeria in the fifties, already concentrated on feminine subjectivity. In *Post coïtum animal triste*, Brigitte Roüan, who plays the leading role, follows the different stages of the love relationship, from infatuation to break up, focusing on her character's emotions. While the young lover remains essentially identical from beginning to end, the mature woman undergoes a wide range of inner states as well as considerable physical upheavals. From the first

scenes, when she is presented literally floating on a small cloud, to the end when she lies unwashed, drunk and desperate on her living room floor, the female character is definitely not *"juste une image."* She is tridimensional. She has an inner volume. Her body goes from ecstasy to agony with a veracity that male directors have never been much interested in capturing. The woman's body in women's film is a continent to discover and to explore.

Although she does not feel that her work differs much from the work of her masculine counterparts, Brigitte Roüan does tackle topics which have not been adequately represented in classic cinema. Both her films offer insights on women's private concerns which her narratives translate visually in crisp and profoundly readable images. For the outsider, Brigitte Roüan presents a glorious image of feminine creativity. While she pursues her career as an actress, she is also preparing a new film. She appears both tremendously busy and happy.

Anne Gillain – You used to be an actress. What made you want to become a director?

Brigitte Roüan – It was by chance. Because I was pregnant. I couldn't act any more so I wrote a script called *Grosse* (so it was quite fitting). I wrote it without any money and I directed and produced it in the same way; without any money.

AG – After this short film you pursued simultaneously an acting and directing career with *Outremer* in 1990 and *Post coïtum animal triste* in 1997. In recent years, quite a few women have, like yourself, directed films in France. In your opinion, what factors have contributed to the current boom in women's cinema?

BR – Yes, it's strange. France is apparently the only country where this is occurring. I think this is due to FEMIS (prestigious film school in Paris) where there are as many female students as male students. So it's logical that there would be as many women directors as there are men in directing.

AG – But there are coed film schools elsewhere, in the United States certainly, where you don't find this phenomenon.

BR – Other countries are perhaps less accepting of women. Here in France there's a tradition. Women have been making films for a long time. Take Agnès Varda for example.

AG – Is there a common denominator among women's films, or do you think this corpus of work is heterogeneous?

BR – Why is it necessary to differentiate among films? This expression, "women's films" irritates me. There is no difference between a film directed by a man or a woman. Each director has his or her own style and it doesn't have anything to do with the sex of the director. They recently counted the number of women directors in France and they found 44 of them. There must be 50 by now. There are as many women as there are men and all these women pursue their own type of work. Each of them has her own particular style, personality. The fact that they are women has nothing to do with anything. I feel closer to a French man than to a Chinese woman.

AG – But wouldn't you say that there is a gendered gaze and that this gendered way of looking engenders difference?

BR – Yes, that's true. In the same way that everything is political, everything is sexual and in this sense everything is different. Yes, you can't deny difference. But there are differences between men and the same is true of women. Between my work and that of Daniel Dubroux, for example, there are as many differences as between Renoir and Buñuel. There are differences among women directors just as there are among male directors. I feel close to Nicole Garcia because we have both been actresses. It's something we have in common. But our work is very different.

AG – It seems to me that men and wo-men are not represented in the same way in these two categories of film. In films by women directors one often finds a biting critique of men whose roles are thrown into question.

BR – Not in my films.

AG – That's true, less in your films than in others, but nevertheless *Post coïtum animal triste* opens with the murder of a man by his wife after 43 years of mar-riage.

BR – Yes, but because it's a crime of passion. A man could have committed this crime. Yes, I should have had a man do it. No, men are not caricatured in my films.

AG – There is the publisher character.

BR – Are you familiar with the publish-ing business? Do you know Francoise Verny?

AG – Just by reputation.

BR – Right, so you see that my publisher is not caricatured.

AG – Okay. Let's talk about the feminine body. Films by women directors seem to offer a representation of it that seems to me to be new. In *Post coïtum animal triste* particularly you portray not only the ravages of passion but also the an-guish of aging or of physical collapse after a break up.

BR – One speaks best about what one knows. A woman is more aware of what

happens to women than a man. Men film the woman's body as a love object. In a woman's film, it is the man's body that is seen as a love object. The gaze is different. As far as the fear of aging is concerned, I do not think that it is a spe-cifically feminine phenomenon. More and more men have recourse to plastic surgery. Aging is not portrayed in films directed by men because, in general, older men take much younger women as mistresses, women who are as much as forty years younger than themselves. Old age is thus much less of an issue. On the other hand, if a woman is with a man who is twenty years younger than herself, it's a much bigger deal.

AG – I saw *Post coïtum* in France and in the United States and I was surprised that in America the film caused a bit of a stir, and even shocked certain viewers. I wondered why since American cinema presents a multitude of sex scenes.

BR – But my film doesn't show anything. If you compare it to *Basic Instinct*, you don't see anything. Your observation really surprises me because I have re-ceived many letters from the United States, some of which are very tender, and in which people wrote, "I recognize myself in your film." I even received a letter from a man. In fact, all sex scenes in movies are all the same. You see a man who grunts over a woman's body and then he collapses panting. On the contrary, my film portrays the woman's pleasure. Even from the very beginning, in the title itself, the human body is com-pared to that of an animal. That's pretty gutsy.

AG – Actually, the credits are accompanied by the sounds of a meowing female cat in heat.

BR – Yes, my cat was the inspiration for this opening scene. I always thought she was so beautiful when she was in heat. She would do things humans would never dare to do. You know, in the first week of its run, I had a friend who would wait in the movie theater lines to hear what people were saying about the film. He noticed that when they would ask for their tickets, they never said the word "coïtum." They would say, "Two Posts" or "Two animaux tristes." A cashier from Provence told me with her southern accent, "you know, they never say "coïtum", but you know that it's because of this that they come to see the film." There was also a black cashier in the United States who yelled, "Post coïtum, enjoy it !"

AG – The title is nevertheless difficult to understand.

BR – Not at all. I found it in *The Art of Loving* by Ovid. I fought for this title and I defended it. Each word is easy to understand. Everyone understands. At first I wanted to call the film *Bon à tirer*, but the title *Tiré à part* was already taken.

AG – I liked the fact that the film presented an esthetic image of maternity: the publisher helps an author give birth to her book. On the other hand, I don't think she's a very good mother. She doesn't cook for her sons. She's is in a drunken stupor on Mother's Day.

BR – But that's because she's having a nervous breakdown. She's a very good mother: she plays soccer with her sons. Do you know many women who can play soccer with their son? She's going through a crisis but it's still a positive portrayal of motherhood.

AG – Are there any directors who have helped you develop your work, who have been role models to you or have inspired you?

BR – No, not really, but there have been certain things they said that have guided and sustained me. Maurice Pialat, for example, told me "you should only do what you really want to do." Claire Denys and Etienne Chatiliez (*La vie est un long fleuve tranquille*) have both told me exactly the same thing: "Stick to what you believe in." There is a certain solidarity among directors.

AG – Do you feel like you belong?

BR – Oh no, I feel horribly lonely, but there are creative exchanges. I've learned a lot with Pialat, watching his work. Pialat taught me credibility. He made me see how important it is to avoid cheating in order to be credible.

AG – What are your future projects?

BR – I just finished writing a script called *Chameau*. The story has nothing to do with women. It's about a group, three women and eleven men, who go on a meharee (a trip on camelback) in the desert. Among the men there are four Saharan nomads, a Serb and an American. The others are French. It's a film about cowardice.

AG – Do you still act?

BR – Yes, I'm going to act in a film by Fina Torrès. I acted in films by Michel Couvelart and Tonie Marshall which are coming out soon, and also in *Pourquoi pas moi?* by Stephanie Giusti.

AG – To finish, what question would you have liked me to ask you?

BR – Oh, that's charming. Let's see. I know, I often wonder: "Why all this for this?" All this work, all this trouble. I think I do it to be loved.

AG – Do you feel more loved when you act or when you direct?

BR – Both give me so much pleasure. Of course, one is more tiring, and takes more time, but acting is wonderful, directing is wonderful.

January 19, 1999

Translated by Tom Pozen

Brigitte Roüan and Borris Terral in *Post Coitum, Animal Triste*, a film by brigitte Roüan

Interview with Françoise Romand:

An

Anne Gillain

Françoise Romand belongs to this new generation of French directors who attended the ID-HEC, the famous and highly competitive – 40 men or women are selected every year among 4000 applicants – film-making school in Paris which has since been renamed the FEMIS. She was not yet thirty when she made her first documentary: *Mix up* (1985) which was followed a year later by *Appelez-moi Madame* (1986). Both received rave reviews and were released in the United States. They have been included in the program of many film festivals all over Europe and North America. Familial, social and sexual identities are at the center of Françoise Romand's work. Her two recent fiction films confirm this recurring concern: *Passé composé* (1994) deals with amnesia and how memories shape and define us, while *Vice vertu and vice versa* (1996) presents the story of two radically different women who exchange their lives.

In her documentaries – she has also done several shorts for French television as well as an 8-hour piece for France 3 – Françoise Romand displays an uncanny gift for transforming reality into fiction, which is to say that her films manage to instill facts with the complex network of meanings one normally associates with products of the imagination. This has certainly a lot to do with the topics she selects. Her films often center around highly unusual situations, the sort, in effect, that a fiction-writer would not dare to invent for fear of being accused of making-up unlikely stories. Caught up between disbelief and sheer emotion, the spectator remains spellbound while watching these all-too-human characters making sense of their life. It is not surprising to learn that Jacques Tati and Jean Renoir have been a source of inspiration for her. Françoise Romand's restrained style often opens up, as in Tati's films, on hilarious insights underlying the absurd dimension

24

of human behaviors. Her humor, however, is never sarcastic and her films always display respect and compassion for their subject matter. There is indeed a Renoirian quality to her intense interest for all manifestations of life. The definition of humanity gains a new dimension with Françoise Romand's films.

Anne Gillain – Could you briefly summarize how you came to be a film director?

Françoise Romand – My great grandfather was one of the first film actors but he never attached much importance to it. He was the waterer-watered (*l'arroseur-arrosé*) in the Lumière brothers film, because he was their gardener at La Ciotat. He was a legend in the family. As a teenager I went to the cinema a lot and I would create little index cards about all the films I saw. It began to give meaning to my life. So why not try my luck in the business? I applied to the ID-HEC right after graduating high school, and to my great surprise, I was accepted. I never really thought I would ever direct films. I would dream about directing films, but for me, it was an impossible dream. If I'm telling you this it's because I think that fifteen or twenty years ago, it wasn't normal (obvious?) for girls to work in certain professions. It wasn't normal especially in our minds. It's well known that in the working world women have a tendency to undervalue themselves in relation to men. Will this ever change? It's not a given. I've noticed in my assistant, who will surely some day be a director, the same psychological obstacles, the same fears

and her propensity to push her brothers, her boyfriend, whereas for herself, even though she is dying to do it, doesn't allow herself to go for it. She keeps putting it off. She keeps doubting.

AG – How do you account for the fact that most women directors are hesitant to differentiate their work from that of men?

FR – It's the fear of having to pay for it. It's better to cover up sexual difference to avoid retribution. We should advance wearing masks.

AG – Do you still think there exists a gendered (*sexué*) way of looking and that this gendered gaze creates different modes of representing the world?

FR – Yes, and that explains the place of women in society. Men react with violence and action, as in the films of Tarantino. Women proceed more with introspection. Many films in the first person, about intimacy, are directed by women. For these women there's an urgent need to situate themselves in the artistic process. Men don't have this need because, for them, it's already there, already acquired, whereas we have to conquer this right. There are exceptions, like Moretti or Cavalier in *La promesse*, but these men have reflected on their place in society and have almost abandoned the will to power.

AG – When you started work on *Mix Up*, your first documentary, what aspect of the subject – it's about two new-borns who, because of an error, were placed each in the other's family – attracted you the most?

FR – What attracted me the most was the impact of the innate and the acquired in a fascinating story. You would think that a child raised in a privileged setting would have more advantages in future life. That's what I thought when I first took on the subject. But I hadn't taken into account the love and the trust that parents give you or withhold from you. So Valérie, raised in a privileged setting goes on to pursue graduate studies which she probably wouldn't have done had she grown up in her biological family, but she suffers a cruel lack of love her entire life and this suffering still torments her.

AG – Almost all your films grapple with issues of identity. Is there a reason for this constant?

FR – On the day I was born, my parents were expecting, without a shadow of a doubt, the arrival of a baby boy, whom they planned to name Serge. However, at that time ultra sound didn't exist yet. They were expecting Serge in my place, which created a last-minute panic about my name. The easiest thing to do: look at the calendar. March 9: Françoise! That's a partial explanation for my interest in issues concerning identity.

AG – You call your documentaries, "fiction documentaries" (*documentaires-fictions*) but recently you made two purely fictional films. How do you distinguish these genres and which one do you prefer?

FR – To make fictional documentaries is to work on the borderline; to question conventions, interrogate the viewer in his relation to identity, make him doubt what he sees. What I like the most is to sew doubt in my films so that the viewer thinks he's watching a fictional film when it's really a documentary and a documentary when it's a fiction. I love documentaries because I love people and their stories which are always richer and more complex than what one could ever imagine in fiction. I'm more curious and more surprised by documentaries and I hope to be able to enrich my fictions with them. I could never do only fictions. I would wither up. I always need to return to the sources and to this enrichment that real people have to offer. But making fiction allows you to stand back, to think about what you're creating because you're far from the whirlwind of life. You put yourself in a covered bowl, a little stifling but quite beneficial.

AG – The character in *Appelez-moi Madame* flirts with lunacy (it's a documentary about a man of about fifty, a family man in a little village in France, who decides to start dressing as a woman). Other characters in your films adopt false identities that dispense with traditional social markers? What is this borderline, this shadowy realm that you attempt to define?

FR – *Appelez-moi Madame* provided a fascinating and disturbing subject. Even if I'm perplexed by Ovida, I can only admire her courage, the nerve, and the self-assurance with which this person acts out her fantasy in the face of a critical society? She dares to show herself just as she is with her share of the truth, her dose of egocentrism, her heaviness and her masculine reflexes. And it's for all these reasons that she demands respect and she stands up to be recognized. I'm attracted to people who cross over lines drawn by society: social cleavages, sexual cleavages. Provocation is my way of torturing generally accepted ideas.

To disturb is to make progress. I don't try to define this shadowy realm, I want to accentuate it in order to live with an uncertainty that is both productive and creative.

AG – What directors have influenced you? Do you have any role models?

FR – No, I don't have any role models, but Tati has marked me as well as Renoir.

AG – What is the most problematic aspect of artistic creation for you?

FR – Production remains the crucial problem for me. I have not found the right person for me, and in each film my relation to the producer demands too much of my energy which should be going entirely into the film. Is it my perfectionism, my inflexibility which causes that? At the beginning of each new project, I feel admiration from the producer which, in the editing stage, turns into a tremendous conflict. I can't help but think that if I were a man, I would not inspire such violence on the part of the producer. It's as if I were putting him personally in danger.

AG – What are your future projects?

FR – Noël Burch is in the process of adapting *La Marquise de Sade* by Rachilde for my next fictional film.

January 20, 1999

Translated by Tom Pozen

A scene from *Appelez-moi Madame*, a film by Françoise Romand

The Turning Point of Feminism: against the Effacement of Women

Sylviane Agacinski

In France today women are in the process of taking feminism to a turning point. In demanding, with *la parité*, the *de facto* sharing of political responsibilities, they are clearly rejecting the *non-differentialist* ideology which, despite equal rights, preserves the ever-persistent male monopoly of power. *La parité* is not a way of letting nature "dictate law" (we know full well that nature in itself never says anything); it is a way of making sense out of human existence characterized by sexual difference (*sexuée*). Nature has never founded anything: neither the hierarchy of the sexes yesterday, nor today the demand for their equality. *All this is political through and through.* On the other hand, that a human being is characterized by its sex (*sexué*), that it is born a boy or a girl, that it can become a father or a mother (but not both at the same time, such is the constraint of the dichotomy of the sexes) is not political - despite what Judith Butler and some others have said.[i]

Moreover, contrary to what we spontaneously think, it is not the natural *difference* between the sexes that has legitimated their *inequality*, it is rather a denial and a reduction of this difference. Throughout our history, women have not been considered "different" beings, embodying humanity on the same grounds as men, they have been defined as *incomplete* and *inferior* men. From Aristotle to Freud, woman has always lacked something to be a man "like any other." She has been humanity's failing figure, its minor form, and not one of two legitimate forms. It is time to understand that this logic of lack and inferiority is not the logic of difference. She alone

29

differed from man, and not he from her. She has not been recognized as half of humanity but as its exotic and "particular" part. We can see this androcentric logic at work all the way up through Kant's *Anthropology*. Abstract universal thought, from the eighteenth century to the present, is in line with this logic, whether it structures political thought or grammatical law. It seems to me that Joan Scott[ii] does not sufficiently explain that it is this paradoxical logic, according to which the universal is masculine and the particular is feminine, that has trapped French feminists and driven them to want to claim their rights sometimes as women, sometimes as human beings, condemned to oscillate between the "particular" and the "universal." The "paradoxes" of feminism have been the counterpart to the paradoxes of androcentrism, identifying the universal with the masculine. Consequently, we can break out of these paradoxes by showing that universal humanity is not *singular*, but *double*, that it must be heard as the humanity of man and woman, on the same grounds.

We can then understand why *conceptualizing sexual difference is a new development*, since it is about finally recognizing the mixed nature of the human race, its existence characterized by sexual difference (*sexuée*) from the outset, without a uniquely singular model. By acknowledging the *universality of difference*, we can escape the aberrant logic of androcentrism that relegates all demands made by women to "particularism."

The impasse of abstract universalism, which neglects sexual difference for the benefit of the sole "human being", has already been pointed out by Simone de Beauvoir in the introduction to *The Second Sex*. It is surprising that we don't remember this. Indeed, she warns us against the temptation, which she believes to be above all *American* (!), to erase the meaning of the word "woman," while she mocks the "highly irritating" ("fort agaçant") work of Dorothy Parker who declared: "All of us, men as well as women, should be regarded as human beings.[iii] " This is an abstract declaration according to Simone de Beauvoir who adds: "It's obvious that no woman, without being in bad faith, can pretend to situate herself beyond her sex".[iv] And why is a woman tempted to erase "her" difference, while a man is not? It is because she feels "in the wrong" being a woman, while a man is "in his right" being a man. The author of *The Second Sex* is thus quite conscious of the androcentric trap of abstraction (even if, all too often, she herself falls into it, notably when she cannot keep herself from scorning all female traits, maternity in particular) and makes it clear that human beings' "inauthentic flight"[v] into abstraction originated in ... the rationalism and philosophy of the Enlightenment. Here we are, then, back in Europe to verify, if necessary, that the effacement of sexual difference equally tempts both sides of the Atlantic. Certain Franco-American disagreements on the question of women are perhaps less simple than they appear.

As we indeed know, certain fiercely anti-*paritaire* French women who take refuge in abstraction and refuse to claim their rights *as women*, pride themselves in universalism and accuse American women of *differentialism*. We must not let ourselves get locked up in this false dichotomy which in reality covers up two harmful ways of erasing sexual difference and of not acknowledging its universal character.

The "French" effacement proceeds by engulfing both sexes in abstract humanism from which the singular model of a sexually neutral human being surfaces. (In reality, as Françoise Héritier[vi] has shown, neutrality is not possible within this model since one of the two sexes takes the place *of both* according to an implacable androcentric logic.)

The "American" effacement proceeds by engulfing women in a generalized particularism where minorities of all sorts (ethnic, religious, cultural, etc.) are grouped together, and both sexes end up being considered pure "constructions" when they are not the result of a "heterosexual matrix", as Judith Butler puts it.

Today, the new French feminism simultaneously challenges both these types of sexual neutralization in affirming sexual duality as the only *universal difference* within humanity. This is why it was able to conceive of the *parité* ideal in politics.[vii]

So, yes, obviously, to the extent that differentiation of the sexes characterizes every human being *a priori*, and is therefore universal, it can be called *natural*. In spite of the historically and culturally variable values and interpretations applied to male/female difference, it structures human existence and, beyond that, the reign of the living. Granted, there are *only uses* of nature - social, political, etc. - that are always interpretations without *ultimate* truth, yet this does not make the differentiation of the sexes, with its history, any less something which we can neither create nor invent, and which we cannot simply deny through a peremptory decision. Our corporeal existence is given to us as such, and it is not because the experience of the body and of death is from the outset historical in nature that we can surmount or get around it. Or even spare ourselves from thinking about it. Like the other beings on this earth, we must eat to survive, we are destined for reproduction and corruption (as Aristotle would have said) and we need both sexes to give life. Claude Lévi-Strauss reminds us that the *most undeniable* characteristic of man is that he is first and foremost a *living being*.[viii] In the name of what idealism should we forget or deny this membership to the world of the living? What would be the use of economy, or politics without the needs and passions of the finite beings that we are? Cultures treat death or the duality of the sexes differently according to their beliefs, their rites or their institutions, and individuals in modern societies are all confronted with the question of the meaning of their sexualy differenciated (*sexuée*) and mortal existence. These questions are not matters for ordinary political science, but require anthropological and philosophical reflection. Sexual difference is a reality at once natural and instituted: necessary for life, male/female differentiation is a natural given, but the taboo that marks incest and the building of kinship and filiation socially establishes sexual difference.

A hasty reading of Sartre often leads us to condemn every allusion to nature in the name of the opposition between nature and freedom. But Sartre uses the expression "human nature" in the philosophical and classical sense of *essence*: he thereby asserts the incompatibility between the idea of "human nature", that is, the idea of an *essence* of man imposing *a priori* his behavior, and the idea that man is free, that is, that he must conceive of his life's purpose without any possible recourse. The principle whereby "existence precedes essence" means that each person must "choose himself" and by himself give meaning to his existence. That does not mean that we can invent our existence and determine the particular or universal conditions in which each person must exert his/her liberty.

Today, blinded by the mirages of technical power, we would like to defeat old age and death, even surmount our condition by changing our sex or by making embryos in the laboratory with genetic material withdrawn from *individuals*. Those who, on both sides of the Atlantic, advocate the effacement of sexual difference no doubt congratulate themselves for this "progress" and for the new liberties that such "progress" offers individuals. That each person can give life *on one's own* and become at the same time father and mother, thanks to the techniques of medically assisted procreation, seems to them to mark progress toward individual autonomy. Even Robert Badinter sees nothing problematic in this, not even the recourse to surrogate mothers, which, in his opinion, is tantamount to "a simple adoption by anticipation."[ix] In fact, those who, through fear of a so-called "naturalism," challenge the recognition of sexual difference in law, are blindly throwing themselves into the arms of applied science, as if from now on it alone were to become the basis of law. With a certain coherence, the same people condemn *la parité* and legitimize the right for couples of the same sex to have "biological or adopted" children.[x] To these people, universal difference between men and women is not worthy of involving the law, while biology carried out in laboratories is justification for all rights. Tomorrow, biology will give us the means, if not to abolish the difference between men and women, to at least make it so that they no longer need each other. "Biological" children will no longer be born of men and women, but will be manufactured with genetic materials, like any craft or even industrial product. This possibility does not signal progress, but rather a disturbing mutation of the species. It should make us conscious of the fact that human societies are not founded on conglomerations of independent atoms.

The existence of both sexes puts each person to a finiteness test which prevents one from considering oneself alone to be the incarnation of "man" and which forces one to coexist with the other (but not necessarily to define oneself as heterosexual). This duality presupposes nothing about the essence of "man" (in the generic sense) nor about the essence of man or woman: it simply confronts each person with the heterogeneity of the human race and leaves the trace of the other in our bodies and in our minds.

Feminism today, like feminism yesterday for Simone de Beauvoir, cannot therefore consist in denying the sexually marked (*sexué*) character of existence - unless we want a feminism without women - but in reversing, theoretically and practically, the old hierarchy of the sexes. This reversal necessarily includes a critique of androcentrism wherever it subsists, particularly in political life - a point to which I will return.

If we can speak of a *turning point*, in comparison with the trail blazed by the first wave of feminism and Simone de Beauvoir, it is because Beauvoir did not see that to realize equality of the sexes women could not simply rise into the world as it was, that they had to transform it, deconstruct it. That it was not enough that a woman become a professor, a philosopher, or a citizen to collapse theoretical or androcentric political constructions. Women's practical and political problem, regarding their place and their status, could not be resolved by their "assimilation," by their accession to the world built and thought by men, for the *male/female hierarchy was still there* in this world, still present, efficient, theorized.

For my part, this is what I discovered by becoming a professor of philosophy. Teaching Plato or Kant, I became aware that I was not dealing with speculations on universal and neutral subjects, but sexually marked (*sexué*) philosophical subjects, whose very concepts were penetrated by the male/ female hierarchical structure. Without imagining *a priori* a systematic divergence of male and female points

33

of view - which still does not exist - we must be able to analyze the androcentrism of theoretical constructions whenever it appears. Why is a considerable proportion of the current innovations in philosophy and the social sciences the work of female theorists? Because they shift attention to the *very basis* of their discipline – from Nicole Loraux to Arlette Farge, from Françoise Héritier to Elisabeth de Fontenay, from Sarah Kofman to Blandine Kriegel (I name these thinkers at random, there are many others...).

It is necessary, for example, to challenge the age-old exclusion in philosophy of the question of procreation. I have tried to do so in my book[xi] by asking why, beginning with Plato's *Banquet*, the *male* philosopher must choose between the love of ideas (and the soul *of boys*), and the desire for progeny (therefore women). Built on a "virile" rejection of flesh and women, metaphysics has left traces in all its conceptual constructs, all the way up to modern oppositions of subject and object or activity and passivity. It is always the feminine that philosophers have *depreciated*, along with the body, matter and nature. If we do not see the relationship between certain conceptual hierarchies and the hierarchy of the sexes, we are applying classical concepts without critical thinking and we remain inside systems marked by androcentrism.

In France (women's circles included), this project has always been hindered by the constant temptation to sacrifice the question of difference to the question of a deceptive universal or abstract legal equality.

Also called "republican," this equality, which implies that the citizen is *neither man nor woman* since both are equal in the eyes of the law, in fact prohibits all claims by women *as women* and forces them to put up with the persistence of the androcentric order. This universalist trap had what it took to seduce feminists eager, early on, to identify with men in order to better emerge from their condition.

After all, this identification has not been only negative: it has allowed women to break with the models in which their mothers had been imprisoned. But while rejecting all "female" heritage, *feminism has fed on misogyny*. Most women of my generation for whom liberty took precedence over everything - and it is for this *that we were passionately Beauvoirians* - opted first for this identification with men and repudiated "maternal models" in every sense of the phrase since it was in the family that the subordination of women was still institutionalizing itself. The choice of economic independence and the critique of marriage very often characterized the way girls of my generation saw things (and the very word "girl" captures the flavor of that era).

Nevertheless, "the feminine" made a come-back, particularly in the body and in sexuality. In the '60s and '70s, the conquest of contraception and the struggle to win the right to voluntarily terminate pregnancy made clear the dissymmetrical reality of the sexes and caused women to become conscious of the specificity of their own liberation. The discourse of women *as women* was no longer taboo, especially since discrimination of all sorts continued to run rampant, despite the equality principle and the dream of the indifferentiation of the sexes. The ideal was therefore no longer to become a man "like any other," but to assert difference in equality.[xii]

The control of reproductive rights also allows us to rethink maternity in a new light: as a strength, as the satisfaction of an essential desire - thus as a freedom - and finally as a privileged experience of responsibility. On this point, Simone de Beauvoir could not guide us, she who wrote that procreation includes "no project" and for whom childbirth was only a "natural function," devoid of meaning and essentially alienating.

But, freely chosen, and emancipated from the male point of view, maternity became not only a freedom but also a privilege. To such an extent that men today find themselves, in a certain way, deprived of the strength that patriarchal domination had for ages assured them: the mastery over progeny. The conditions necessary for men and women to establish new relations, founded on respect for their difference and equality, are perhaps now in place.

On the political scene, the idea of *la parité* has represented, since the beginning of the '90s, a way of giving new content to political equality. In a representative democracy, save for cases of referendum, representatives normally exercise the sovereignty that belongs to the people. If in both governmental assemblies, the National Assembly and the Senate, 90% of the seats are held by men, we notice, without even mentioning other governmental bodies, a male quasi-monopoly of power that deprives women of their *right to exercise sovereignty*.

This deprivation does not exist because French women do not want to become candidates, nor because people do not vote for them, but because political parties, traditionally male or even "macho" territory, do not nominate them as candidates. They perform a *constant positive discrimination* towards men, prolonging the heritage of a Republic long ago inspired entirely by ancient models. The question of what a democracy should be with women, which has never been addressed, poses itself today in France with particular urgency.

Up until now, the Constitutional Council (*le Conseil Constitutionnel*) has always considered that the Constitution of 1958 did not allow the law to distinguish between men and women in matters, for instance, of electoral lists. Law was thus supposed to remain neutral with respect to the sexes, while society was not.

Conversely, if we grant that *both* sexes constitute humanity *universally*, it is legitimate to rethink the sovereignty of the people by taking into consideration the double composition of the people. In this case, women should be able not only to elect representatives, but to also represent, the people on the same level as their fellow male citizens. (It is obviously not a question of men's and women's *separate* representation.) Women must therefore have increased access to the status of political candidate, contrary to what takes place in political parties today. What is at stake in modifying the Constitution today is the ability to break free of a false universal in acknowledging that men and women must have equal access to mandates and elective functions and in allowing law to correct the effacement of women in our democracy.

Translated by Mary Schwartz

Notes

i   Judith Butler, *Gender Trouble*. New York: Routledge, 1990.

ii   *Only Paradoxes to Offer*. Cambridge: Harvard UP, 1996.

iii   *The Second Sex*. New York: Vintage Books, 1989. p. xx.

iv   My translation of "Il est clair qu'aucune femme ne peut prétendre sans mauvaise fois se situer par-delà son sexe" (*Le Deuxième Sexe*. Paris: Gallimard, 1976. p. 13). This sentence is curiously missing from H.M. Parshley's English translation of *The Second Sex*.

v   My translation of "fuite inauthentique" (*Le Deuxième Sexe*. Paris: Gallimard, 1976. p. 13).

vi   *Masculin/Féminin, la pensée de la différence*. Paris: O. Jacob, 1996.

vii See in particular Blandine Kriegel, *Philosophie de la République*. Paris: Plon, 1998.

viii *Structural Anthropology*. Trans. Claire Jacobson and Brooke Grundfest Schoepf. New York: Basic Books, 1963. pp. 47-8.

ix   My translation of "une simple adoption par anticipation". *Le Débat*. 36 (Paris 1985). p.10.

x   See Evelyne Pisier's "PACS et Parité: du même et de l'autre" in the October 20 1998 issue of *Le Monde*.

xi   Politique des sexes. Paris: Seuil, 1996.

xii This change was set in motion in particular by Antoinette Fouque. See: *Il y a deux sexes: essais de féminologie, 1989-1995*. Paris: Gallimard, 1995.

La Parité *in Politics:*
From a Radical Idea
to a Truncated Reform

Mariette Sineau

"Nous (les femmes) sommes
le Tiers-Etat de la République."
("We [women] are the Third
Estate of the French Republic.")

Edith Cresson, *France 2 Radio*, June 9, 1996

"Hemiplegic", "one-legged", the metaphors are not lacking to qualify the French version of democracy and the monopolization of political power by males. Still today, France is placed next-to-last in the countries of the European Union in terms of percentages of women elected to the Lower House (10.9%). If France seems inept, most notably compared to Scandinavian countries, at feminizing its instances of political decision, it owes this to certain historical burdens. The "Salic Law," which under the monarchy prohibited women from succeeding to the throne of France, was taken up by the revolutionaries of 1789. Political equality among all citizens thus accommodates the exclusion of women from all political rights. This sidelining of women would last more than a century and one-half, until the ordinance of April 21, 1944 would make women full-fledged citizens. To the weight of these historical factors are added institutional brakes. For instance, certain aspects of the Fifth Republic (such as a uninominal voting system for the election of deputies, widespread use of accumulated mandates, etc.) have blocked the entrance of women into the electoral or parliamentary scene.

To break the deadlock, a radical idea has blazed a trail through the 1990s: the idea of political parity. Defined as "l'égalité quantitative garantie pour l'accés à certaines fonctions électives"[1] ("guaranteed quantitative equality for access into certain elective functions"), *la parité*[2] marks an unexpected return to the legal battle. The concept of *la parité*, which is presented both as "une demande d'égalité" ("a demand for equality") and as "la reconnaissance d'une altérité socialement construite"[3] ("the recognition of a socially-constructed alterity"), allows for an escape from the classic dilemma raised by the citizenship of women in democracy: the dilemma of the choice between equality and taking into account sexual difference. This is why it has had the beneficial effect of making everyone rethink abstract universalism and otherwise analyze the question of the political representation of women.

Taken up by numerous associations, who have thus contributed to an awareness of the invisibility of women in the arenas of political decision-making, this claim has been able to remobilize a feminist movement that was previously disinterested in electoral affairs.[4]

1. *La parité* under debate: universalists vs. differentialists

The analysis of the debates which have taken place as a result of the battle for *la parité* reveals the existence of tension caused by different conceptions of equality and democracy. On one hand, universalist republicans oppose *la parité* today just as they have opposed all categorical rights in the past. In the opposing camp can be found all those (women and men) who underline the limits of formal egalitarianism, who distance themselves from any fixed interpretation of the law, and who refuse to characterize as "democratic" any democracy without women.

A universalism indifferent to differences

If numerous legal experts and male politicians are opposed to *la parité*, it is because, they say, of their attachment to the principle of universality posed by the French Declaration of the Rights of Man and the Citizen of 1789, which does not recognize any sexual distinction among individuals. Furthermore, the enactment of a democracy organized on the basis of *la parité* would bring harm, in their eyes, to the republican principle of national sovereignty, which does not lend itself to any breakdown of suffrage, nor to any distinction between voters by category.

Qualified by legal experts as an infringement upon the right to impartiality, *la parité* is expressly denounced by a number of acting political "republicans" as a breach which puts democracy in peril. Thus François Mitterrand, during his second term as president, declared himself shocked that one could want to "découper la démocratie en tranches" ("cut up democracy in slices"). The former president of the Constitutional Council, Robert Badinter, also places himself among the unconditional unversalists, and sees in the putting into action of *la parité* an intolerable menace of "communitarianism."[5]

The tenants of republican universalism have often been supported in their opposition to the idea of *la parité* by militant feminists. Certain women see in it a way to reintroduce, or even essentialize, gender difference in politics. It is thus that Eleni Varikas denounces a "solution magique qui prétend traiter l'exclusion des femmes par des mesures qui perpétuent et institutionnalisent la répartition sexuée qui fonde leur exclusion"[6] ("magical solution which proposes to treat the exclusion of women by the same measures which perpetuate and institutionalize the sex-based distribution upon which their exclusion is founded"). Others, notably of the extreme left, criticize the pertinence of an alliance of all women on the theme of *la parité* which makes no reference to a societal undertaking that would throw into question social inequalities and division of labor according to sex.

In the press, journalists, analysts, and essayists from all sides tirelessly denounce the malignity of the idea of *la parité*. They point out the dangers which would be inherent in the concept of *la parité*, or the misguidance to which it opens the door. As such, Olivier Duhamel perceives *la parité* as a veiled menace to democracy, the destructive effects of which (ethnicism, nationalism, and a shuddering fall-back upon difference) would not fail to follow. He holds out that "l'acte de parité est parfois indispensable, mais que le principe de parité serait déplorable" ("the act of parity is sometimes indispensable, but the principle of parity would be deplorable") (*L'Express*, November, 1993). Like an echo of her husband's voice, Elisabeth Badinter cries out against the idea that "les paritaires ne proposent rien moins que de changer de système politique et d'imposer la démocratie communautaire des quotas importée des Etats-Unis" ("proponents of *la parité* propose nothing less than to change political systems and to impose the communitarian democracy of quotas imported from the United States") (*Le Monde*, June 12, 1996). Lastly, in a chronicle bearing the revealing title, "La violence des faibles" ("The violence of the weak"), Jacques Julliard explains that the principle of *la parité* in politics would place women "dans une situation d'assistance perpétuelle c'est-à-dire d'infériorité réelle" ("into a situation of perpetual assistance, that is of real inferiority"). "A force d'insister sur l'identité au détriment de l'universalité, les faibles ou les minoritaires scient la branche sur laquelle ils prétendent s'asseoir : leur appartenance à un droit commun valable pour tous" ("As a result of their insistence on identity at the expense of universality, the weak or the minorities saw off the branch upon which they claim to be seated: their eligibility for a common right that is valid for all") (*Nouvel-Observateur*, June 27-July 3, 1996).

Women as a danger to democracy: so goes an often-recurring theme in the French political debate. Under the Third Republic, radicals and radical socialists refused to grant women full political privilege, reasoning that their vote would threaten the fragile Republic which was at that time up against royalist attacks. Today, universalists, whether they lean toward the left or the right, often push to the extreme the potential deviations of the principle of *la parité*, arriving at the same conclusions as their forefathers: women, by claiming *la parité*, are going to destroy the foundations of the republican and democratic ideal.

As a case in point, partisans of the current legal status quo invoke the jurisprudence of the Constitutional Council. They remind us that by a decision passed on November 18, 1982, supreme jurisdiction invalidated that article of municipal law which instituted a maximum quota of representation by each sex (of 75%) on lists of candidates in municipal elections (in communes of more than 3,500 inhabitants). The invalidation was delivered in the name of equality among all citizens in the eyes of the law, guaranteed both by Article 3 of the Constitution of 1958 and Article 6 of the Declaration of the Rights of Man and the Citizen. It was thus in the name of principles assuring formal equality that the constitutional judge opposed a measure which aimed to assure real equality in municipal assemblies. It was to universalism and to the philosophy of the rights of man that he pointed in order to thwart a policy for the rights of women founded on the principle of positive actions.

Adversaries of the principle of *la parité*, try as they might to entrench themselves in this jurisprudence, cannot bury the debate on democratic parity. They invoke constitutional rights as a way of refusing any voluntarist policy for the feminization of nominees and of the elected.

Unequal rights for unequal people

Other authors have lent themselves to different readings of the law, which, moreover, go hand-in-hand with another conception of the right and the principle of equality. This reading emanates most often from activists engaged in the fight for *la parité*, but also rallies certain legal experts. It consists in affirming that there would be no constitutional obstacle barring the enactment of a law on *la parité*, and underlining that one may even find concrete textual elements from which to draw support. These authors base their reasoning mainly on that phrase of the preamble of the Constitution of 1946, taken up by the Constitution of 1958, which reads: "La loi garantit à la femme, dans tous les domaines, des droits égaux à ceux de l'homme" ("The law guarantees woman, in all domains, rights equal to those of man"). Following this line of argumentation, there would be no reason to revise the Constitution to impose *la parité*. It would suffice to lay claim to this equality of legal status, as guaranteed by the legislature of 1946, in order to draft a law on *la parité*. Such a law would be a measure of real equality, coming into existence from the formal legal equality posed by the Constitution.

Other authors go even further. They affirm that national legislation does not respond to the legal norms contained in the Constitution. Such is the position held by Gisèle Halimi (founder of the feminist movement, Choisir-La Cause des Femmes), who says, "Plus qu'un constat, plus qu'une déclaration, voire une proclamation, il y a garantie, obligation du passage de la liberté formelle au droit réel" ("More than a realization, more than a declaration, or even a proclamation, there is a guarantee, an obligation to pass from formal liberty to real rights") (*Le Monde diplomatique*, October 1994). These authors emphasize that the principle of *la parité* is quite different from the principle of the quota, and thus that the jurisprudence of the Constitutional Council does not apply. If a quota, contrary to equality, is unconstitutional, then *la parité*, which proposes perfect equality, is constitutionally necessary. If they see no legal obstacle to the enactment of *la parité*, many supporters of *la parité* nonetheless consider that a revision of the Constitution is absolutely imperative for political reasons.

Defenders of *la parité* see themselves as supported by philosophers and political scientists, who insist on questioning the very principles of current republican citizenship. To show in the notion of *la parité* a valid basis, the politicist Jean Vogel questions the construction of democratic universalism and recalls that "l'institution de la citoyenneté procède d'une auto-définition arbitraire du corps politique"[7] ("the institution of citizenship proceeds from an arbitrary self-definition of the political body"). He continues, "Ainsi la décision de limiter, au siècle précédent, la composition du corps électoral aux électeurs censitaires, ou celle de considérer pendant des décennies le suffrage universel masculin comme identique au 'suffrage universel' tout court, étaient des faits arbitraires, dont aucun juriste n'arguera cependant jamais pour démontrer l'illégitimité des lois adoptées par les représentants élus par les électeurs de l'époque" ("So the decision, last century, to limit the composition of the electoral body to the eligible voters, or the decision to consider, for decades running, universal masculine suffrage as identical to 'universal suffrage' period, these were arbitrary facts, which no lawyer would nonetheless ever argue to demonstrate the illegitimacy of the laws adopted by the representatives elected by the voters of that period"). From that point on, if there be anything arbitrary, it can be changed at any moment, and the political body can, in light of new values (such as *la parité*), decide to redefine itself, to open itself up.

Certain female philosophers, including Jeannette Colombel, are for their own part glad to remind us that the notion of situation – which is at the center of the Sartrian concept– has come to "dérégler la première, l'universalisme en philosophie comme en politique... Sartre évite le piège du repli communautaire ou d'affirmation identitaire tout en parlant de différences – 'l'Autre en Histoire' – espérant cependant en des 'universels concrets', des 'universels singuliers'" ("be the first thing to upset universalism in philosophy as in politics... Sartre avoids the trap of communitarian withdrawal or of identity affirmation, all the while speaking of difference – 'The Other in History' – putting hope nonetheless in 'concrete universals' or in 'singular universals'") (*Libération*, December 31, 1995). Similarly, Françoise Collin points out that it is about time to "penser l'un en même temps que le deux, ou que le plusieurs, et non en dehors l'un de l'autre" ("think the one at the same time as the both, or the several, instead of separating them one from another"). In this sense, *la parité* in politics would permit to "sortir de la logique des contraires" ("escape the logic of opposites"), countering universality and specificity "selon une pensée dichotomique d'héritage cartésien" ("according to a dichotomic idea of Cartesian heritage"). ("Les hommes ont toujours été à la fois des êtres humains, et des êtres masculins, sans que cette double qualification leur apparaisse comme un dilemme"[8] – "Men have always been both human beings and masculine beings at the same time, without having this double qualification appear to them as a dilemma.") Finally, in response to the article by Elizabeth Badinter, the philosopher Sylviane Agacinski examines in these terms the value of universalist abstraction: "Si l'universalisme consiste à ignorer absolument la différence sexuelle, l'essentielle mixité du genre humain, alors, il faut faire la critique philosophique et politique de l'universalisme" ("If universalism consists in absolutely ignoring sexual difference, the essential mixture of the human race, then the philosophical and political critique of universalism must be made") (*Le Monde*, June 18, 1996).

French universalists are also taken to task by certain legal experts. Over the course of a long theoretical work, Eliane Vogel-Polsky threw herself into an elaborate critique of the legal theory on the equality of the sexes, which constitutes for her an "inaboutissement programmé" ("programmed non-outcome"). Shocking, and heretofore rarely denounced, evidence: "L'égalité des sexes est la seule qui ait été et qui soit encore conjoncturelle, fragmentaire et diachronique, c'est à dire qu'elle a été intégrée dans les systèmes juridiques contemporains par une succession de textes séparés visant des domaines spécifiques : l'égalité des hommes et des femmes n'a jamais été consentie, reconnue et accordée en une seule fois pour tous les domaines de la vie en société..." ("Equality between the sexes is the only kind which has been and which is still today related to economic fluctuations that are fragmentary and diachronic; that is to say that it has been integrated into contemporary legal systems by a succession of separate texts targeting specific domains: the equality of men and woman has never been consented to, recognized, and accorded at one time and for all the domains of life in our society...") In her eyes, legal systems which recognize "l'égalité des citoyens et des personnes de manière abstraite et neutre en l'assortissant de l'interdiction de discriminations fondées sur le sexe, la race, la couleur..." ("equality of citizens and of people in an abstract and neutral manner, by adding it to the prohibition of discrimination based on sex, race, color..."), leads necessarily to an impasse. To get out of this rut, it is necessary to change tools and to adopt a legal system which "reconnaisse le droit fondamental autonome – existant per se et non par incidence – de l'égalité de la femme et de l'homme. Et ce droit fondamental doit se traduire par *la parité*" ("recognizes the fundamental autonomous right – existing per se and not incidentally – of the equality of woman and man. And this fundamental right must be translated through *la parité* ").

As for specialists in social code, they note that this branch of the law "articule volontiers égalité et différence" ("willingly articulates equality and difference"), emphasizing that "le discours juridique de l'égalité a longtemps été le discours de l'égalité formelle qui n'est pas refus des différences mais plutôt indifférence aux différences"[9] ("the legal discourse on equality was for a long time the discourse of formal equality which is not the refusal of difference, but rather in-difference to differences"). Jean-Jacques Dupeyroux, for one, does not hesitate to say "Non au principe d'égalité" ("no to the principle of equality") if it leads to rich and poor alike having the same claims to state-allocated family benefits (*Libération*, November 10, 1995).

These remarks demonstrate, in the eyes of some, that the best argument there may be to support the claim of *la parité* is to say, "For unequal people, there must be unequal rights." Or, on the contrary, to say, "To grant to women and to men the same legal treatment leads to denying justice to women." This critique of formal equality, moreover, has some illustrious antecedents. It is the logic of the criticism that Marx was already directing at the agenda of German socialists. Using this logic, Guy Braibant opportunely recalls that, if the principle of inequality has constitutional value, it also has political value. He writes, "Les assemblées juridiques ne sauraient s'opposer aux évolutions nécessaires et entraver la marche vers l'égalité réelle au nom d'une conception de l'égalité juridique... Des discriminations considérées aujourd'hui comme justifiées ne le seront peut-être plus demain – par exemple à l'égard des étrangers. D'autres seront au contraire considérées comme fondées pour mieux assurer l'égalité des chances et des conditions"[10] ("Legal assemblies would not be able to oppose the necessary changes and hinder progress toward real equality in the name of one conception of legal equality... Some types of discrimination which are today considered justifiable may not be so tomorrow; for example, with respect to foreigners. Others will, on the contrary, be considered as founded to better assure equality of opportunity and of conditions").

This "instrumentalist" vision of the law – in the service of an equality that is up to politicians to define – is shared by Francine Demichel. She says, "Sans intervention sur le terrain même du droit, les femmes sont condamnées, pour très longtemps encore à n'être désignées par celui-ci qu'à la condition d'être assimilées aux hommes, conjuguées au masculin. *La parité* est seule à même de remplacer cette identification unilatérale d'un sexe à l'autre par une réelle égalité des rapports entre les sexes." ("With no intervention in the very arena of law, women are condemned for a long time to come to be designated by the law only under the condition that they be assimilated with men, conjugated with the masculine. *La parité*, and *la parité* alone, is able to replace this unilateral identification of one sex with the other by a real equality of relationships between the sexes.") This legal expert insists on the conception of abstract citizenship which emanates from the Constitutional Council, as from a majority of jurists, as excessively "dogmatic" or "absolutist." In her view, sex must be taken into account by the theory of representation, because it contributes to defining "l'identité même de l'individu et du corps social" ("the very identity of the individual and of the social body"). Was it necessary to wait for a woman lawyer to intervene and write a chronicle in the Recueil Dalloz before reading such conclusions?

2. *La parité* as a stake in politics: taking back the idea

Political figures have not remained indifferent to the debate on *la parité*. Witness the multiplicity of reform proposals which have succeeded one another since 1994. Over the course of time, the number of both right- and left-wing male politicians to seriously consider the principle of *la parité* has been increasing.

Electoral preoccupations are no strangers to this state of affairs. In the midst of a crisis in political representation, political leaders understood that it was time "d'entendre la société sous peine que bientôt celle-ci ne les écoute plus"[11] ("to hear society, lest it soon stop listening to them"). Moreover, opinion is shown to be more and more favorable to the feminization of the instances of political decision, including at their peak.[12] Thus, the IFOF survey published in *L'Express* of June 6, 1996 reveals that a strong majority of French people of both sexes approve of a whole series of reform measures that would be taken to achieve male-female equality in the political arena: 84% of those surveyed were in favor of an "interdiction pour les hommes politiques d'occuper plusieurs postes à la fois" ("restriction prohibiting male politicians from occupying several positions at the same time"); 82% gave favorable responses to the "organisation d'un referendum sur les mesures permettant d'atteindre l'égalité hommes-femmes" ("organization of a referendum on measures permitting male-female equality to be reached"); 79% said yes to the "nomination d'autant de femmes que d'hommes aux postes importants qui dépendent de l'Etat et du gouvernement" ("nomination of as many women as men to high-level State and governmental positions"); and 77% said yes to "modifier la Constitution afin d'introduire *la parité* hommes-femmes comme principe générale" ("modifying the Constitution in order to introduce male-female parity as a general principle").

In 1994 numerous reform projects come to the fore. This was due to the European elections in June having included *la parité* on the agenda in the form of several lists composed of equal numbers of male and female candidates (among which were the Socialist and the Ecologist lists). Simone Veil, then Minister of Social Affairs, of Health, and of Urban Affairs, under the Balladur administration (RPR[13]), proposes a reform aimed at the institution of a progressive quota for representation of women at municipal, regional, and European elections (all of which are votes using a list system of proportional representation, which lends itself better than a uninominal system[14] to the application of numerically-perfect parity). Furthermore, six legal proposals (of parliamentary origin) were brought forth. One of them, drafted under the initiative of the association Choisir-La Cause des Femmes and presented by three deputies of the Mouvement des Citoyens ("Citizens' Movement"), has the objective of modifying Article 3 of the Constitution by adding the following clause: "L'égal accès des femmes et des hommes aux mandats politiques est assuré par *la parité*" ("Equal access for women and men to political mandates is guaranteed by *la parité* ").

In 1995 – a presidential election year – three new legal proposals saw the light of day. One of the most surprising outcomes of the campaign will be to see the main competitors address the question of the division of power between the sexes. Several candidates have explicitly developed the issue of *la parité* and have put forth reform projects in order to achieve it. On behalf of the Green Party, Dominique Voynet has rallied support for a modification to the Constitution and drafted a legal proposal to that end. The Communist Party candidate, Robert Hue, declared himself in favor of a referendum to implement *la parité*. The Socialist Party candidate, Lionel Jospin, made several proposals in order to "faire avancer cette grande idée de *la parité*" ("further this great idea that is *la parité*"), among which are a limitation on the accumulation of mandates and a reform of the ballot system used in legislative elections. "Un scrutin mixte en France (majoritaire et proportionnel) serait la manière de réaliser une meilleure égalité hommes-femmes" ("A mixed ballot system [using both majority rule and proportional representation] would be the only way to reach better male-female equality") (*Le Monde*, March 10, 1995). On the right, Edouard Balladur declared himself in favor of the implementation of quotas for women ("disons 30% pour base" – "let's say 30% to start") and promised to organize "dans les cent jours" ("within the first hundred days"), if he is elected, a constitutional revision by referendum. As for Jacques Chirac, he declared his desire to link party financing to the feminization of each party's list of election candidates and promised to create a National Observatory of *la parité*.[15]

In 1996, six new legal proposals relating to *la parité* were brought forth. In June, an article entitled the "Manifeste des dix" ("Manifesto of Ten") was published in *L'Express*. The article was signed by ten, female ex-ministers – left-wing, moderate, and even right-wing – all of whom were ready to get beyond partisan politics in order to realize *la parité*. The publication of this text, which has the impact of a bombshell in the political arena accelerated a shift among those in charge on the question of *la parité*. On the right, Alain Juppé (RPR) – then Prime Minister – declared himself clearly in favor of revising the Constitution. On the left, the unconditional conversion of Michel Rocard to the idea of *la parité* marked a milestone. For the ex-Prime Minister, only this radical, yet not "undemocratic," solution will allow for an end to the current situation which makes it so that "c'est la communauté des mâles qui gouverne" ("it is the community of males that governs") (*L'Express*, June 20, 1996). The Socialist Party Secretary himself, Lionel Jospin, also made great strides on the issue of *la parité*. In 1996, he recognized that the "temps de la contrainte est bel et bien arrivé" ("time for constraint has come once and for all"). This willingness to change things is reflected in the text ("Les acteurs de la démocratie" – "The players in democracy") which was adopted by the Socialist Party during the National Convention on Democracy, gathered in Paris on June 29 and 30, 1996. There, activists pronounced themselves in favor of a revision of the Constitution which would establish the principle of male-female parity. The Socialist Party also affirmed its determination to at least double the proportion of women elected over the course of the elections, and decided to apply a quota of 30% to the number of female candidates at the next legislative elections.

The President of the Republic, Jacques Chirac, having decided to dismiss the French National Assembly, the legislative elections would take place in anticipated fashion in May and June of 1997. During the course of the campaign, Lionel Jospin made renovation and feminization of the political arena one of the central themes of his platform. He firmly declared himself in favor of parity between women and men in the political arena. After the victory of the socialists – who presented nearly 30% women, of whom some 17% were elected – Lionel Jospin, having become Prime Minister, renewed his promise. In his statement of general policy, on June 19, 1997, he proposed to the French a new republican pact founded on the modernization of France's democracy: "Il faut d'abord permettre au Françaises de s'engager sans entraves dans la vie publique... Une révision de la Constitution, afin d'y inscrire l'objectif de *la parité* entre les femmes et les hommes, sera proposée" ("We must first of all enable French women to engage in public service without hindrance... A revision of the Constitution, in order to inscribe in it the objective of parity between women and men, will be proposed").

This promise was kept, at least by all appearances. On June 18, 1998, the government brought before the office of the French National Assembly a project of constitutional law related to equality between women and men. The result of ten years of debate, the proposal was unanimously adopted by the National Assembly on March 10, 1999 by the French deputies. After having triomphed over the opposition of the right wing and the Senate (which, faithful to its tradition of misogyny, had swept the project aside after a first reading), the constitutional reform requires only a vote by the two Chambers together at the Congress of Versailles[16] to become permanent.

3. The Constitutional Modification: Consensus on Minimal Reform

What does the reform consist of? The legal project adopted is short, if not laconic. On one hand, Article 3 of the Constitution (which forms the basis of the principles of indivisibility, sovereignty, and universality of suffrage) is completed by the clause, reading: "La loi favorise les conditions dans lesquelles est organisé l'égal accès des femmes et des hommes aux mandats électoraux et fonctions électives ("The law favors the conditions under which is organized equal access of women and men to electoral mandates and elective functions"). On the other hand, Article 4 (which relates to political parties) is completed thus: "ils contribuent à la mise en œuvre du principe énoncé au dernier alinéa de l'article 3 dans les conditions déterminées par la loi" ("they contribute to the enactment of the principle set forth in the last clause of Article 3 under conditions determined by the law").

One fact which, upon first reading, does not fail to amaze is that the term *"la parité "* appears nowhere in the wording, although it is the very object of the reform. Why is this? The reasons put forth relate, we are told, to the practical difficulties of its realization. *La parité*, which evokes the idea of perfect equality "renvoie à un déterminisme mathématique impossible à mettre en oeuvre"[17] ("implies a mathematical determinism that is impossible to put into action"). Other than its symbolic aspect, the project has a precise legal objective: to authorize the legislature to take positive discriminatory measures in favor of women, without risking (as happened in 1982) the censure of the Constitutional Council. In other words, it is left up to Parliament, in the application of this reform, to take the correct voluntarist measures to attain the objective of *la parité* in the political arena. Such measures would include imposing quotas on candidates, deciding financial compensation for parties that feminize their candidate lists, etc. It represents a reform that is necessary (from a legal standpoint) but insufficient – a kind of an empty shell that must be filled with concrete proposals.

The project elicited various commentary, some of which, it must be said, is somewhat negative, including some coming from legal experts. Georges Vedel, former member of the Constitutional Council, was the most severe, qualifying the project as "marivaudage législatif ("legal gallantry"): "Et voilà aujourd'hui que le pouvoir constituant, ce souverain, dans un débat fondamental dit qu'il n'a rien à dire, que c'est au législateur de se débrouiller et au Conseil constitutionnel de prononcer le dernier mot" ("And we see here today that in a fundamental debate, the constituent assembly, that sovereign power, has nothing to say, that it is up to the legislature to find its way and up to the Constitutional Council to say the last word" (*Le Monde*, December 8, 1998). In the same vein, Danièle Lochak remains "tout de même assez sceptique sur la portée de cet article" ("nonetheless fairly skeptical regarding the scope of this article").

A number of women politicians and activists have similarly expressed a rather critical view, from Gisèle Halimi to Roselyne Bachelot (RPR) and Yvette Roudy (PS),[18] without forgetting Muguette Jacquaint (PC).[19] Many emphasize that the project will not reach its full meaning until the articles of its application have been adopted. And that these articles stand to pose serious problems, most notably because the uninominal voting system makes for an awkward fit with the principle of equal access for women and men.

Why did the government choose to present such a lukewarm text, reflecting the idea of minimal reform, and thus take the risk of "disappointing?" This choice was not accidental. It results from a necessity imposed by the Constitution, according to which the Prime Minister and the President of the Republic may not present a project for the revision of a fundamental law without being in agreement. Moreover, Jacques Chirac would not have accepted wording that might have represented the views of "paritarist" radicals. The revision was thus the result of a compromise reached (in June 1998) between the two executive heads of state, who both, by turns, continue to up the ante on the subject of feminization in politics with the presidential election in sight (which could take place in anticipated fashion before the scheduled date of 2002). It is, it would seem, upon the express request of the Elysium that in the wording of the legal project the term "*la parité*" was carefully avoided in favor of the term "equality," Jacques Chirac having pointed out that right-wing deputies would oppose voting on a reform authorizing 50/50 quotas. As Georges Vedel has very well pointed out, the bill notes a consensus on the objective of equality, but does-not come down in favor of any of the diverging views regarding the modes of enacting this egalitarian objective. "Le flou est commode. Salut les artistes !" ("What convenient ambiguity. Hello creativity !") The project contains the advantage, Danièle Lochak further tells us, of "pouvoir rallier les suffrages de tous ceux et toutes celles, dont bon nombre de mes amis, qui, au nom de l'universalité, critiquent *la parité*. Je ne vois vraiment pas qui pourrait s'opposer à cette formule qui respecte parfaitement l'objectif d'universalité"[20] ("being able to rally the suffrage of all those men and women, a great number of whom are my friends, who, in the name of universality, criticize *la parité* . I really cannot see who could oppose this clause which perfectly respects the objective of universality"). If the revision of Article 3 is a revolution of customs, one could say that it is a negotiated revolution.

Has the mountain, then, given birth to a molehill? Is this a trompe-l'oeil reform we are dealing with here? Or rather, as certain people suggest, can we see in it a base for incentive measures to come, one that may before long result in parity among women and men in the elected assemblies? The future alone will tell.

We may only point out that for the first time in France a process of change is underway, which, in an inescapable and irreversible manner, is going to drive the major parties to practice a veritable mix in their nominations or else run the risk of losing all credibility in the eyes of the electorate. Already, two votes have served as tests of the (good) will of male politicians to open up politics to women. On one hand, the regional elections of March 1998 (which were carried out by integral proportional representation) were marked by an explosion in the number of women candidates, both nominated and elected (the proportion of candidates rose from 27% in 1992 to 37% in 1998, that of elected women from 13% to 26%). Everything happened as if the policy of quotas, applied with success by the Socialist Party to the legislative elections of 1997, had a spreading effect. All the parties, including those on the right, had to resign themselves to presenting women in good positions for fear of disappointing an electorate hoping to see its elite be feminized. On the other hand, the composition of lists for the European election of June 13, 1999 shows that, for this type of ballot, being conducted by the list system of proportional representation on a national scale, *la parité* has, for the most part, penetrated the political mores of our time. The Socialist, Communist, and Green parties have strictly enforced the practice of alternating between men and women on their lists. Only the parties on the right and extreme right have taken some liberties with the principle of *la parité*, all the while giving in to the principle of feminization. If they show 50% women (or more) on their lists of candidates, these women do not occupy very crucial positions among the open slots. Undoubtedly, the movement toward a more equitable division of power between the sexes has been launched in France, even if the road will be long and riddled with pitfalls.[21]

Translated by Heidi Kyser Genoist

Notes

1. Francine Demichel, "A parts égales : contribution au débat sur la parité", *Recueil Dalloz Sirey* (Paris: March 21, 1996), p. 95.

2. Translator's Note: In France, the movement which has grown up around the concept of political parity as it is defined here, and which has involved the efforts of politicians, activists, scholars, writers and journalists, has itself come to be known as "*la parité*." The varying translations of "parity" and "*la parité* " herein have attempted, respectively, to account for the concept as such, at its most objective, versus the school of thought at large, along with its products, though there is always necessarily some measure of overlap between the two.

3. Françoise Gaspard, "De *la parité* : genèse d'un concept, naissance d'un mouvement," in *Nouvelles Questions Féministes*, vol. 15, no. 4 (Paris), p.31.

4. Different stages have punctuated the increase in power of this claim: 1. September 1989, the European Council organizes a Seminar on Democratic Parity; 2. Spring 1992, the release of a work, *Au pouvoir citoyennes ! Liberté, Egalité, Parité*, contributes to the diffusion of the idea of *la parité* in France; 3. November 1992, the Declaration of Athens is adopted on the occasion of the premier European summit on "Women and Power"; 4. November 1993, the Manifesto of 577 for Democratic Parity is published in the daily newspaper *Le Monde*; and 5. May 1996, the Charter of Rome is signed promising the promotion of "la participation égale des femmes et des hommes à la prise de décision" ("equal participation of women and men in decision-making") on a European level.

5. In an interview with the daily newspaper *Figaro* of March 9, 1995, he stated his position with perfect clarity: "Nous entrons dans un monde où... nous verrons s'opposer deux conceptions de la démocratie. L'une est celle dans laquelle les citoyens se pensent d'abord en termes de comunautés, considérées comme des composantes structurelles de la nation. L'autre vision qui, elle, me paraît véritablement républicaine, fidèle aux pères fondateurs, est celle de la nation française, de tous les citoyens français, quels que soient leur origine, leur sexe, leurs affinités culturelles, leur religion, leur race" ("We are entering a world where (...) we will see two conceptions of democracy at odds. One is that in which citizens think of themselves first in terms of communities, considered to be like the structural elements of a nation. The other vision, which I myself see as truly republican, loyal to the founding fathers, is that of all French citizens, regardless of their origin, their sex, their cultural affinities, their religion, or their race").

6. Elni Varikas, "Une représentation en tant que femme? Réflexions critiques sur la demande de parité des sexes," in *Nouvelles Questions féministes*, vol. 16, no. 2 (Paris: 1995), p. 118.

7. Jean Vogel, "La citoyenneté revisitée," in Eliane Vogel-Polsky, *Les femmes et la citoyenneté européenne, European Commission, European Network*, "Les femmes et la prise de décision," (Brussells: direction générale V, multigraphié, 1994), p. 43.

8. Françoise Collin, "La raison polyglotte ou pour sortir de la logique des contraires," in *EPHESIA, La place des femmes, L'enjeu de l'identité et de l'égalité ou regard des sciences sociales* (Paris: La Découverte, 1995), p. 675.

9. Antoine Lyon-Caen, "L'égalité et la différence dans l'ordre du droit," in *EPHESIA, La place des femmes, l'enjeu de l'identité et de l'égalité au regard des sciences sociales* (Paris: La Découverte, 1995).

10. Guy Braibant, "Le principe d'égalité dans la jurisprudence du Conseil constitutionnel et du Conseil d'Etat," in *Conseil constitutionnel, La déclaration des droits de l'homme et du citoyen* (Paris: PUF, 1989).

11. National Assembly, Report No. 1240: Rapport fait au nom de la Commission des lois constitutionnelles, de la législation et de l'administration générale sur le projet de loi constitutionnelle (no 985) relatif à l'égalité entre les femmes et les hommes (December 1998), p. 45.

12. See lecture by Mariette Sineau entitled "La féminisation du pouvoir vue par les Français(es) et les hommes politiques : images et représentations," in *La parité. Enjeux et mise en oeuvre*, Jacqueline Martin, ed. (Toulouse: Presses de l'Université du Mirail, 1998), pp. 61–81.

13. Translator's note: "RPR" stands for "Rassemblement pour la République" (usually translated as "Rally for the Republic"), the Republican party, or the "right," as it is called, of France.

14. In France, two assemblies are elected by ballot in a uninominal system consisting of two rounds: the French National Assembly and the General Councils (or departmental assemblies).

15. By decree of the President of the Republic dated October 18, 1995, an "Observatoire de *la parité* entre les femmes et les hommes" ("Observatory of *La Parité* Between Women and Men") was instituted. On January 15, 1997, the Observatory placed in the hands of the Prime Minister, Alain Juppé, a report drafted by Gisèle Halimi which proposed various solutions to arrive at *la parité*. Subsequent to this report, a debate on the presence of women in the political arena took place at the French National Assembly on March 11, 1997. This debate did not result in a vote.

16. According to the stipulations of the Constitution of 1958, in order for a constitutional reform to be adopted it must be voted on in the same terms by the National Assembly and the Senate, then ratified by a majority of three-fifths by both Chambers of Congress together.

17. Report of the National Assembly No. 1240, cited above, p. 95.

18. Translator's Note: "PS" stands for "Parti Socialiste" or the Socialist Party.

19. Translator's Note: "PC" stands for "Parti Communiste" or the Communist Party.

20. Report of the National Assembly No. 1240, cited above, p. 52.

21. Some think that the Constitutional Council could invalidate the clause concerning *la parité* which appears in the law on the new regional electoral system, particularly if it is attacked before the constitutional reform of Article 3 can be definitively adopted.

References

Conseil d'Etat. *Rapport public 1996. Sur le principe d'égalité*. Paris: La Documentation française, 1996.

Demichel, Francine. *A parts égales: contribution au débat sur la parité*. Paris: Recueil Dalloz Sirey, March 21, 1996.

"Femmes en politique." Special edition of *Pouvoirs*, No. 82, September 1997.

Gaspard, Françoise, Claude Servan-Schreiber, and Anne LeGall. *Au pouvoir, citoyennes ! Liberté, Egalité*, Parité. Paris: Seuil, 1992.

Halimi, Gisèle. *Rapport de la Commission pour la parité entre les femmes et les hommes dans la vie politique*. Paris: Multigraphié, 1996.

Jenson, Jane and Mariette Sineau. *Mitterand et les Françaises. Un rendez-vous manqué*. Paris: Presses de Sciences Po, 1995.

"La parité 'pour.'" Special edition of *Nouvelles Questions Féministes*, November 1994.

"La parité 'contre.'" Special edition of *Nouvelles Questions Féministes*, May 1995.

Martin, Jacqueline, ed. *La parité. Enjeux et mise en œuvre*. Toulouse: Presses Universitaires du Mirail, 1998.

Mossuz-Lavau, Janine. *Femmes/Hommes pour la parité*. Paris: Presses de Sciences Po, 1998.

Sineau, Mariette. *Des femmes en politique*. Paris: Economica, 1988.

Voguel-Polsky, Eliane. "Les impasses de l'égalité ou pourquoi les outils juridiques visant à l'égalité des femmes et des hommes doivent être repensés en termes de parité." In *Parité-Infos*, supplemental edition to the series. Paris, 1994.

The Politics of PACS in a Transatlantic Mirror: Same-Sex Unions and Sexual Difference in France Today

Éric Fassin

1989 was not only the year the Berlin wall finally collapsed. In France, 1989 was primarily the year of the Bicentennial of the French Revolution – *i.e.*, at long last, the Revolution was over (at least, according to François Furet). This meant that, henceforth, instead of opposing 1776 to 1789, a (good) liberal Revolution to a (bad) radical Revolution, French "neo-liberals" could invoke de Tocqueville to denounce the perils of democracy in America – thus turning around the transatlantic mirror: in contrast to a French tradition of civility fortunately inherited from a happy combination of the Old and New Regimes merging in the *"République"*, "democratic passions" (meaning the immoderate love of equality) jeopardized the American nation. This became intellectual commonsense in Parisian circles in the following years, in response to American (so-called) "political correctness," and shortly thereafter, to (so-called) "sexual correctness."

In France, 1989 was also the year of the *"affaire du foulard"* : should young Muslim women be allowed to wear a veil in public schools? The political choice was generally presented as an alternative between the principle of *"laïcité"* and a (somewhat unprincipled) cultivation of cultural difference. Language notwithstanding, this debate was not so much about religion: in fact, it reflected a growing concern about the "integration" of immigrants, or rather second-generation immigrants, in French society. The defense of a national model against the perils of ethnic fragmentation was elaborated by public intellectuals such as Elisabeth Badinter, Régis Debray, and Alain Finkielkraut – in the name of the *"République."* Resisting *"ghettoïsation,"* they identified the French nation with what they defined as a universalist model of individual integration. In the process, they too drew on a transatlantic contrast: American differentialism (*i.e.* the *"communautarisme"* of identity politics) was the mirror image of French universalism (*i.e.* the *"individualisme"* of Republican politics).

In France, 1989 may then have been the moment when "liberal" intellectuals (*à la Furet*) and defenders of the "nation" (*à la Finkielkraut*) united under the banner of the French *"République"* against the American countermodel, as they identified the critique of egalitarianism with the critique of identity politics. After the final collapse of Communism, America became the new Other (or should one say that America was, yet again, the other Other?). This political alliance largely defines the intellectual climate of the 1990s in France – for the beauty of this rhetorical construct of a contrast between national political cultures is that it applies equally well (or poorly, depending on one's perspective) to extremely diverse issues: not only ethnicity, but also gender, and sexuality.

Indeed, not only does the "Republican paradigm" define French public debates in the recent period about "immigration" (with the transatlantic contrast generally presented as one between the French "melting-pot" and American "multiculturalism"), but it has also been used to discuss the politics of feminism (for example, in Mona Ozouf's essay *Les mots des femmes*), and the politics of homosexuality (in particular, in Frédéric Martel's essay *Le rose et le noir*).[1] In each case, the authors define, in contrast to the "disuniting of America," the so-called *"modèle républicain."* For example, gay counterculture is rejected in the name of individual integration: the yearly Gay Pride demonstration is according to this view but another example of "Americanization."[2]

*****

Given this universalist framework, one would expect French "Republicans" of all stripes to embrace wholeheartedly the issue of same-sex marriage: it would seem to be the culmination of a universalist agenda. Or at least, so it has been recently, in the United States – precisely where French universalists look not for a model, but rather for a counter-model. This is how Hannah Arendt's "Reflections on Little Rock" could be recently updated for contemporary

American purposes – from the Civil Rights movement to the Gay Rights movement, from the late 1950s to the late 1990s: "The right to marry whoever one wishes is an elementary human right compared to which [...] nearly all other rights enumerated in the Constitution are secondary."[3] Indeed, whereas the Supreme Court of the United States started racial desegregation in schools, with *Brown v. Board of Education* in 1955, it did not complete its work until desegregation applied to marriage as well, with *Loving v. Virginia*, in 1967: only then was the old logic of *Plessy v. Ferguson*, in 1896, finally and completely overturned – races could not any longer be deemed equal while they remained separate. Desegregation can be the most powerful weapon against discrimination – especially within marriage.

One essential question remains – whether the shift from race to sexual preference is legitimate. Does the same logic apply in both cases? Can one extend the argument – from one kind of discrimination to another, from one minority to another? Paradoxically, the answer may be easier to provide in France than in the United States: since 1985, French law (in contrast to American federal law) has explicitly rejected discrimination based on "sexual orientation" (or rather, literally, "mores"), alongside other forms of discrimination – based on race, sex, national origin, religion, and so on. The parallel between miscegenation laws and the issue of same-sex marriage should thus be even more obviously convincing in France than it is in the United States.

Of course, as many have pointed out, not every legal distinction can be considered a form of discrimination: equal treatment only applies to comparable situations. For example, we find it obvious that children and adults should not be entitled to the same rights – in France as well as in the United States. The legal distinction only reinforces that which we usually consider to be an acceptable social distinction. However, not every social distinction is given legal reinforcement. For example, class differences, or religious differences, are not legally established – neither in France, nor in the United States. Thus, giving legal status to a social distinction does require powerful justifications; otherwise, it is appropriate to call such legal distinctions a form of discrimination. Women are a case in point: in France, women are entitled to a pregnancy leave: they are the ones who give birth to children. However, parental leave is not for mothers only – women do not have a monopoly over prime education. In a word, although the legal system may legitimately distinguish between different categories of citizens, it may only do so for good, strong, or (to use the language of American law) "compelling" reasons; otherwise, the law only serves to justify what could be called (to use the language of the French political tradition) "privileges."

Homosexuality is indeed different from heterosexuality; but is the difference such that they should be legally distinguished – with different rights attached to each? And in this case, what are the "compelling" reasons that could justify maintaining homosexuality outside of marriage laws, especially once discrimination against homosexuality is illegal, as is the case in France (contrary to the United States)? Or, conversely, why should the political principle of equality not apply within the family – why should it not extend to marriage law? And how can one say that this not about homosexuality, but about marriage, and the family – and not see that marriage and the family do have something to do with discrimination against homosexuals?

Indeed, the family as an institution is not merely the last bastion of discrimination against homosexuals in France; it is also at the heart of this discrimination. Not only because all families play a primary role in socialization – in families, values are taught, as well as prejudices. But also because while this institution is defined as heterosexual by nature, it remains legitimate to exclude homosexuals from their families. It is no wonder that even today parents should reject their own child, and children their own father or mother, when they first discover his or her homosexuality – in both cases ensuring that homosexuality stays out the family. It is no wonder that in Fance courts should deny custody of a child to the gay parent after a divorce, or reject adoption demands by single homosexuals, even though the law says nothing about a person's sexuality for purposes of divorce or adoption. In all these cases, judges, parents, and even children, simply draw a logical conclusion from a general principle: if the family is defined as heterosexual, then homosexuals do not belong in the family.

How can one not see this? The answer, of course, is simple. Not that discrimination is invisible. Actually, people do not see what they do not want to see – they are blind to what they refuse to acknowledge. In the same way, in 1980, the French Constitutional Council, reviewing laws that go back to Vichy establishing a different age of consent for heterosexuality and homosexuality, refused to invalidate them. The argument was that "for the sake of minors, the law may distinguish, without disregard for the principle of equality, between sexual acts based on whether they involve persons of the same sex or not." Within two years, the National Assembly was to repeal this law: discrimination was then in full view. Today, many in

France argue that toleration for homosexuality should not lead to its inclusion within the family: but discrimination may soon cease to be invisible. Or so it would seem, given the contemporary emphasis, among intellectuals, on universalism as a defining feature of French political culture.

*****

Logically, both "liberal" and "national" Republicans should have applauded as same-sex marriage became a public issue. Indeed, a bill granting some kind of a (limited) legal status to same-sex couples originated in the early 1990s with political figures claiming a universalist logic – such as Jean-Pierre Michel, a gay Assemblyman politically affiliated with the arch-Republican Minister Jean-Pierre Chevènement. However, once the PaCS *(Pacte Civil de Solidarité,* formerly known as *Contrat d'Union Sociale,* or *Contrat d'Union Civile – C.U.S.* or *C.U.C.)* was under attack, for the most part, Republican intellectuals either remained silent, or joined in its denunciation. Politics has its own logic, which may not always coincide with intellectual logic – and this is also true of intellectual politics.

Those who are willing to grant a certain number of social rights to same-sex couples in France today, through something like the minimal "*concubinage,*" often reject more legitimate forms of domestic partnership, such as the *PaCS.* The real issue, beyond the *PaCS* (even though the bill currently discussed in Parliament makes no reference to the topic whatsoever), is in fact access to adoption as well as reproductive technologies – both of which currently legally exclude same-sex couples in France. The real problem is that, while not objecting to gays and lesbians as individuals, nor even as couples, many refuse the perspective of gay and lesbian families.

It is not exactly surprising that this should be a problem on the Right – traditionally, the Right has defined the family in a traditional fashion, indeed, as the bulwark of tradition. The question is then: why should this also be a problem on the Left – as evidenced by the embarrassing absence of most left-wing "*députés*" when the *PaCS* was first put to the vote on October 9, 1998? Two answers then come to mind. The first is "cultural" – and not altogether surprising. While the persistent misogyny of politicians is more frequently discussed today, in light of the "*parité* " debates, homophobia is hardly absent either in these circles, and should not be overlooked. And it is only in the last few years that in France what might be called (in comparison with the United States) the Old Left has started opening somewhat to the (French) New Left, in order to consider not only class but also minority issues – both inequality and discrimination. And there is yet a long way to go.

The second answer is "historical," and it probably requires a longer explanation. When the Left returned to power under the leadership of Lionel Jospin in 1997, the idea expressed by the new government was to reclaim the family in the name of a *"politique familiale de gauche"*: whereas, according to an opposition inherited from the Republican tradition, the French Left had always been suspicious of the (private) socialization that takes place in families, and preferred to rely on the (public) socialization of schooling, now at last the phrase "left-wing family policies" (or "politics," for that matter) would not be an oxymoron. This means that the image of the family had to be transformed: instead of opposing legitimate to illegitimate families, one should extend the definition of a legitimate family. These "brave new families" rehabilitated by left-wing politics are complex families, composed and recomposed, but not decomposed, through marriage, divorce, and remarriage – not to mention unmarried couples with children. The left-wing modernization of the family was in fact the acknowledgement of complexity in contemporary family life, as analysed, for example, in the work of sociologist Irène Théry.

The Left thus opened up the definition of the family. But how open should it be – *i.e.*, how far should one go in the direction of complexity? For all throughout the 1990s, the issue of same-sex couples had been raised on the Left: should these couples be granted a status? And if so, since the question was not any longer merely of toleration, but actually of recognition, should one not go a step further and grant legitimacy not only to same-sex couples, but also to gay and lesbian families? This was the new question raised when the Left regained power in 1997, as gay and lesbian organizations joined in support of (beyond the much more moderate version of the *PaCS*) same-sex marriage itself – not only the *A.P.G.L.* (*Association des Parents et futurs parents Gays et Lesbiens*), but also the *Centre Gay et Lesbien, AIDES*, and even *Act-Up Paris*.

The Socialists in government then tried to resist this pressure by occupying a political position which might be defined as *"juste milieu."*[4] This "middle ground" logic applies both to family, and to homosexuality issues (and indeed, to others as well, such as immigration). On the former front, the idea is that one should open up the definition of the family – but not go too far: marriage need not be stable for the family to survive; but in order to preserve stability for the children, at least, the principle of sexual difference should remain at the foundation of the family. On the latter front, the idea is that discrimination against homosexuals should be opposed. It is true that this was already established by the Socialists in the early 1980s, after the election of François Mitterrand. But in the 1990s, they argue, it is possible to go further, though not too far – halfway between toleration and recognition, halfway between homosexual individuals and gay and lesbian families: a semi-recognition for same-sex couples.

One problem only remains. The middle ground strategy is clearly a politically shrewd choice, as it may gain support in the center, and thus remain popular: this is why the French Socialists define their position in a contrast to both "extremes" – in simultaneous opposition to homophobic militants, and... homosexual militants. But obviously, the risk is that framing this contrast as an equivalence may also have a political cost: the center may not be on the left, after all. How could the *"juste milieu"* characterize the Left? And then, how can the French Socialists still claim to be on the left?

*****

This is the point where intellectuals play a crucial part: they provide arguments to justify this political choice. Not that this is very new: in France, the relative power of intellectuals also implies that they tend to be closer to power – their influence in public space is sometimes purchased at the expense of independence from public opinion. This is the key function of public intellectuals in France: they provide arguments for public debate. But the easiest way for intellectuals to influence politics is to use the language of politics – their political language is more likely to be reflected in the public sphere if this language itself reflects preexisting positions in the political world.

What is remarkable in this case, is that French opponents of same-sex marriage, especially on the Left, shift from the political language of universalism to other languages, in order to justify their position: universalism can hardly justify the *"juste milieu"* as a left-wing position. Given the difficulty of coming up with a political justification, the first solution is to look for a foundation outside of politics – hence the recourse to the social sciences; hence the importance of "experts." Sociologist Irène Théry, in particular, first through an article published by the (*"juste milieu"*) think tank Fondation Saint-Simon, and then through a report on family reform ordered by the Socialist governement, provided arguments to establish the intellectual legitimacy of middle ground politics.[5]

In her work, "sexual difference" (*"la différence des sexes"*) is not presented as a political issue, but rather as an anthropological foundation: this *"ordre symbolique"* (a notion that combines French intellectual traditions in social anthropology and psychoanalysis) is not open to political negotiation – it is a given. Of course, one can dispute the anthropological data: as anthropologists have known for a long time, "sexual difference" is hardly the universal definition of marriage and the family. One can also dispute the idea that anthropology (or psychoanalysis, or any other "science") should predetermine our political choices – as if marriage and the family were outside of the political realm, beyond the democratic pale of public debate. But the political choice of the middle ground is still granted more legitimacy when intellectual discourse resonates with conventional wisdom in order to establish sexual difference at the heart of marriage and the family.[6]

Scientific legitimacy in and of itself is not sufficient to justify the *"juste milieu."* Political justifications are required to show that "sexual difference" is not only a scientific necessity, but also a political imperative. And this is where the debate about *"parité"* comes in: it contributes the left-wing aura of feminism to the politics of the middle ground. In order to avoid the stigma of Americanization, the inventors of *"parité"* in politics were willing to say that it had nothing to do with (American-style) "quotas": women were no minority, since sexual difference was no ordinary difference, like class or ethnic differences: it was an essential, universal difference. This potentially essentialist argument served a strategic purpose: at first, it worked powerfully in the direction of equality – between men and women. But in the context of the debate surrounding gay and lesbian couples and families, it could also work, quite powerfully too, against equality – between heterosexuals and homosexuals. This is what Prime Minister Lionel Jospin's wife, philosopher Sylviane Agacinski, suggested in a book on the "politics of the sexes," which is also about the politics of sexuality, and developed in later interviews and articles: according to her, Simone de Beauvoir notwithstanding, "sexual difference" is not merely a social construct – it is, through motherhood, a biological reality. This philosophical argument translates politically: "sexual difference" is a political necessity for the women's movement; therefore, it should not be given up for the sake of gay and lesbian families[7].

The paradox is that this reformist view of feminism (progressive in terms of gender, conservative in terms of sexuality) finds echoes in France among radical feminists, and radical lesbians. Of course, it is not altogether surprising: these radical critics of patriarchy find it difficult to fight a political battle in favor of marriage and the family – even if it means the inclusion of gays and lesbians in these institutions. The fact that gay leaders should support same-sex marriage does not always help, as the gender tensions have obviously not vanished in a gender-neutral politicization of homosexuality. The result is that radicals may be tempted by the arguments of women like Irène Théry and Sylviane Agacinski – not because they want to preserve a "symbolic order" that excludes homosexuals from marriage and the family, of course, but because they advocate (from the outside) a countercultural vision of homosexuality. Middle-ground reformists prefer "disorderly conduct" among homosexuals: as long as homosexuality remains subversive, it will not subvert the "symbolic order" of heterosexuality.

The symmetrical paradox is of course the price that intellectuals have to pay for this *"juste milieu"*: they now have to oppose, and sometimes in the name of Foucault, the "assimilation" of homosexuals within society, through marriage and the family. In order to provide an intellectual and political justification for the *"juste milieu"*, they have to recant, both intellectually (by invoking *"la différence des sexes"*) and politically (as they reject the logic of equality) their professed universalism.

*****

These debates raise numerous questions. We may conclude with a political one. Today, in France, "universalism" is the name of the game. This means that the question of being in favor of or opposed to universalism is politically irrelevant: universalism is the common language within which disputes about "minorities" take place – this is obvious in the case of *"parité,"* and it is becoming visible in the case of the *PaCS*. The relevant question is then: how can we make use of this rhetoric to contribute to social change? How can we appropriate it in a politically satisfactory fashion? My suggestion is that today in France it is possible (though difficult) to articulate the claims of the women's movement and of gay and lesbian liberation by using the language of equality, instead of sexual difference – for sexual difference is today the language with which the interests of women and homosexuals are pitted against each other. Paradoxically, when French Republicans are forced to abandon the language of universalism in order to resist minority claims, it may be wise to appropriate this rhetoric in order to fight for equality – not for homosexuals, not for women, but for all.

Notes

1. Mona Ozouf, *Les mots des femmes, essai sur la singularité française*, Fayard, Paris, 1995. Some of the reactions are to be found in a dossier published by *Le Débat: "Femmes: une singularité française?"* (n° 87, November - December 1995). Frédéric Martel, *Le rose et le noir, les homosexuels en France depuis 1968*, Seuil, Paris, 1996.

2. On this recent history of French intellectual (and political) history, I have written two pieces in English: *"'Good to Think'. The American Reference in French Discourses of Immigration and Ethnicity,"* *Multiculturalist Questions*, Steven Lukes and Christian Joppke, eds., Oxford U.P. (to be published); and "The Purloined Gender. American Feminism in a French Mirror", *French Historical Studies*, 22:1, Winter 1999 (to be published). They expand on what is only sketched here.

3. Hannah Arendt, "Reflections on Little Rock", *Dissent*, 6, n° 1, Winter 1959, excerpted in Andrew Sullivan's reader: *Same-Sex Marriage: Pro and Con*, Vintage, New York, 1997, p. 144.

4. I have developed a political history of these recent developments in *"PaCS Socialista:* la gauche et le 'juste milieu'", *Le Banquet*, n° 12–13, dossier "Mariage, union et filiation", October 1998, pp. 147–159.

5. Irène Théry, "Le contrat d'union sociale en question", *Esprit*, 10, October 1997, pp. 159–187, and the report *Couple, filiation et parenté aujourd'hui. Le droit face aux mutations de la famille et de la vie privée*, Odile Jacob / La Documentation française, Paris, 1998.

6. I have developed a critique both of the arguments (what I call *"l'illusion anthropologique"*) and of the intellectual stance (what could be called *"l'illusion de l'expertise"*) in two articles: "L'illusion anthropologique: homosexualité et filiation", *Témoin*, n° 12, May 1998, pp. 43–56, and "Le savant, l'expert et le politique. La famille des sociologues", *Genèses*, n° 32, September 1998, pp. 156–169.

7. Sylviane Agacinski, *Politique des sexes*, Seuil, Paris, 1998; see also, for example, her interview (and the critical review by Michel Feher) in the gay and lesbian magazine *Ex Aequo*, July 1998, pp. 22 - 25, and her recent (controversial) article on the front page of *Le Monde*, February 1999, against *"l'effacement des sexes."*

La féminisation des noms de métier, un crime de lèse-masculin

Benoîte Groult

Les Français ont généralement tendance à penser que leur langue, mise en forme par Vaugelas dès 1647, puis constamment rectifiée par des grammairiens successifs et rappelée à l'ordre par cette gardienne du beau langage qu'est l'Académie Française, constitue un trésor à protéger. Or, la sociolinguistique l'a démontré, le langage n'est pas seulement un outil, un moyen de communiquer. Le vocabulaire n'est pas neutre. Il est le miroir d'une société dont il reflète les préjugés, les tabous, les fantasmes et il a pour fonction de perpétuer ses structures et ses hiérarchies. Le langage est un pouvoir.

Il ne faut donc pas s'étonner de retrouver dans le vocabulaire ce subtil réseau de discriminations qui tend à l'effacement ou à la marginalisation des femmes, tout comme les discriminations dans les lois ont tendu à faire d'elles des citoyennes de seconde zone. Le patriarcat qui s'exerçait dans nos structures sociales s'est exercé également ment dans nos manières de parler.

Certains prétendent que cet aspect particulier de l'oppression des femmes est secondaire et sans importance. Mais c'est oublier le rôle fondamental d'une langue pour la formation d'une identité, qu'elle soit nationale, culturelle ou sexuelle. Comment les femmes parlent, comment on leur parle, comment on parle d'elles, tout cela est déterminant pour l'image qu'elles auront dans la société et plus encore pour l'image qu'elles se feront d'elles-mêmes.

Cette discrimination langagière n'est d'ailleurs pas un phénomène nouveau. Déjà au Ve siècle avant J.C. Hérodote signalait que dans nombre de pays d'Afrique et d'Orient qu'il avait visités, il existait des parlers distincts pour les hommes et pour les femmes, que ce soit dans la phonologie, la syntaxe ou le vocabulaire. Avec les siècles et quels que soient les régimes, (toujours exclusivement masculins), la situation n'a guère évolué. Au XVIIe par exemple, on se souvient de l'ironie dont Molière accabla les *Femmes Savantes* et les *Précieuses Ridicules*, dont le crime était - déjà! - de vouloir accéder au même langage que les hommes. Longtemps une femme érudite a été considérée comme un "bas-bleu", terme qui n'a pas d'équivalent masculin, alors qu'un homme érudit était un "honnête homme", terme qui n'a pas de féminin! (La formule "une honnête femme" ne se référant qu'à ses mœurs). De même un homme cultivé est un savant respecté alors qu'une femme instruite n'est "qu'une guenon qui cherche à imiter son maître". (Proudhon). C'est par le langage aussi qu'on remet une femme à sa place.

Nous devrions d'ailleurs éprouver quelque reconnaissance pour les précieuses, car elles ont représenté la première tentative faite par des femmes pour prendre la parole et s'approprier le beau langage. Tentative sévèrement réprimée par la suite grâce à des méthodes implacables: le refus de toute instruction constitua le principe de base de l'éducation des filles jusqu'à la fin du XIXe. Pendant la Révolution française un député, Sylvain Maréchal, déposa même un projet "portant interdiction d'apprendre à lire aux femmes".

Pourtant la féminisation des noms de métiers n'avait jamais posé problème. Si peu de femmes avaient exercé des fonctions dans le passé! Au Moyen Age par exemple, on féminisait sans états d'âme. On disait une tisserande, une venderesse, (mot qui est toujours en usage dans le langage juridique), ou une tapissière. Même l'Eglise féminisait: diaconesse, prieure, supérieure, abbesse, etc.

C'est au XXe siècle qu'est apparu le blocage, quand l'accession de femmes de plus en plus nombreuses dans des métiers jusque là réservés aux hommes commença à menacer le monopole masculin. Il fallut réagir par tous les moyens: interdiction aux jeunes filles d'entrer dans les Grandes Ecoles, d'exercer une profession libérale; refus (jusqu'en 1945!) du droit de voter et de celui d'être élue etc. Et, conséquence logique, refus de les faire apparaître dans le langage. Si elles s'obstinaient à "envahir" les métiers masculins, elles seraient contraintes de renoncer au féminin!

Qu'il s'agisse d'une question de pouvoir ne fait aucun doute puisque l'acceptation de formes féminines devient inversement proportionnelle au prestige de la profession! Les exemples sont éloquents: pour les standardistes, informaticiennes et autres opératrices, le féminin s'appliquerait selon les règles habituelles sans émouvoir, même l'Académie.

En revanche, dès qu'il s'agit de professions haut de gamme, ajouter un e muet au masculin, changer le suffixe -teur en -trice, ou utiliser un déterminant féminin tel que *la* ou *une*, (ex: *la* ministre, *une* députée) apparaît comme un crime de lèse-masculin! Un abus de pouvoir qu'on a imputé aux féministes alors qu'il s'agit tout simplement d'appliquer une règle de grammaire élémentaire: "Le nom change généralement de forme selon son genre, masculin pour les êtres mâles, féminin pour les êtres femelles. Le nom en Français a perdu le genre neutre si fréquent en Latin" (Grammaire Hamon). On a presque honte d'avoir à rappeler cette évidence!

Les obstacles se situent d'ailleurs rarement dans les mots, ils sont dans les têtes comme le démontrent quelques exemples aberrants: si vous êtes centenaire, vous avez droit au mot *doyenne*. Mais si vous entrez à l'université, vous serez Madame *le doyen*.

Si vous êtes au service d'un patron, vous êtes *la secrétaire*. Mais en entrant au gouvernement, vous deviendrez *Madame le secrétaire d'état*.

Vous pouvez vous dire *directrice*, si c'est d'une école maternelle. Mais à la Recherche Scientifique, on vous appellera *Madame le directeur*.

Et que dire de tous ces noms de métiers qui se terminent par un e muet et pourraient donc être épicènes[i], comme ministre, juge, peintre, poète? Au nom de quoi refuser de les faire précéder d'un déterminant féminin, alors que nombre de mots se terminant également par un e muet s'emploient sans problème aux deux genres: photographe, concierge, téléphoniste et bien d'autres. Mais encore une fois, ces métiers-là ne portent pas ombrage aux hommes. On en revient toujours à cette question de prestige...

Cette résistance à l'évolution normale de la langue est d'autant plus inacceptable que *tous* les grammairiens sans exception sont d'accord pour condamner "l'affreux *Mme le* qui gâte tant de nos textes". C'est ce qu'écrivait Ferdinand Brunot, déjà en 1922. Et un autre éminent linguiste affirmait dans le *Guide du bon usage* en 1955: "Quand on aura persuadé les femmes que le féminin n'est pas une déchéance, au contraire, le terrain sera libéré d'une lourde hypothèque... La femme qui préfère pour le nom de sa profession le masculin au féminin accuse par là même un complexe d'infériorité qui trahit ses revendications légitimes. Dérober son sexe derrière le genre adverse, c'est le trahir. Dire *Mme le directeur, Mme le docteur*, c'est proclamer la supériorité du mâle dont le genre masculin est l'expression grammaticale".

Damourette et Pichon, auteurs de l'essai *Des mots à la pensée*, allaient plus loin encore: "La facilité du français à former des féminins différenciés devrait détourner les femmes adoptant des professions jusque là masculines de ridiculiser leurs efforts méritoires par des dénominations masculines écœurantes et grotesques, attentatoires au génie de la langue".

Enfin Robert Le Bidois, autorité en matière de langage, approuvait la féminisation, optant pour les féminins en -eure, comme au Québec, (proviseure, docteure, ingénieure) pour mieux inciter les usagers à utiliser le déterminant féminin.

La situation restant bloquée malgré tout, Yvette Roudy, la ministre des Droits de la Femme dans le gouvernement socialiste de 1981, sous la présidence de François Mitterrand, décida de créer une "Commission de Terminologie pour la féminisation des noms de métiers, de grades et de fonctions" afin de proposer des formes acceptables par le maximum d'usagers. Dans les années 80 s'étaient créées de nombreuses commissions de terminologie chargées d'adapter le vocabulaire aux réalités nouvelles dans les domaines médicaux, scientifiques, techniques etc. C'est ainsi que furent forgés des mots comme stimulateur cardiaque pour remplacer pacemaker, logiciel et ordinateur pour computer, hardware et software, et bien d'autres néologismes. Il fallait lutter contre l'invasion des termes américains qui paraissent souvent plus prestigieux que leurs homologues français. Nombre de ces mots, proposés par des spécialistes de chaque discipline sont aujourd'hui entrés dans l'usage. Mais à côté d'une aliénation par le snobisme, il existe également une aliénation par le sexisme, les termes masculins paraissant plus honorifiques que leurs homologues féminins. C'est d'ailleurs sous le prétexte de ne pas dévaloriser la profession qu'elles exercent que les femmes refusent de la féminiser. Elles se croient plus respectables en avocats qu'en avocates et plus prestigieuses en se désignant comme Mme *le* docteur. Une réaction désolante car elle montre à quel point les femmes ont intériorisé la dévalorisation du féminin.

Désolante aussi l'attitude de notre Académie Française, dont l'action en faveur du féminin s'est bornée, rappelons-le, à refuser depuis 1634, date de sa création, de recevoir une femme sous la Coupole. Et quand enfin en 1980 ils ont élu Marguerite Yourcenar, les 39 académiciens l'ont accueillie par un barbarisme; "Madame l'Académicien!" Lors de sa mort, quelques années plus tard, le communiqué à la presse signalait "le décès de notre cher *confrère* Marguerite Yourcenar".

L'anomalie dans le langage souligne bien l'anomalie de la présence d'une femme dans un lieu aussi auguste qu'une académie.[ii] Tout cela fait partie de ce que Luce Irigaray appelait la "stratégie d'effacement du féminin".

Pourtant, depuis peu, on voit craquer la banquise du traditiona-
lisme français: dans le gouvernement de Lionel Jospin formé l'an
dernier, les 5 nouvelles ministres ont annoncé à la presse qu'elles
souhaitaient désormais mettre leur fonction au féminin: Mme *la* ministre, Mme *la* Garde des sceaux, etc...

L'Académie, piquée au vif, adressa alors un message solennel au
président Jacques Chirac, protecteur de la dite Académie, par l'en-
tremise de 3 de ses membres: Maurice Druon, son secrétaire perpé-
tuel, Hélène Carrère d'Encausse, *directeur* en exercice, (sic) et
Hector Bianciotti, chancelier... Les Immortels y affirmaient sans
rire que cette décision irréfléchie mettaient en péril la langue française. Position d'autant plus difficile à défendre pour ceux qui se
veulent les gardiens du purisme que la formule Madame *le* constitue
un contresens grammatical et de plus un témoignage d'élitisme bien
irréfléchi... Les académiciens admettent en effet que des formes féminines "se sont établies dans l'usage pour les métiers de négoce, ex.
boulangère, charcutière, épicière... mais qu'il n'est pas souhaitable
d'en former de nouveaux". Comment avouer plus clairement qu'on
peut tolérer le féminin dans les métiers de service mais pas dans les
hautes sphères?

Le temps est heureusement révolu où l'Académie faisait la loi et
impressionnait les Français. Ils commencent à s'apercevoir qu'ils
sont les derniers des francophones à accepter que leur langue suive
l'évolution de la société! Déjà en février 90 le Conseil de l'Europe
publiait une circulaire sur "L'élimination du sexisme dans le langage", recommandant à tous les Etats membres "d'adapter le vocabulaire à l'autonomie des deux sexes, le principe de base devant être
que les activités de l'un et de l'autre soient visibles au même titre".

Ce n'était pas un brûlot féministe, on ne peut soupçonner le
Conseil de l'Europe d'être un repère de pétroleuses... Mais l'opinion
n'était pas mûre et la presse passa sous silence cette circulaire qui
rappelait une fois de plus "l'interaction entre les mots et les comportements", notant que "l'utilisation du genre masculin pour désigner
les personnes des 2 sexes est génératrice d'incertitudes souvent gê-
nantes".

Suite à la recommandation européenne, la Belgique francophone faisait adopter un décret féminisant les noms de métiers, de grades et de fonctions dans tous les documents administratifs, au motif
que "la langue constituait un instrument de pouvoir sexiste qui em-
pêchait les femmes de s'intégrer normalement dans la société".

Seule la France refusait d'entendre ce langage. Pire, Maurice
Druon, se jugeant seul propriétaire du Français, rappelait vertement

à l'ordre la Communauté Wallonne, déclarant cette décision "aberrante et choquante!"

De son côté, le Grand Conseil suisse, arguant lui aussi que le refus de féminiser "occultait l'existence des femmes qui sont la moitié de l'humanité", décidait de moderniser la rédaction de ses textes officiels.

Enfin, on sait que le Québec, pour qui la sauvegarde de sa langue constitue une preuve de son identité, face au monde anglo-saxon qui l'entoure, a depuis longtemps féminisé l'ensemble des métiers, optant, pour les mots en -eur, (cas difficile car il n'y a pas ici de règle de formation de féminin) pour un ajout d'un e muet. On lit couramment dans la presse, une auteure, une docteure, une professeure, une ingénieure, sur le modèle de prieure. Nous étions tentés par cette solution, ne serait-ce que pour harmoniser l'usage du Français dans les différents pays, mais il fut rappelé à notre Commission en 86 que les mots terminés en -eure s'étaient formés à partir de comparatifs et qu'on ne pouvait ajouter un e muet à des mots comme docteur ou ingénieur qui n'étaient pas des comparatifs! On sait que les grammairiens sont gens tatillons! On ajouta que les Français n'avaient pas à prendre exemple sur leurs cousins paysans du Québec, que leurs origines ne prédisposaient pas à légiférer sur notre belle langue. C'est donc l'usage qui décidera, étant entendu que dans tous les cas ces noms de métiers devront être précédés d'un déterminant au féminin: une professeur ou professeure.

Cependant il se produisait en 96 un fait nouveau et encourageant: l'apparition dans le Larousse d'un certain nombres de métiers au féminin... Le quotidien *Le Monde* a d'ailleurs salué "ces heureuses féminisations qui permettent d'échapper au masculin forcé". On trouve pour la première fois *la juge, la ministre, la sculptrice* et quelques autres. Je signale que *factrice* et *inspectrice* sont dans le *Littré* depuis 1967 et *agricultrice* depuis 82.

Les restrictions dont on assortit l'entrée des femmes juges ou ministres en disent long sur l'épaisseur des préjugés qu'il a fallu vaincre. *Le Larousse* n'avance ici qu'avec des précautions de Sioux. En fin d'article et entre parenthèses, on lit, "ce féminin s'emploie parfois en langue familière", ou bien, "La graphie *députée* serait acceptable". Pour avoir participé pendant 2 ans, en tant que Présidente de la Commission, à des débats entre linguistes, j'imagine aisément les discussions déchirantes qui ont abouti à ces formules prudentes, presque honteuses. Mais l'essentiel est d'être entrées dans le Noble Livre, fût-ce par la petite porte.

Je voudrais pour conclure aborder ce problème de la féminisation qui a fait couler tant d'encre depuis 10 ans, sous un jour différent: celui de la singularité française.

Pourquoi le féminisme français, quand on le compare aux formes qu'il prend sous d'autres cieux, a-t-il cette démarche mesurée, je dirais même timorée, qu'ont déplorée si souvent les féministes anglo-saxonnes?[iii] Pourquoi ne se montre-t-il jamais agressif, combatif et manque-t-il de cette dimension militante qui transforme les récriminations individuelles en lutte positive, débouchant sur des actions solidaires et des progrès tangibles?

Cet effacement, cette soumission des femmes sont une vieille tradition en France. Elle remonte au XVIe siècle, quand Henri IV exhuma la Loi Salique[iv] qui datait de l'an 511 et qui codifiait l'héritage des terres pour en écarter les femmes. Il en fit une loi politique interdisant aux femmes d'hériter du Royaume de France. En conséquence, nous n'avons jamais eu de reines régnantes, mais des épouses royales, régentes pendant la minorité de leur fils, ou bien des favorites et autres courtisanes. En 1789, malgré les 2 seuls députés féministes de la Convention, Condorcet et Goyomar, la Loi Salique fut réactivée par la Révolution française. Et en Mai 1870, Napoléon III la faisait réinscrire dans la Constitution!

Dans la mesure où le Pouvoir relève du Sacré, (la monarchie se transmettait de Droit Divin), il est évident que la Loi Salique fonctionne aujourd'hui encore puisque, malgré la démocratie, les femmes n'ont toujours pas réussi à conquérir des places au plus haut niveau ou à faire pression sur les gouvernements. L'exemple le plus frappant: les Françaises n'ont obtenu le droit de vote qu'en 1945, après les Indiennes ou les Turques, et les avant-dernières d'Europe! Et pour la représentation au Parlement, elles sont également la lanterne rouge: moins de 10%. Seule la Grèce fait plus mal.

Enfin les Françaises ont été handicapées par leur éducation, la "bonne éducation" que l'on donnait aux jeunes filles. Ici les femmes se montrent polies jusqu'au ridicule. Polies en se taisant, en n'insistant jamais. En admettant les grivoiseries et gauloiseries typiquement françaises ou, pire, en feignant de les trouver spirituelles. La grande peur des Françaises: perdre leur séduction, passer pour agressives, c'est-à-dire non féminines. La Parisienne, la séductrice sont un des piliers de l'imaginaire masculin. Contrairement à ce qui se passe aux Etats-Unis, on ne constate pas chez nous cette hostilité de principe à l'égard des hommes. Ils ne sont pas considérés collectivement comme des oppresseurs ni les femmes comme des victimes. Très loin de la codification un peu maniaque des rapports entre les sexes en Amérique, il reste ici une longue tradition du commerce entre hommes et femmes, qui s'est inaugurée au Moyen Age avec l'Amour Courtois. Elle s'est poursuivie au XVIIIe dans les fameux Salons qu'on aurait tort de prendre pour des boudoirs, et où s'est débattue la philosophie des Lumières entre hommes et femmes souvent également cultivés, (Mme de Staël, Mme du Deffand, Melle de Lespinasse, Mme du Chatelet, physicienne et compagne de Voltaire, etc.).

Le résultat est que le fossé ne s'est pas creusé entre les sexes comme aux Etats-Unis mais c'est aussi cette misogynie rampante qui maintient les femmes dans des positions subalternes loin des lieux de pouvoir politique, économique ou religieux.

Où en sommes-nous en 1998? Rappelons que notre Commission de terminologie a conclu ses travaux en 86 par une Ordonnance signée du premier ministre Laurent Fabius et qui a paru au Journal Officiel. Elle établissait que le féminin existe de droit et doit se marquer, sinon par une forme différente du mot, au moins par la présence d'un déterminant féminin. Cette proposition n'a été suivie que par des initiatives courageuses mais individuelles. Se dire écrivaine continue à susciter des sourires apitoyés! Mais la récente décision des femmes ministres, prise au plus haut niveau, est en train de modifier le climat... J'en donnerai pour preuve la circulaire que vient d'adresser Amnesty International à tous ses bureaux à travers le monde, annonçant que la formule Droits de l'Homme serait désormais remplacée par celle moins ambiguë de Droits de la Personne ou Droits Humains, inspirée de Human Rights, le but étant d'éradiquer le sexisme dans le langage et de se conformer à l'Ordonnance française de féminisation.

Il semble donc que l'effort des féministes et de nombre de femmes médecins, pharmaciennes, avocates ou députées, soient en train de porter des fruits.

En France, les femmes ont toutes les audaces quand il s'agit de leur corps. Il y a longtemps qu'elles n'hésitent plus à montrer leurs seins. Pourquoi auraient-elles encore honte de montrer leur féminin?

Notes

i   Mots qui ont la même forme au masculin et au féminin.

ii   Il y a maintenant 3 femmes sur 40 membres.

iii   Lire à ce sujet *Les mots et les femmes*, Essai sur la singularité française de Mona Ozouf, Ed. du Seuil.

iv   Edictée par les Francs Saliens.

W omen in Politics

Madeleine Cottenet-Hage

"La politique est un club où les hommes aiment vivre
entre eux."
Simone Weil quoted in *Cordon*, 190.

"[...]une femme de pouvoir est-elle encore une femme?"
Ségolène Royal, 83.

"L'admission des femmes en politique serait la marque
la plus sûre de la civilisation."
Stendhal quoted by Michèle Barzach, 145.

When, in 1989, Michèle Barzach wrote in *Le paravent des égoïsmes*
that she was "scandalisée par l'absence des femmes dans la vie politique en France," and that "[l]a politique est sans doute le milieu le
plus machiste que l'on puisse imaginer" (144), she was neither the
first nor the last to express what is one of the many regrettable manifestations of the "French exception."[1] Eight years later, Elisabeth
Guigou can still write, in *Etre femme en politique*, "En France les
femmes sont exclues de la vie politique" (33). Indeed, the present
debate (1998) surrounding *la parité* suggests that the position of
French women in politics has not improved much since Françoise
Giroud's *La comédie du pouvoir* and Françoise Gaspard's *Madame
le...*, both published in 1977. In 1993, when women comprised only
5.7% of the elected assemblies, France still ranked... seventy second

in the world, twenty-sixth in Europe and fifteenth in the European Union. True, in 1997, that percentage for the National Assembly rose to 10.9%. With 63 women elected – 42 socialists among them – the number of "*députées*" doubled. Furthermore the inclusion of five women Secretaries or *Ministres*, one Assistant Secretary or *Ministre Déléguée*, and three *Secrétaires d'Etat* in today's cabinet would seem to undercut Barzach and Guigou's assertions.[2] But let us not forget that only 5.6% of senators are women 7.5% mayors, 5.5% "conseillers généraux," and 12.1% "conseillers régionaux." These statistics still place France well below the nearly 20% across the board in European representation by women.

So I turned to an unusual flurry of testimonies recently published by several "femmes *en tête*" in politics [3] for an answer to some of the questions which the statistics beg: why are there not more women in politics? What in their background, education, character, or career choices helped these women "break the glass ceiling" in a field where others fear to tread or fail? And what has their experience been living "en rupture" with current societal norms?

Among abundant material, I chose to look more specifically at six books: five by past or present *Ministres* in French cabinets, Martine Aubry's *Le choix d'agir* (1994), a more dispassionate exposition than a militant exposé; Frédérique Bredin's personal and warm testimony penned during an electoral campaign, *Députée: journal de bord* (1997)[4]; Elisabeth Guigou's controlled yet angry *Etre femme en politique* (1997); Michèle Barzach's outspoken *Le paravent des égoïsmes* (1989); and Ségolène Royal's *La vérité d'une femme* (1996), the most virulent of the five. I decided to also include Nicole Notat's combative, forceful and most enlightening *Je voudrais vous dire* (1997).[5] As head of the large CFDT confederation of unions, Notat is one of the few powerful women in the singularly male world of unions closely linked to political decisions and action. Though passing reference will be made to several of the biographies and studies of women in politics published recently, this analysis – necessarily brief and therefore devoid of nuances – will focus on *direct testimonies*.

By publishing these testimonies, the authors were, presumably, pursuing several goals, some more explicitly then others. Making public their vision of society and political objectives was obviously one of them (certainly in Martine Aubry's *Le choix d'agir*). Exposing the difficulties of women in high-ranking politics was an other objective, usually reflected in the titles' gender marks. At the same time, convincing their readership that women approach power differently, and that a stronger presence of women in government might/would change the way politics is conducted, became an important concern. Finally, by recounting or reframing their own stories, albeit with great restraint, the authors were seeking greater legitimation not only for themselves but for women in politics in general, and hoped to encourage a younger generation follow their steps. Between the covers, stories of exclusionary tactics, and mean fights, the difficult balancing of private and public lives, and of femininity and power tell us that reaching the top still requires unusual talents, determination and moral strength.

Family and Education

Whatever scant information the testimonies provide on family backgrounds, they paint an interesting and mostly congruent picture.[6] Raised in supportive family backgrounds – not necessarily upper class or moneyed – most women grew and developed *with*, not *against*, their immediate environment.[7] They were not rebels[8] but products of liberal-minded families which viewed girls as equal to boys, and encouraged them to pursue their own paths. "…[A]vant d'entrer en politique," writes Guigou, who grew up in Morocco in public and co-ed schools, "je ne me suis jamais sentie brimée en tant que femme" (14). Says Nicole Notat, whose parents lived in a small community in Northern France, "Ni dans mon enfance ni dans mon adolescence, je n'ai eu à déplorer une quelconque incidence de mon sexe sur mon indépendance personnelle" (146). Nothing, then, in the family background prepared these women (Royal excepted) for their future encounters with male sexism in the larger context of society, although Guigou does makes passing remarks on the discrimination other girls were subjected to in Moroccan schools which she attended. For most of them, then, feminist awareness – and militancy – would come later.

In these families, formal education was a firmly held parental belief, and girls were encouraged to excel at school; marriage was not presented as the inevitable future of women.[9] While credit is sometimes explicitly given to strong maternal figures in the family history – as in the case of E. Guigou whose grandmother came to Marrakech at the age of eigtheen to open the first post-office – the role of fathers in creating a space for these young girls to develop their potentials fully and harmoniously is acknowledged more explicitly still (perhaps because most of these mothers, like Barzach's, did not work outside the home and therefore contributed in diffuse ways more to the shaping of their daughters' sense of self than to their career decisions).[10] Sometimes substitute father figures replace what we may conjecture was a missing real father. Thus a twelve-year old Barzach was taught by a fifty-year old doctor whose concern for suffering, joy of life, and sensitivity, in her own words, "fascinated" her. "Je décidai alors de vivre comme lui" (16). She would study medicine, and become a gynecologist.

Several of the authors stress their ties to a rural community, and to a specific region, crediting them with the transmission of values such as work, realism, and empathy for "simple people." Guigou has links with the southeast where her family settled after they left Morocco, Royal with Lorraine, Notat with the northeast. "Je porte en moi l'instinct rural" writes Royal, who would become the representative of a rural western *département*. But even the "Paris-bred" Bredin and Aubry emphasize their links with the provinces: Bredin with Normandy, Aubry with the South-West, perhaps responding to the traditional French myths that invest goodness in "le terroir" and "le peuple."

As we know, in France, access to the upper ranks of government is greatly facilitated for graduates of the *Grande Ecole*, "l' ENA". Though discrimination does make it more difficult for women to pass the entrance examination, and to graduate, as statistics show and Martine Aubry comments,[11] four of these six women, Martine Aubry, Frédérique Bredin, Elisabeth Guigou, and Ségolène Royal graduated from ENA. Michèle Barzach graduated from medical school.[12] Nicole Notat alone, as is generally the case with trade-union leaders, had more modest beginnings as a secondary school teacher.

Parental commitment to and involvement in political causes was rare, with the notable exception of Martine Aubry. So why did these young women choose to go into politics? Or did they *choose* to do so? Certainly the fact that commitment to service in one form or the other was a strong family value, therefore learnt early, explains, at least partly, why, when given a chance to go into Public Service, they were ready. D. Bredin suggests that her catholic school education imprinted a desire in her to serve others.[13] The same is true of Nicole Notat whose desire to effect change was also critical to her choice of involvement in a union. But prestigious as their assignments might have been, Guigou at the Treasury and in the Ministry of Finance, and Aubry in the Ministry of Labor, and Conseil d'Etat, and great as their abilities are, their political careers were helped by their connections as ENA graduates, and then their proximity to the centers of political power. A President's attention seems to have done the rest. Thus, Giscard d'Estaing, and later François Mitterand must both be credited for bringing them to positions in that inner sanctum, the Elysée Palace, where they served in various guises, as aides and counselors. This, incidentally, conforms to a very French pattern for gaining access to power: being part of an elite network, rather than being selected through the democratic process. François Mitterand, however, knowing that their ultimate legitimacy could be secured only through an electoral vote, urged his female aides to seek election as representatives and gave them his full support.[14]

The promotion of women on the part of both presidents was a calculated political move, but probably also reflected a sincere belief in the equality of talents. This very promotion, however, by two notorious womanizers, not unmoved by the feminine charm of a gifted crew, both hurt as well as helped these women (some more than others !). Rumors circulated that some of them enjoyed too close a relationship with the President, but, as a French proverb says, "On ne prête qu'aux riches." The rumors, tactfully denied in Elizabeth Guigou's book, highlight the dangers to women of venturing into the political arena, where exposure is maximum. On the other hand, there is little doubt that their being recognized and appreciated by the two presidents was determining in pushing these women to the forefront and ensuring their successful progression to the top positions, which they might not have been able to achieve on the strength of talents only.[15] (For it is still true that women need to be twice as good as their male colleagues in order to succeed.) The four women ministers in the present Socialist cabinet acknowledge their gratitude to the last Socialist President with an elan that Edith Cresson – the first woman chosen as Prime Minister by Mitterand in May 1991 who exercized her power under the most difficult conditions before being forced to resign ten and a half months later – would likely not share !

Laure Adler, relying on earlier studies, notes that, since the thirties, being appointed to a Cabinet position has, paradoxically, been a woman's surest and easiest path to political power. Customarily, the sexism of the French electorate has been invoked as a reason why access to an elected position was much harder for women. But studies on women in French politics show that sexism exists less in the electorate than in the parties and the Assemblies supposed to represent the views of their constituents.[16] Reading about parliamentary opposition and its delaying tactics in giving women the right to vote in the twenties and thirties is enlightening, though not necessarily surprising. But the testimonies of the late eighties and nineties show, only too clearly, that, until very recently, the obstacles to women's progress in politics were still in place within the parties themselves, whether they be on the left or on the right.[17] Some of the most passionate and acrimonious discussions in these testimonies bear on sexism in political parties. Access for women to the upper ranks of party organizations was hindered deliberately, and women were often confined to menial tasks. Even when women reached the higher ranks, they had great difficulty being selected as candidates to the Assembly and a male candidate was preferred, unless the battle were deemed lost in advance. When victory was considered hopeless, women were sent into the battle, although prognostications were sometimes wrong and the woman won. Once elected, women *députées* were severely punished for not aligning themselves along party lines. Barzach's fall from grace is memorable: she was perceived as too "encombrante" by her RPF colleagues.[18] In this context, it is difficult not to side with those women – and this includes the women discussed here – who believe that government intervention, in the form of a constitutional amendment, is necessary to ensure "*la parité.*" In response to the lack of women candidates and representatives, a 1996 organization of women from the left and the right, Mouvement des Femmes pour la Démocratie, called for women to by-pass the present party structures, "present candidates themselves," "encourage women candidates to come forward," and "support the candidacies of women and men that share their views." Among the women signing the call for action were M. Barzach, F. Bredin, and two of the most visible and active women in politics in the last two decades, Yvette Roudy and Simone Veil.

Women and Power

Women, most authors agree, have a different relationship with power than men do – a different way of *using power*, and of *participating in politics*. Their argument goes as follows: 1) Because of their experience, women are closer to daily realities, and therefore more concerned with and more able to devise and implement concrete actions to improve the lives of both women and men. While it is difficult to manage both private and public lives, the women's involvement with daily realities is therefore seen as a major asset. A corollary, according to Edwige Avice,[19] is the ability of women to synthesize a multiplicity of "odd pieces" and different voices. Avice has this lovely comparison: they are like a music director. 2) Women are less ideological or dogmatic, and more pragmatic in decision-making. 3) Consequently, they *want results* and have little patience with endless and useless committee discussions. Martine Aubry's 1994 title says it clearly: *Le choix d'agir.* That same desire to act, that same positive outlook on the possibilities of change, that same refusal to bow to counterforces of scepticism, passivity, fear, this "frilosité" which has become one of the journalistic *clichés* in France today, makes Nicole Notat's passionate testimony both convincing and uplifting. She entitles her fourth chapter, "Je voudrais vous dire que la résignation n'est plus de saison." 4) Women speak a different language, they "say it as it is," and dislike "*la langue de bois*" used by their male counterparts. 5) Some of the women politicians are of the opinion that they respond more emotionally to the needs of their constituants, which creates better communication with them; arguing, however, – and as they are fully aware – that there is an emotional bond between women representatives and their constituants, risks reinforcing the stereotypical view of women, that women are more influenced by sentiment than by reason. 7) Although women have a different relationship to power, they are not necessarily less ambitious. But they are less enamoured with the image and the trappings associated with power, and more inclined to look upon it as a means to effect changes, not as a gratifying end in itself. Younger women seem to have less difficulty than an older generation of women owning up to their ambition, being less vulnerable to the common view that ambition is not a feminine value.

A survey taken and reported by F. Bredin in 1995 confirms that voters, both men and women (although with slightly different percentages) support the view that political women do exercise power differently than men: they are credited with using a different discourse, thought to be closer, more responsive to daily problems, and believed to be more pragmatic than dogmatic, less vain and less arrogant (Bredin, 108).

Finally, and characteristically, all the authors report having experienced self-doubt when first asked to take on a position with high responsibility. Can I do it, is their immediate response, and they may have to be reassured before they consent.[20] In this, too, they differ from men who, if they are beset by self-doubt, are much less likely to admit it publicly. Rather than view these admissions as a regrettable internalization of a social attitude according to which women are less qualified for high office than men, I would suggest that these indicate instead that women are more honest with themselves, and approach their job with a more realistic and healthy awareness of the difficulty of the tasks to be performed, as well as the sacrifices which will be required.

Private/Public lives

Why are women more concrete, and more interested in action than in prestige? The authors offer the same answer: their private lives act as a safety valve to balance their public lives. The emotional demands and rewards of their families keep them from investing as much in the pursuit of political power. At the same time, they confide how difficult it is to manage both their public and private lives simultaneously. "C'est un fardeau," writes Notat. At the center of their concern are conflicting schedules that are particularly disastrous for women with young children. Barzach and Bredin are most eloquent on this topic. *Le Conseil des Ministres* is scheduled on Wednesdays, when young children are home. Disorganization on the home front may catch you off guard. Other meetings go on well into the night or are scheduled on week-ends. Political campaigns require them to be on the road for weeks. All offer as one of the reasons for the lack of women in the higher political ranks women's reluctance to take time away from their families, and write of their feeling of guilt. "Si généreuse que soit la cause, le soupçon d'égoïsme au détriment des enfants rôde. Les femmes, en politique, s'en veulent un peu" (Bredin, 27). "*Super Woman* n'existe pas et chacune bricole comme elle peut" (*Ibid*).

Some author hint that relationships with partners are problematic particularly when there is status difference, but there is no real discussion of this sensitive issue. "Il arrive, writes Bredin tersely, que le compagnon en prenne ombrage" (26). On the other hand, Guigou gives credit to her husband for his unwavering support.

These testimonies are more open and direct about the risks associated with public exposure: slander, sexist attacks, verbal, graphic and even physical abuse (as in the case of Nicole Notat who was attacked physically in a demonstration in October 1996). One understands why they so strongly feel the necessity to preserve the boundaries between their private and public lives, if only to protect their own families, not always successfully, from the brutality and smouldering violence of the political stage. At the same time, because politics is so dependent upon "images," there is considerable pressure to allow photo opportunities, to give interviews, (cf. Martine Aubry in *Paris-Match*, 12/3/98 or Ségolène Royal, on her maternity bed in the same magazine several years before), and to reveal personal details in the vain hope that they will close the gap between leaders and citizens (Aubry, 62).

"En politique, les femmes sont regardées avant d'être entendues," writes Guigou (190) and she advises women to "remiser la séduction au placard" (*Ibid*). Coming from a woman minister whom a colleague described – admittedly in private ! – as "bandante," the advice is weighty. A variation on the image of the "placard" or closet was recently offered by Françoise de Panafieu in a radio debate on women and politics, when she said that these women must leave "une moitié d'elles au portemanteau."[21] Memories of Edith Cresson drawing lewd and crude comments from some men on the benches of the Assembly the day she delivered a speech in a tight dress are still rankling. In France, where, in the words of Kathryn Hall-Jamieson, "wombs [and] brains" are not necessarily viewed as an oxymoron, women in public roles, whether they be plain or good-looking, still run the risk of unleashing repressed sexual male fantasies, as many of the anecdotes illustrate, to one's ceaseless amazement. How to hold on to one's feminine identity, "être femme/en politique," including being free to choose the external signs of femininity, is one of the two questions encoded in Guigou's title, and one she devotes several pages to (while the other question addresses the difficulties of woman as a social role, or how can one "être/femme en politique").

The potential abuse to which these women may be exposed is undoubtedly one of the reasons why they insist so firmly on the right to their privacy, as a refuge from a stressful life in a conflict-driven, male-dominated space where appearances and power games too often matter more than substance and results. There they can plunge themselves once more into daily chores (!) and be reminded of the simple, pleasant, or harsh reality of "normal" people's lives.

Is it easy? After reading these testimonies, we know it is certainly not. Is it exciting to be in public life? Yes, says Ségolène Royal, and one has the impression that the others agree. Most of all, they welcome the chance they are given to test, through action, their own visions of a better society. So let me speak very briefly to the issue of a woman's political vision.

When Women Dream of a Republican Society

Brief I will be, indeed, by singling out two of the most recurrent and salient concerns which underlie all the other, specific recommendations these women make for shaping or re-directing, our society. Of the three words that compose the French republican motto, the six women authors would likely give their preference and attention to *justice* and brotherhood, amending this loaded term into the neologistic *humanhood*.

Though their training (often in economics and finance) and their careers contradict, or at least subvert, the traditional notion that women are by nature caretakers and social workers, it is nonetheless striking that, among the dominant values that inform their visions for the nation, concern for the disenfranchised, the needy, and the excluded ranks first. All could subscribe to Michèle Barzach's political agenda, the backbone of her 1989 publication, which systematically examines issues of health, hospital management and care, drug addiction, delinquency, crime and punishment, the rights of children, and the aged, and changes in the family structures. Two words best qualify her social program: "respect" and "dignity" of the individual. Not surprisingly, her plea for equitable treatment of women – and children – is one of the five points she lists as a reason to be in politics. Perhaps more unexpectedly, her positive analyses of today's societal changes constitute a refreshing rejection of the stereotypical (in France) discourses of gloom and doom. Her message is that we can do something to ensure a more just and caring future. Would she be saying the same now that she has been compelled to return to private practice? We may wonder.

At the same time, Barzach's passionate call for an end to policies which, based upon national and international selfish interests, contribute to the widening gap between the rich and the poor affirms not only the preeminence of humanitarian over economic and industrial concerns, or, as Aubry writes in her chapter, "Avoir plus ou vivre mieux," the quality of life over the quantity, but also the necessity of politics of *solidarity*. Solidarity, for these women in leadership positions, is not only a goal for society; it is a privileged mode of conduct in politics. All the authors stress the importance and necessity of relating, listening to others, consulting, working with and within the community for communal well-being, entering into *relationships* with all social partners in society, irrespective of their colors, political or ethnic. For Nicole Notat, power is enjoyable not only because she likes overcoming obstacles, and finding solutions, but, and as importantly, because it gives her a chance to meet and understand *the Other*.

A related notion attached to solidarity is that of *service*, which takes us back to the reasons mentioned earlier why these women went into politics in the first place. A documentary film on today's French political women – of whom several are included here – which aired on television in December 1998, confirms the importance they all attach to the notion of *service* as a goal for their action. Once again, such emphasis on *consultation, attention and inter-action, and service* may be looked upon with some suspicion, because it sounds so much like what women are traditionally socialized to do, and perceived as doing best.[22]   But one of the differences is the much larger scope of these women's programs. It may be that, as

Evelyne Sullerot's once claimed, women focus on individual events and stories to draw energy and motivation to act. This is certainly made very clear in F. Bredin's journal. But contrary to what Sullerot also believed, these women are investing this energy into serving *collective well-being*, not just individual lives. And "collective" here extends well beyond national boundaries, to embrace the globe.

I know, we are back to where we started: women's socialization. But if this socialization means that women's presence in politics benefits both men and women, and directs our society towards "humanhood," then we have answered Guigou's question: "Les femmes changeront-elles la politique?"

Conclusion

A reader of these testimonies is likely to conclude that, despite their small numbers, these women have already left an imprint on the political scene. Certainly, if we add the records of Simone Veil and Yvette Roudy, to name only two of the most effective women politicians in the two previous decades, then the evidence is strong on the social advances implemented because of their actions. The question is, how long are women condemned to remain an exception in politics? In 1995 Yvette Roudy, in her book, *Mais de quoi ont-ils peur?*, invited women to come down into the ring. "Allez les femmes ! On vous attend," clamored this former Ministre, – now to be "declined" in the feminine – who, as the present mayor of Lisieux, has helped more women occupy public positions than any other leader in the nation (for Roudy has always put her actions where her mouth is). So let us not be hood-winked by pessimist pronouncements,[23] but rather be encouraged by evidence that more women are interested in working for change, whether at the local or national level. In the recent debate on *"parité"* already mentioned, F. De Panafieu commented that women's representation in *"la vie associative,"* which covers associations of various kinds, political, cultural or service-oriented, has increased nationally and is now strong. Hopefully, these associations will supply a larger pool of women for our future democratic institutions. Bredin's account of her own election campaign, and of her years as mayor of Fécamp (Normandy), already sketched the image of an involved, devoted "équipe des filles," as she called them, on the local political scene.

Finally, one of the most encouraging signs of change in France in 1998 may have been the active and very visible role young girls played during the October 1998 strikes of "lycées." These girls on television, in the newspapers, in radio broadcasts, stood up as mouthpieces for other *lycéens*; *they* were the ones who attempted to organize the spontaneous movements into orderly and focused demonstrations, and to keep away those intent on disturbing the orderly process. They handled themselves with poise, spoke with assurance and clarity. Most remarkable still, was the number of "beur" women among the female leaders. All this speaks for a better future for women in politics. Young men stand up and take notice. Here they come.

Notes

1. Michèle Barzach was the Minister of Health and Family in the cabinet of Jacques Chirac (1986) during the "cohabitation" period. Her independence of mind, and her refusal to follow party lines, made her one of the scapegoats of the RPR. At the time her book was published, she was still in politics, and her worst moments were still to come, which left her very bitter. Cf. Laure Adler, *Les femmes politiques*, 202–204.
2. Here are the women in the 1998 cabinet listed according to the official protocole: Martine Aubry, Ministre de l'Emploi et de la Solidarité is number 2, after Lionel Jospin, Elisabeth Guigou, Minsitre de la Justice and Garde des Sceaux, Nicole Perry, Secrétaire d'Etat aux droits des femmes et à la formation professionnelle, Ségolène Royal, Ministre déléguée, chargée de l'enseignement scolaire, Marylise Lebranchu, Secrétaire d'Etat chargé des PME, du Commerce et de l'Artisanat, Michelle Demessine, Secrétaire d'Etat chargé du Tourisme, Catherine Trautmann, Ministre de la Culture et de la Communication, Dominique Voynet, Ministre de l'Aménagement du Territoire et Marie-George Buffet, Ministre de la Jeunesse et des Sports.
3. Cf. Françoise Barret-Ducrocq and Evelyne Pisier's book, *Femmes en tête*, Flammarion, 1997. I am using the term "testimonies" for lack of a better term, since all of them mix personal and political reflexions in various dosages. Aubry's *Le choix d'agir*, for instance, reads more like a political treatise, while Bredin's presents itself as a journal.
4. F. Bredin is the representative for Seine-Maritime.
5. Written with the editorial help of Hervé Hamon.
6. Ségolène Royal's background was totally different.
7. Interestingly, three of them grew up outside France, Guigou and Barzach in Morocco and Royal in Dakar then in Martinique. It is tempting to speculate that there is a positive corrolation between belief in action and change and the fact of having once been outsiders and looked at this society with more "distance." The case of Norwegian-born Eva Joly in justice would be another case in point.
8. This was not the case for Edith Cresson, whose political drive, according to her biographer, E. Schemla (*La femme piégée*), seems to have been nourished by resentment against her upper-classbackground.
9. Biographies of political women confirm that emphasis was placed on education in families of future female political figureheads. Cf. for instance Murielle Szac's *Dominique Voynet, une vraie nature* (Plon, 1998).
10. The role of a strong maternal figure is paramount in Dominique Voynet's case.
11. Cf. *Femmes en tête*, p. 364.
12. So did Dominique Voynet. Interestingly, the traditional American career path to a political appointment, the law, does not apply in France, especially not in the case of women.
13. Dominique Voynet's biographer, too, stresses the importance of a Catholic tradition of service in the Voynet family. In addition, the parents were committed union members.
14. Aubry is representative for a district in Nord, Guigou in Vaucluse, and Royal in Deux-Sèvres.
15. One might object that the same is true of men. In the corridors of power, connections, and being recognized by those in power are essential. But there is a difference between "cronyism," or networking, and more or less subtle sexual politics at that level. While

it is true, however, that institutional sexism has thwarted many women's political career, it is also true that paradoxically it may have served others in previous decades, when fewer were available. "Il fallait trouver des femmes, alors on en a pris une là où elle était," said Simone Veil about her beginnings in governement (Sarazin, 108).

16. This is confirmed by Anne-Marie Couderc, *Ministre déléguée à l'emploi* in 1996: "le blocage se situe davantage dans les structures politiques que dans l'opinion publique."

17. Many women – and some men – have been pushing for an amendment to Article Four of the Constitution that would "favoriser l'égal accès des femmes et des hommes aux mandats et aux fonctions" (text of the latest version). Whether the debates about "parité" indicate a fundamental change in "mentalité," and not simply an opportunistic strategy forced upon the party leaders, is debatable. At this date (January 1999), the National Assembly has voted in favor of the amendment, while the Senate is using delaying tactics to prevent its becoming a law, and is denouncing "une politique des quotas." They argue that this is an internal party matter, not a national one. Interestingly, the rightwing senators are drawing ammunitions from Elizabeth Badinter's opposition to what she calls a "texte de régression" that goes against republican equality.

18. Cf. Françoise de Panafieu's comment that, "D'autres ont trahi Chirac, mais avec elle [Barzach], ils se sont permis de tirer à vue. Parce que c'était une femme..." (Barret-Ducrocq, 361).

19. Quoted by Cordon, 153. She was a former Minister under Mitterand.

20. Edith Cresson and Dominique Voynet's biographers recount similar moments of uncertainty. Cf. Also F. Giroud's 1977 *La comédie du pouvoir.*

21. France-Inter, 12/08/98.

22. Of course, we hear men politicians use similar language but the focus of their action could be subsumed under different terms: efficiency, economic development, international power, even when they agree – as the Left does – that a more just society is their goal.

23. Cf. Josyane Savigneau who, in a recent, more emotional than tightly reasoned article "La grande dérive des femmes" (*Le Monde*, 12/08/98) argues, after Susan Faludi, that a backlash has hit France. Or Christine Delphy, editor of *Nouvelles Questions Féministes*, who shares the same pessimistic view of the nineties in France (cf. *Le Monde*, 01/19/98).

Women and Popular Genres in France (1980s-1990s)

Brigitte Rollet

In September 1977, the weekly *Le Film Français* devoted a special mini-dossier to women filmmakers in France. Although Claude Gautheur, the author of the article, expressed his satisfaction that between 1973 and 1976, around 15 female directors had made their first films, he also conceded that there should be even more, writing "c'est peu. C'est insuffisant. Et scandaleusement." Apart from the feminist publications of the time, the interest from mainstream and specialized media for Alice Guy's successors was reserved to say the least. More than twenty years later, there would probably be not enough pages in the same journal to write a report about a similar topic. Moreover, the success of the films made by French women is now expanding beyond France and Europe: according to film specialist Anne Gillain (1995), the *New York Times* published in April 1995 an article devoted to French films made by women and their contribution to the renewal of French cinema. She also mentioned the recent interest shown by American film producing companies in buying these films for an American audience. Even if box office receipts as such are not valid criteria for judging the quality of a film, it is however worth noting that most women filmmakers have now succeeded in escaping the "ghetto" of limited audiences. Encouraged by the recent success of some women's films, such as *Y aura-t-il de la neige à Noël?* made by the unknown young film neophyte Sandrine Veysset in 1996, some producers seem to be more willing to back up film projects by women. Similarly, more and more women's applications for the coveted *avance sur recettes* (advances on benefits) are successful.

When considering what preceded this and the recent release of successful and innovative films made by French female directors over the past five years, it would be easier to gain a wrong impression of women and film making in France. The current situation of women filmmakers in France, however exceptional and unique it could be[1], and especially when compared with other Western countries, is slightly misleading and often paradoxical when examined in detail. It is true that since the mid-1990s, there has been a regular flow of young female directors (most of whom were born in the late 1950s early 1960s), with a similar educational background (the majority graduated from the FEMIS[2]), whose films (and more especially their first long length feature film) brings a much needed originality and sometimes impertinence to a rather repetitive and often uncreative French cinema. Far from making films within the unofficial boundaries traditionally erected to contain women's contribution to artistic creations, the new and older generations seem to claim back their share in the "gender-related" distribution of cinematographic genres. After Tonie Marshall's "thriller" *Pas très catholique* (1994) and Marion Vernoux's road movie *Personne ne m'aime* made the same year, some film directors have now started making "heritage" or historical films,[3] alongside "mafioso thriller"[4] and comedy,[5] proving that there are now no genres closed to woman directors. Moreover, most of the directors opting for traditionally "male" cinematographic genres, have succeeded in renewing them, if only by rewriting their unwritten rules and by successfully breaking the boundaries between one genre and the other, offering hybrid creations which escape all attempts at classifying them. Whatever film they make, they attract attention many of their predecessors longed for. Their "visibility" is today much more obvious than a few decades ago when years would pass without the release of a single film made by a woman.

Although it is always difficult to assess the direct impact of one career over the other, it is however true to say that the success of some of their elders such as Coline Serreau, Diane Kurys and Josiane Balasko from the mid and late-1970s onwards, contributed greatly to the visibility of films made by women on the one hand, and to the reappropriation by women directors of popular genres on the other. By challenging the notion of what films made by women could be, these directors indirectly showed a way more and more of their successors are now willing to follow.

The 1970s represents a key moment in women's contemporary history. As far as French cinema is concerned, the decade after May 68' saw the arrival of more women filmmakers than in the fifty years which followed the invention of cinema.[6] The situation was not much better in the 1950s and 1960s. While the New Wave was hailed among other things for allowing the discovery of new – male – film directors (more than a hundred new directors made a film in five years),[7] not a single woman started a career as a filmmaker at the time (Varda is not really an exception since her first film had been released in 1954). According to both Paul Lejeune's (1986) and Annie Blondel's research (1981), there were around sixty women filmmakers during the 1947–1980 period. From the long list of directors who made their first – and, for some, only – film in the 1970s, most have fallen into oblivion, if only because their names are regularly absent from film encyclopaedias.[8] A handful, however, are now well-known in France as well as abroad. Coline Serreau, Diane Kurys and Josiane Balasko are the most successful trio of contemporary film makers, and their success is due to various reasons. Although their films are all different in form and in tone, their authors have a lot in common. The three directors are baby boomers (all were born in the late 1940s)[9] whose career started around the same time (mid or late 1970s). They all started their artistic career as theatre and film and television actresses. They all contributed to the *café-théâtre* creations and shows, sometimes playing with the same stand-up comedians, like Serreau and Balasko making their theatrical debuts with the radical stand-up comedian Coluche in the early 1970s, or on the same stage of one of the most popular *café-théâtres* of the time, the *Café de la Gare*, although not at the same time[10]. Like many of their contemporaries, they were soon disappointed with the limited range of roles offered to actresses and moved on the other side of the camera. Both Serreau and Balasko had previously written the screenplay of a film they did not direct but in which they played the main part.[11] Their early career was in one way or the other directly linked to some major changes in French culture and society as well as in women's lives.

While Kurys's first autobiographical films were seen as typical *films de femmes* (films made by women), a label she, and others like Serreau were quick to reject, the two other directors opted for what was then very much considered as a male-dominated genre. Autobiographical texts which concentrate on family matters, domestic problems and close relationships have long been associated with the "feminine," while texts such as the memoirs and other subjective accounts by historical figures of matters of national and international width are often seen as on the masculine side.[12] Kurys's trilogy, started in 1977 with *Diabolo menthe/Peppermint Soda* and which includes *Cocktail Molotov* (1980) and *Coup de foudre* (1983) does not escape the unwritten rules of woman film making in the 1970s that on the one hand, the first film made by a woman is always autobiographical and on the other that these autobiographical films offer the rare perspective of one or more female protagonists.[13] Like so many of her contemporaries, Kurys did put in practice the feminist statement according to which "the personal is political." Indeed, her own history which is at the core of her first films from *Diabolo menthe* to *La Baule les Pins* (*C'est la vie*) included (1990), goes beyond the strict boundaries of personal recollections and gives her female audience a reflection of their own experience of growing up as a woman in post war France. Unlike Serreau and Balasko who do not necessarily chose a female perspective in their films, Kurys' early films are woman-centered narratives where the female gaze predominates. Although as stressed by Carrie Tarr, there is an "ambivalence in the way gender and sexuality are constructed" in Kurys' films (1999: 148), her earlier films gave her female audience insights of the lives of little girls, young and mature women and filmic representations of many dilemmas women face at all age, which were rarely shown in French cinema before. The various portrayals of mother-daughter relationships, the depictions of sisterhood and female friendship Kurys offered in her earlier films, also hits home and contributed to their success with female audiences.

Although Serreau's first film followed another path, it could also be seen as complying with another "rule" regarding women's choice of genres. Documentaries were a recurrent choice of women filmmakers in the 1970s for economic as well as for ideological reasons. Serreau's *Mais qu'est-ce qu'elles veulent?* (1975–1977) was a major contribution to the feminist movements of the time, although Serreau had no direct links with them.[14] From her first fiction film *Pourquoi pas* ! (1978) onwards, Serreau opted for a genre few before her had chosen. Despite Alice Guy's (1873–1968) early contributions to what was – and still is – the most popular cinematographic genre in France, her successors were rare in making comedies. Nelly Kaplan's anarchical comedy *La fiancée du pirate* made in 1968 with Bernadette Laffont as the female protagonist, did not attract many followers. For reasons that recent research has made obvious,[15] women filmmakers and audiences alike were not necessarily at ease with such a woman-unfriendly genre. Serreau's reappropriation of the genre in her very personal way allowed a renewal of a genre which had not changed much since the end of the silent era (despite

Jacques Tati's and Pierre Etaix's innovative attempts in the 1950s and 1960s).

Serreau made what could be defined as philosophical comedies which were always (and in her view still are) a vehicle to express her views on several issues, many of which are class, "race" and gender related. A strong believer in feminism and Marxism which are in her view "des instruments de lutte et de travail qui ont tous remis en question et dont on ne peut se passer" (1978: 29), Serreau has also followed the tradition initiated by 18th-century writers whose aims in their writing were both to entertain and enlighten their readers. Her use of humour is often reminiscent of Voltaire's and Montesquieu's who under the pretense of light tales gave much food for thought to their readers regarding social, political and religious issues of their time. Serreau's social comedies go well beyond the mere entertaining function aimed at by her predecessors and they often suggest alternatives to dominant thoughts and beliefs. Far from indulging in the caricature-like mode of earlier French comedies regarding gender issues, her films use humour as both a catalyst and a trigger. After the utopian *Pourquoi pas* ! (which is seen by some critics as the indirect "model" of Balasko's *Gazon maudit*), and the "revolutionary" *Qu'est-ce qu'on attend pour être heureux*? (1982), Serreau's films continued to witness the changes in French society and culture. Although perhaps less "committed" than her first films, her following films continue to express her beliefs. Her biggest success so far, *Trois hommes et un couffin* (1985) attracted more than 12 million viewers and gave the director the third place on the list of the most successful films since the beginning of the Fifth Republic (1958).[16] Serreau is also the only woman in the top 20 names of the same list, proving, if proof is needed, that major commercial success is still uncommon for films made by women. The general reluctance of most women directors to be seen as making "commercial" cinema has a lot to do with the unofficial hierarchy put in place since the New Wave between *auteur* and non *auteur* (i.e.commercial films). Although, as shown by Geneviève Sellier (1997), the *auteur* in question is undoubtedly male, it is very common to use the word as "gender-neutral," an option often chosen by female directors themselves.[17] Serreau's career shows an interesting blurring of the boundaries since her definitely auteur films were also commercially successful. Let's remember here that the auteur-weighting of a film seems to be in France in inverse proportion with the popular success it attracts. Interestingly, the so-called universalism extremely vivid in France since the French revolution not only influences women's own conception of their art but also the way their films are received.

What was at stake was Serreau's success, whatever one thinks of the film itself.[18] More important it seems was the fact that for the first time, a woman succeeded in a male genre.

The second woman's name on the list mentioned above is Josiane Balasko's whose successful *Gazon maudit/French Twist* (1995) was the second most successful films of the year. It was Balasko's fourth film since she started directing ten years earlier and the first to be released outside France. Unlike Serreau and Kurys who struggled to finance their first films, Balasko's debut as a director was influenced by the success of the screen adaptation of the plays initially written and performed by the *Théâtre du Splendid*, a theatre band she helped to create in the 1970s. Balasko's cultural and artistic inheritance comes directly from the *café-théâtres* which flourished in France – and more especially in Paris – in the 1970s. These places allowed the emergence of female stand-up comedians writing and performing their one-woman show, a premiere in France, even if the cabarets of the late 19th century welcomed female performers (such as Thérésa and Yvette Printemps) who would be described today as unruly and carnivalesque women.[19] Many comic actors and some actresses come from the Splendid.[20] The success on stage of their first hit, *Le Père Noël est une ordure* in the late 1970s, led to a film version with the comedians playing their stage role (1982). Almost unknown abroad, the film soon becomes a *film-culte* in France in the 1980s. The success of the film led many to believe in a renewal of the French comedy, which is in a sense true. The strong disrespect for institutions as a whole partly generated by May' 68, the satirical and cruel mood of the Splendid brought a much needed renewal of a genre which had been endlessly repeating the same formula during the previous decades. The interest in the *café-théâtres* contributed to the financing of films made by or with comedians from the Splendid, whose popularity (both as individuals and as a group) since *Le Père Noël est une ordure* was growing. Michel Blanc had no problem finding a producer for his first film *Marche à l'ombre* in 1984. Similarly, Balasko could finance her film *Sacs de noeuds* in 1985 with Isabelle Huppert and herself in the leading roles.

Although Serreau's comedies borrow from, among other sources, some aspects of the café-théâtre tradition, her comedies have little in common with Balasko's. Far from the relatively "contained disorder" of Serreau's films, Balasko opts for excess, a tendency she shares with her former fellow comedians from the Splendid. A rare example of female unruliness in a French context, Balasko could be seen as a French version of Britain's Jo Brand and/or America's Roseanne, breaking taboos and endlessly pushing the boundaries of taste. A carnivalesque woman *par excellence*, she follows the parodic and satirical tradition of French *café-théâtre*, using the self-derision typical of one-woman shows to denounce a wide range of issues from racism to sexism, homophobia and prostitution. Her strong sense of irony led her to move from one parody of a genre to the next. After the police story (*Les Keufs* made in 1988 where she plays a policewoman going under cover as a prostitute to dismantle a prostitution ring), and the fantasy/gothic narrative (*Ma vie est un enfer* made in 1991 where the boring life of the character she performs is changed with the unexpected arrival of the devil himself played by Daniel Auteuil), Balasko opted for the French tradition of the farce which she radically transformed. Her continuous sense of transgression as a director and an actress led her to create and perform the third role in the classic love triangle, thereby representing probably the only cuckold in the history of French cinema whose rival is a woman. Despite the important arrival of female comic stand-up in French cinema on both side of the camera[21] and on stage, she occupies a unique position within French cinema, both as a comic actress and a film director.

Beyond their individual successes, Serreau, Kurys and Balasko have shown how to rewrite genres and to make them a valid and efficient vehicle for wider issues. The new generation exploits the genre with various aims: from the bittersweet comedies of Laurence Ferreira-Barbosa dealing with mental breakdown (*Les gens normaux n'ont rien d'exceptionnel*, or Aids (*J'ai horreur de l'amour*, 1997), to Tonie Marshall's exploration of family troubles (*Enfants de salaud*), or more recently women's relationship with their body in *Vénus Beauté Institut*, their films not only add another meaning to the already polysemic "comedy" but they also prove their authors' skills in creating laughter. Moreover, some directors tend to develop a different approach to film making, creating a female solidarity between filmmakers and actresses and/or between filmmakers themselves, therefore indirectly suggesting a "third way" in film making. Sandrine Bonnaire accepted to be paid only with the percentage of the film's benefits in Patricia Mazuy's *Peaux de vaches* (1989) following the director's problem in financing her project. This led to a critic talking of the film as a "film de copines," an expression which could be easily applied to other films since. It is indeed not rare to see filmmakers appearing in each other films in roles which go far beyond the cameo appearance: Dominique Cabrera rather ironically plays the minor role of a psychoanalyst in Judith Cahen's *La révolution sexuelle n'a pas eu lieu* (1999), a film whose concern between political and sentimental commitment, and between the personal and the political echoes some of Cabrera's films. Similarly, Claire Denis[22] and Brigitte Roüan appear in Tonie Marshall's *Vénus Beauté Institut* (1999) while Catherine Corsini thanks Laurence Fereira-Barbosa in the credits of her latest comedy *La nouvelle Eve* (1999). At a time where parity in politics is very much talked about by female politicians who opt for what could be read as a form of female solidarity going beyond the strict boundaries of their political parties, it is interesting to notice another form of cooperation, albeit minimal, between women in French cinema.[23]

Notes

1. Women filmmakers since the beginning of the 1990s, represent between 17% and 20% of the overall number of filmmakers in France. The average annual number of films made by women in France since 1990 (including co-productions of French-speaking film) is 17.

2. Formation et Enseignement aux Métiers de l'Image et du Son. The FEMIS replaces the IDHEC and is considered the best school of Film in France. None of the directors who started making films in the 1970s studied at the IDHEC where women accounted for only 4% of the overall number of students in 1974. The female students were at the time discouraged from taking the film direction option.

3. See Agnès Merlet's *Artémisia* and Vera Belmont's *Marquise* both released in France in 1997.

4. See Mima Esposito's *Toni* (1999).

5. The recent release of Tonie Marshall's and Catherine Corsini's latest films (see below) tends to suggest a growing interest by women in the "genres of laughter."

6. See Rollet B., 1999. "Femmes et Cinéma en France. L'après mai 68", in *Clio. Femmes. Histoire et Société*, no 8, (forthcoming).

7. See Sellier G., Fall 1997. "La Nouvelle Vague: un cinéma à la première personne du masculin singulier", in *Iris*, no 24, pp. 77–90.

8. Françoise Audé's book (1981) remains the best reference in this regard.

9. Balasko has two dates of birth: 1950 and 1952.

10. See Rollet B., 1997. "Two women speak out: Serreau and Balasko and the inheritance of May 68'", in *Voices of France*, M. Cross and S. Perry (eds), London Pinter, pp. 100–113.

11. Serreau played in Jean-Louis Bertuccelli's *On s'est trompé d'histoire d'amour* in 1974 and Balasko in Jean-Marie Poiré's *Les hommes préfèrent les grosses* in 1979.

12. See Estelle C. Jelinek (ed), 1980, "Women's autobiography and the male tradition" in *Women's autobiography*, Indiana University Press, pp. 1–20.

13. See Tarr C., 1999. *Diane Kurys*, Manchester University Press.

14. Except the money Antoinette Fouque gave her the first time they met to help her financing her film. See Rollet b., 1998. *Coline Serreau*, Manchester University Press.

15. See Rowe K., 1995. *The Unruly Woman. Gender and the Genres of Laughter*, Austin, University of Texas Press.

16. Following the recent success of Poiré's *Les visiteurs* (1991) with more than 13 millions spectators, Serreau's film is now 4th on the list.

17. The idea "je ne suis pas une femme qui fait du cinéma, je suis quelqu'un qui fait du cinéma" is recurrently expressed by women filmmakers in France.

18. The reception of her film by American feminists was very critical. See Moldeski (1988).

19. See Pillet E., 1995. "Thérésa et Yvette: à propos du comique féminin au café-concerts", in *Féminin/masculin. Humour et différence sexuelle*, G-V. Martin (ed), Cahiers de recherche de CORHUM-CRIH, no 3, p. 29–47.

20. Other members include: Anémone, Marie-Anne Chazel, Christian Clavier, Thierry Lhermitte, Michel Blanc and Gérard Jugnot.
21. See Valérie Lemercier's directing debut with *Quadrille* (1997). She is currently shooting her second film, a comedy where she plays a woman whose father is gay.
22. The director of *Chocolat* (among other films) also played a secondary part in Laetitia Masson's *En avoir (ou pas)* made in 1995.
23. At another level, women directors were very much involved in the reaction against the Chevènement law in February 1997.

References

Audé F. 1979, *Ciné-modèle, cinéma d'elles*, Lausanne, L'Age d'homme.

Blondel A., 1981, *Cinéma des femmes, cinéma féministe ou cinéma féminin*, Doctorat de 3ème cycle, EHESS.

Gautheur C., 9/9/1977, "Elles ont touné tout l'été", in *Le Film Français*, No 1689, pp. 24–28.

Gillain A., Fall 1995, "Films de femmes", in *Femmes Info*, No 74, pp. 24–26.

Lejeune P., 1987, *Le Cinéma des femmes*, Paris, Lherminier.

Moldeski T., (1988). "Three men and baby M", in *Camera Obscura*, May, pp. 69–81.

Serreau C., February 1978, "Coline Serreau, une contestataire tranquille:, interview in *La Revue du cinéma. Image et son*, no 325, pp. 27–9.

Mina Tannenbaum *or* *Something Happened*

Sylvie Blum-Reid

"J'ignorerai toujours à quoi elle passait ses journées, où elle se cachait, en compagnie de qui elle se trouvait pendant les mois d'hiver de sa première fugue et au cours des quelques semaines de printemps... C'est là son secret. Un pauvre et précieux secret que les bourreaux, les ordonnances, les autorités dites d'occupation, le Dépôt, les casernes, les camps, l'Histoire, le temps – tout ce qui vous souille et vous détruit – n'auront pas pu lui voler."

Patrick Modiano, *Dora Bruder*

This article explores Martine Dugowson's 1994 film *Mina Tannenbaum*. The film depicts the story of two young Jewish girls growing up in France during the 1960s. The inscription of a feminine Jewish identity is rarely illustrated in French cinema and literature. One of the most recent examples that come to mind is Patrick Modiano's portrait of a young girl during the occupation in *Dora Bruder* (1997). In French film history, filmmakers Diane Kurys inscribe Jewish female characters in, for example, *Entre nous* (1983), *Coup de foudre*, *Cocktail Molotov* (1980) and *Diabolo Menthe* (1977) as well as Charlotte Silvera in *Louise l'insoumise* (1985) and *C'est la tangente que je préfère* (1998).

Dugowson in her first feature film creates an unusual style, combining interesting cinematographic and narrative techniques, such as dissolves to red or white, the superposition of doubles for both protagonists, the intervention of "angels" in the sky, the use of

97

interior voices, and a questionable narrator. Furthermore, Dugowson posits unusual exaggerated representations, one, traditional, of woman as a vamp, and the other, totally delirious, of a young woman cross-dressing as a Hasidic male Jew. The use of popular music icons reinforces the Jewish positioning of the two future young women in French society from the 60s through the 90s.

I will use the "marrano experience" as the guiding thread to explain Mina's position and farther push my interpretation of a film that was not marketed as a "Jewish film."[2] Marks' analysis of "the Jewish presence in French writing can be understood through close textual reading linking it to gender and sexuality" (Ungar, 107).[3] As the dominant character, Mina's fate is already cast during the opening sequence. My reading of Mina as a "marrana" helps excavate otherwise hidden layers of the narrative and draws a psychologically multi-dimensional, multi-faceted, complex character. *Mina Tannenbaum* can be considered as a filmic text haunted by the specter(s) of the Holocaust. Constructed in a classical sense, with a prologue and an epilogue, the plot is located successively in the 60s, 70s, 80s, and 90s. It consists of a series of flashbacks on Mina's life, some of them technically very innovative, some of them embedded flashbacks (flashbacks within flashbacks).[4] *Mina T.* articulates post-Auschwitz; but also post-68 concerns and a feminist sensibility. Questions arise once the screening is completed: How can one create art after Auschwitz, to borrow from Theodor Adorno? How can one live and carry one's parents' burden of the Holocaust? How can Mina Tannenbaum, a baby girl born a few hours after Ethel Benegui, at the same clinic, become so different and ultimately self-destructive? How can Ethel, her best friend, socially rise and adapt herself to the male-dominated world of journalism while Mina's aspirations slowly collapse?

Most critics have devoted themselves to studying feminine friendship as the overall thematic concern of the film. I wish to over-interpret the film by reading its traumatic historical positioning. The film contains none of the nostalgic associations with and fascination for the retro mood (la mode rétro) that took place in France in the mid-seventies, save for the characters' clothes, hats, and platform shoes – a return to the seventies that is still taking place in contemporary fashion. Martine Dugowson, (a relative to filmmaker Maurice Dugowson) playfully stirs up some controversial and stereotypical representations of Jewish people but also of women as seen in French and American cinema. Jewish representations on screen have tended to fall into what Alain Finkielkraut calls "juifs à l'ancienne" or "résidus médiévaux" – images that the filmmaker here suggests but instantly perverts.[5] Vignettes and direct references to Hollywood films are inserted in a few sequences to echo the heroines' inner dialogue.

My analysis of the film combines the inscription of femininity and Jewishness which is never discussed or mentioned directly, as part of the structuring elements in both Mina's and Ethel's lives and friendship. Yet the ways they each identify with Jewish/and female identity differ essentially and cannot be reduced to one static position. *Mina T*, follows two girls growing up in Paris, France from the 60s all the way into the 90s. Chronological markers delineate the script in a linear fashion that, after a few witnesses and the narrators introduction in a prologue opens with the birth of Mina and Ethel, on or around April 5, 1958. Contemporary French history weaves itself into the script, in light touches. For instance, May 68 is mediated by the sound of television broadcasts overheard in the background. It is also present in graffiti. History, as part of the larger narrative, remains peripheral to the film yet catches up with it. The primary focus is on the immediate lived experience of the female protagonists, and centers on the introspective mood of Mina, an artist striving to make a name for herself in a predominantly male-dominated, businesslike "art world." Popular culture is the preferred material that filters contemporary French history.

French pop songs are most important elements here and constitute a shared generational memory for any spectator who grew up at that time in France and for whom these very songs evoke private and collective moments. The music comes closest to being Dugowson's "thirty something" autobiographical signature. These songs constitute the film's diegetic music and are formally embedded within the narrative. In silent films, music was used to cover sounds of the projection, but as Claudia Gorbman remarks "it had important semiotic functions... it provided historical, geographical and atmospheric setting, it helped depict and identify characters and qualify actions. Along with intertitles, its semiotic functions compensated for the characters' lack of speech" (Gorbman, 53). Next to the eastern European musical score that Peter Chase composed for the film, the different songs in *Mina Tannenbaum* inscribe and identify each protagonist's racial and cultural background. Additionally, the performers or musicians are linked to each of the protagonists' racial/ethnic/cultural heritage. Most artists referred to – singers and musicians – are either Jewish or ethnically and culturally different and have recognized their differences.

Enrico Macias, a Franco-Algerian singer, who represents the pied-noir "exilic" experience, is heard in Ethel's home. Ethel, played by Elsa Zylberstein, who appeared earlier in Pialat's *Van Gogh*, (1991) is clearly designated as a North-African Jew by the use of this singer. The first time we see Ethel in her familial setting at a bar-mitzvah, we hear the song "Ah qu'elles sont jolies les filles de mon pays !" Serge Gainsbourg, a.k.a. Lucien Ginsburg (1928–1991), the Ashkenazic Jew and artiste maudit, is linked with Mina. Mina is played by Romane Bohringer, whom Dugowson had seen in Cyril Collard, *Les nuits fauves* (1992). Mina's fascination for Gainsbourg spans the entire film. When they both are invited to a party in April 1974, Mina sulks about going to a party, something she dislikes, when they did not even play any Gainsbourg songs. An enlarged close-up of Gainsbourg's eyes adorns the wall next to her door in her 90s studio. Gainsbourg has written lyrics where his Jewish origins figure ostensibly.[6] Gainsbourg is the perfect embodiment of the 60s in France and became a cult figure in the late 80s and early 90s. His lyrics were extreme plays on words and language in the tradition of the French "chanson." Such semantic games are not absent from Dugowson's film which is loaded with play on words, such as the allusion to Gainsbourg and Gainsborough, the English painter and child portraitist. The textual reference is Gainsbourg's composition of a song on that motif, about his relationship with British actress Jane Birkin. Gainsbourg died in March 1991. *Mina Tannenbaum* produced by IMA films, (Institut du Monde Arabe) was released a year after to the day of Serge Gainsbourg's death in March 91.

The Egyptian-born musician Dalida is also profiled, and returns twice on the soundtrack with the song that becomes Mina's motif but is at the root of an argument with Ethel during the café sequence (in 1974) and at the end. That song "Il venait d'avoir 18 ans" ("He just turned 18") is a bold essay on the sexual relationship between a 36-year-old woman and her 18-year-old lover. Dalida, of Italian origins came to France in the 50s and became an international star whose success still reverberates despite her suicide in May 1987. She ranks as one of the most important French singers of the century and denotes interchangeably "the Napolitan… the Montmartrois child, the realist or the oriental singer." She has had the celebrity of Brigitte Bardot, and is still a cult figure in France.

Mina and Ethel's argument revolves around the interpretation of that song, which Ethel rejects as "stupid" whereas Mina criticizes her for not understanding anything. The role of language and words and their signifiers plays a large part in Mina and Ethel's friendship. They are constantly analyzing words and sentences, trying to make sense of them, and sometimes overinterpreting people's intentions.

For example, the word "dégueulasse" recurs several times, and acquires new meaning toward the end of the film. Its use is a direct reference to Godard's *Breathless* sequence: "Qu'est-ce que c'est, dégueulasse?" The final message between Mina and Ethel is probably misinterpreted by Mina as well.

Ethel and Mina's friendship is constantly seen as that of doubles or twins, part of the same (split) persona. I suggest instead that the film strives to see them as different. The narrator, Mina's cousin, reflects on the day the two friends met: May 2, 1968. The two Jewish patriarchs, ancestors or angels, seen hovering over the Montmartre sky contest that instance. That humorous skit is reminiscent of Woody Allen's short film "Oedipus Wrecks" included in *New York Stories* (1989) about an overbearing Jewish mother who is seen floating in the sky above New York. From the contested or unreliable date of their first meeting – May 2, 1968, when it should have been April 2, 1968 – the spectator quickly gathers that they met at their ballet lessons: "Dans les années 60, toutes les petites filles veulent faire de la danse."

The friendship evolves in Montmartre, on the Right Bank. Their encounter is geographically circumscribed to the bench, at the top of Montmartrois staircases, around Lamarck-Caulaincourt where they will meet for years, where the passing of time takes place, sometimes in full 180 degree panning shots. Montmartre is the privileged site where friendship develops and persists: the original Montmartre, away from the hordes of tourists, an area that lent itself to the Surrealists' explorations inside Paris. The physical and symbolic crossing over to the Left Bank, framed at first by a shot of the Seine waters, is a major event. Mina registers at an art school to take drawing lessons, and walks across the Pont des Arts, leaving behind the Right Bank. She meets François, who eventually asks her if she is from the "quartier." Female bonding is explored under a new light, and exposed in its authenticity. In many ways, the film rings of the extraordinary female characters' complicity presented by Jacques Rivette in *Céline et Julie vont en bateau* (1974).

Mina has been painting since the age of seven. She met Ethel at the ballet lesson, where she brought her portfolio of paintings, one of them being a copy of the portrait of the English painter Gainsborough's two daughters. Ethel tries first to steal the painting from her at this first meeting. By April 15, 1989, Mina has grown into a "consecrated" artist as the opening of the art exhibit featuring some of her work would have us believe. Ethel at that time is still struggling to "become someone" as a journalist and art critic. The difference between the two is further strengthened by the use of Jewish iconography pairing Mina with a Hasidic male Jew or Rabbinical student, complete with "papillotes"(sidelocks) as her alter ego while pairing Ethel with the classical cinematic image of femininity found in the American vamp Rita Hayworth. Dugowson adeptly uses the concept of the doubles, and projects them as fighting each other at a café in the April 1974 sequence. Ethel ascends the social ladder, and becomes a trendy journalist, after a pathetic beginning where she impersonates Mina and obtains an interview with a famous Parisian artist. By the end of the movie, Ethel has a career and a baby girl called Mina. She skillfully adapted to the demands of journalistic reportage in an oppressive milieu by playing the femininity card. Mina is more reticent to accept some of the demands of the outside world that she sees as corrupted. She prefers to starve rather than to compromise. She comes across as a Balzacian character. She despises her friends' first journalistic ventures, where Ethel is cast in the "feminine" subservient role – a role Ethel reluctantly adopts in her journalistic career.

Both women conflict with their mothers. This aspect was, according to film historian Ginette Vincendeau, widely criticized by the Franco-Jewish community, especially because of the overbearing role of the Jewish mothers: "Mina Tannenbaum's depiction of the Jewish petite bourgeoisie of the Montmartre area provoked strong reactions in France. It is not difficult to see why, since the mothers, the traditional central figures of Jewish culture, are turned into monsters."[7] However, it is questionable which segment of the Jewish community in France was polled since the film was endorsed by Radio Juive and Tribune Juive in Paris.[8] ... Dugowson develops a clearer portrait of Ethel's mother, a dictatorial woman who is constantly blaming Ethel for everything, and who herself was a victim, since she was, according to the script, "sold for six camels," hinting at some horrendous market transaction. Ethel's mother is representative of what Aldo Naouri calls the "Yiddishe mama" in Jewish tradition.[9] Mina's mother does not express herself in private, but instead chooses the national broadcasting channels to vent her frustration with her daughter. Mina's fragmented portrait, as told by her untrustworthy cousin, who claims the right to tell her story, but who is hardly seen next to Mina during the entire film, contains many ellipses and disclaimers, once by Mina herself, returning from the dead and contesting the authenticity of some episodes. It turns out that the cousin wants a part of Mina's fame and possibly to star in the film in the making. Many references to a film within the film are made, until the end, when the lights are turned off by the film crew.

In the last part of the film, Mina's parents are revealed to be both survivors of the Holocaust, children of parents who did not return from concentration camps. Yet, the film never discusses the trauma. Like many survivors, they choose not to reveal the traumatic past. As documented in Claudine Vegh's interviews "most of those who were left orphans never talk about their past, it is taboo … they do not want to, above all, they cannot talk about it."[10] If the family's memory of the past has been muted throughout the film, it cannot be erased. Vladimir Jankélévitch has commented extensively on the irrevocable memory of those who lived through that time, and continue to somehow live in it. According to Jankélévitch, one can recognize such individuals by their gaze. His reading of the gaze is crucial here in my reading of Mina's life as an artist and child of survivors,

> le rescapé d'Auschwitz peut, au fil des ans, avoir perdu tout souvenir de son calvaire, n'y plus penser et n'en parler jamais, ne tenir nul compte, dans sa vie présente, d'un passé maudit enseveli ; la marque indélébile imprimée sur son bras par les bourreaux immondes s'est peu à peu effacée… Seulement un air lointain, je ne sais quelle lueur étrange et fugitive dans le regard: cette indéfinissable lueur est comme le reflet métempirique de l'inexpiable, c'est-à-dire de l'impardonnable, c'est-à-dire de l'irrévocable.[11]

One telling episode evocative of the past occurs when Mina's friend has German high school correspondents visiting Paris. Her mother reacts violently and forbids her to receive any Germans in their apartment. In that episode, Mina's mother is literally changed into a little girl, wearing a Jewish star on her lapel. In a role-reversal, Mina's mother and later her father become "her" children. Such regression anticipates the father's future state. In 1991, Mina visits her father in a psychiatric ward, where he is totally delusional. That dramatic episode takes place at the very end of the film, prior to Mina's death.

Death imagery repeatedly surfaces in the film that is otherwise composed of comedic elements and "magical realist" or surreal moments. The opening sequence of the birth of the baby girls at the Rothschild clinic is a tilt shot representing a layer of soil filled with worms. The same sequence closes with a ballet of nurses dancing with babies in their arms, provoking laughter and disbelief within the spectator. This juxtaposition, mixing birth and death motifs, quite uncanny for any happy occasion, mysteriously connects with the last cemetery sequence. It also reflects the tragicomic spirit of the film. At the end, earth returns to earth. Mina's stone-faced mother and her friends Serge, Jacques, and her cousin throw some earth on her coffin in the Jewish section of a cemetery. Mina's suicide takes place after Ethel's call canceling their date. In filmic time, sex and pleasure are paralleled with death. After leaving the telephone message, Ethel has sex with her husband, while Mina's expiring body is shown in a fetal position in a red fade out. The two sequences, framed in different spaces, are parallel, and both feature television images, one showing a Gainsbourg song for three seconds, and the other a repeat of Dalida's performance of "Il venait d'avoir 18 ans."

Two different Jewish traditions are explored in the film. Mina is implicitly linked to the Ashkenazic traditions through her parents while Ethel is explicitly linked to Sephardic traditions, with the emphasis placed on accents, sentimentality, burial rites, and the naming. Mina is in the marrano tradition of someone who has Jewish origins, yet does not follow the religion, and is essentially like most of French Jews since the nineteenth century, assimilated. Her Jewish origins are never discussed, but given de facto. Her mother appears in the prologue and quotes the Talmud, mentioning how it despises unmarried women like her daughter.

The narrative eliminates Mina's story since she dies, unmarried, without any children. Ethel, however, is a successful career woman living with her gentile boyfriend Gérard, with whom she has a little girl called Mina. She writes Mina's obituary for her magazine. Mina T. will live on in her arts, as the final irony mentioned by the narrator-cousin is that after her death in poverty, her tableaux started selling. "Mina Tannenbaum? Depuis sa disparition, ses toiles se vendent de mieux en mieux." She has become a star, posthumously.

The composition of France's Jewish population has changed over the last 30 years, and is noticeably more Sephardic than Ashkenazic, a turn of events that took place progressively after 1962 and the end of the French presence and colonization in the North African colonies. Ethel's family name, Benegui, designates her North-African Jewish origins. As Elaine Marks writes "In the France of the early 1990s Jews seem to be most recognizable through their names… What's in a name? In France, a monolithic, unchangeable identity perceived as otherness is thought by some to be revealed in names. In the absence of distinctive clothing and conformity to a physical stereotype… to be Jewish is to have a Jewish name. The making and reading of lists of names has become in France, a significant activity carried out both by anti-Semites… and by Jews who attempt to fight against silence and to encourage remembering" (72).

Jewish rituals are respected in Ethel's family. Her mother transmits the tradition. She has been obsessed with Ethel's marrying within the religion ever since Ethel was five years old, threatening her with "don't marry a goy, or I'll kill you." Casting for a Jewish husband, Ethel attempts to fulfill her mother's deathbed wish and life-long desire, in an extremely parodic scene, reminiscent of Spike Lee's style in *She Gotta Have it* (1986).

Mina's family is more introverted and full of angst. Darkness pervades their apartment in direct contrast to Ethel's profusely sunlit apartment(s). Earthtones mark Mina's childhood as a child of holocaust survivors. An uncanny flashback, using color and light changes, goes back in time to the year 1942, the locus of an unnamed event, a "lieu de mémoire" never spoken of in the film. A young girl, possibly the mother, is seen sitting on a chair, waiting or left alone, with a yellow star sewn on her coat, while the song "J'attendrai" is playing.

My reading of *Mina Tannenbaum* is inspired by Elaine Marks' description of the marrano within French culture. Marrano, originally a Spanish word for pig, is defined by Marks as "secular Jews in France, Western Europe, and the United States, particularly in urban areas, throughout most of the nineteenth century and all of the twentieth, although they were Europeanized and Christianized, remained crypto-Jews in the same way that many of the Jews who converted to Catholicism in Spain and Portugal in the fifteenth century, known as Marranos" (129).

Mina has two faces, metaphorically. She is constructed as marked and different. Ethel's difference is that she is cast as "Oriental" and tied to Jewish religious rituals. Mina does not have access to any religious rituals. Mina is a haunted character before she was born because she carries her parents' past: "Mina vit au sein d'une famille traumatisée par la Shoah."[12] Although she belongs to the post-war generation, her angst resonates with the same preoccupations that are found in Finkielkraut's essay *Le Juif imaginaire*, a controversial portrait of Jewish identity that describes "the dilemma of the affluent children of Holocaust survivors who sought their own political identity in the years following the student revolt of 1968."[13] "Ce monde assassiné me concerne et me hante, mais dans la mesure où j'en suis tout à fait exclu. Ce n'est pas moi-même que j'y cherche, c'est ce que je ne suis pas, ce que je ne peux plus être."[14]

Mina's inability to communicate finds an outlet in her paintings, ranging from large dark to reddish hued canvasses, depending on her state of mind. In the second part of the film, she will accidentally bear the difference on her face. I choose to read the accident that leaves her "scarred" as emblematic of what has so far not been said, but yet has always differentiated Mina as Other. Her face, not unlike the narrative, is split in two: before and after the "accident" and the scar that she has to live with. After the accident, Mina's life becomes a descent into hell.

Two years after the accident (April 2, 1991), Mina is now a copy artist and lives in isolation. Reluctant, but unable to sell her paintings, she is reduced to compromise her talents in copying "famous" paintings and portraits. Mina has become another anonymous copy artist in a world where "the uniqueness of the work of art," to borrow Walter Benjamin's terms, has become a meaningless term and where art works are reduced to reproductions. Walter Benjamin's essay combines a fitting discussion of both painting and film, to present the concept of the aura. The sarcastic film epilogue turns Mina into a bestselling artist after her death, a position she would have contested. "The cult of the movie star, fostered by the money of the film industry, preserves not the unique aura of the person but the 'spell of personality,' the phony spell of a commodity."[15]

Mina's facial scar, resulting from the unexplained accident, (she ran into a car, after a dispute with Ethel) alters the entire perspective that people (mostly men) have on her. She has become an outcast, and broken off her friendship with Ethel. Yet we must assume that part of this change stems from her subjective vision. The shots tend to sustain this analysis: we are inside Mina's head, and see the others' gaze through her point of view, and their different reactions to her "cicatrice." Whether there is a literal or figurative disfigurement, the physical sign of her exclusion and difference has been mounting throughout the narrative. Her scar sometimes appears real. Dugowson underlines the ambiguity of the film here, by showing a visible but also sometimes invisible scar and drawing a teardrop on Mina/Bohringer's cheek, reminiscent of a Pierrot clown figure.[16] This facial scar figures prominently in one of George Perec's traumatic dreams entitled "La Dénonciation." Perec, in a psychoanalytical session, dreamt years after his parents' disappearances, that in 1941, he and his father were denounced to the S.S. who came to arrest them. Perec is immediately spotted by the scar he apparently has underneath his chin. "Ils s'apprêtent à arrêter aussi le patron, mais celui-ci me relève la tête et me désigne en montrant la petite cicatrice que j'ai sous le menton" (p. 124).[17]

The film's essential problematic is that of the gaze. The second episode in the chronology of events after the birth follows Mina at the optometrist's, on April 5, 1963. From then on, she has to wear glasses, altering her entire vision of things and people. A little boy mocks her by cruelly calling her "serpent à lunettes." It's not so much Mina's vision of the world that is explored but also her desire not to be seen as ridiculous and out of place. Her relationship with men is impaired by her lack of self-confidence. This is something that she shares for a while with Ethel. The two teenage love-stories they have with men were both failures and missed happenings. The film is paved with such missed events, such as the encounter between Mina and her art professor, Mina and François, Mina and Jacques Dana. Mina does not outgrow this. Her long-term relationship with Serge is destroyed when she indirectly admits that she loves the art gallery collector and ends up in total isolation.

Ultimately, the parents' past and history catch up with Mina. Her final days have reconciled her with her ten-year-old self, whom she encounters by the elevator while leaving the "maternal" apartment. Her mother is moving out to the provinces, abandoning the apartment, while the father is hospitalized. This constitutes a traumatic moment for Mina, yet her mother appears unmoved by the change of place. When Mina crosses path with her own self as a child, it is her feisty ten-year-old self, the same one that Ethel met in 1968, enraged by imposed ballet lessons and creatively copying but altering Gainsborough's portrait of his two daughters in that they both whisper to each other. As a child, she was in a battle with the world. As a thirty-three-year old woman, she is alone and unable to express her true feelings to men such as her hidden love for the art gallery owner. Mina is truly unhappy, according to her mother's testimony broadcast on National television during a special program, devoted to Holocaust survivors. Her mother publicly denounces her daughter's inability to find happiness, forcing history back into the narrative.

The Holocaust, fifty years later, is not just a conversation piece, as mentioned once in Mina's interior monologue, next to Vietnam and drugs. Mina's final drug overdose is discreet, and all we see of her is a fetal position, in a crane shot ending in a red dissolve. It is now for friends and family (and spectators) to perpetrate her memory and story within the larger historical narrative.

Mina's death occurs during the month of April, a month that runs through the film as a core moment – forcing the inevitable question, what happened in April? Most encounters between Mina and Ethel occur in April, starting with the birth of Mina and Ethel, twins at birth, but separated by death in April 1993.

Jorge Semprun's autobiographical narrative *L'écriture ou la vie* (1994) constantly crisscrosses the month of April, as the central knot that slowly reveals its true meaning in time and space. April for

Semprun is the eternal date he has with memory, death, and remembrance. The month of April is a painful reminder tying memory, death, and liberation, all at once, as the camp of Buchenwald where he was interned was finally liberated by the Allied forces, on April 11, 1945. *L'écriture ou la vie* goes back and forth to the last days at the camp, which Semprun was to leave April 26, to return to Paris, ultimately. Semprun does not know if he really came back from death "Car je n'avais pas vraiment survécu à la mort... je n'y avais pas échappé. Je l'avais parcourue, plutôt d'un bout à l'autre... j'étais un revenant en somme" (24). His "Lazarus" gaze is unbearable for those who see him then. "Une nouvelle fois, sans l'avoir prémédité, du moins apparemment, j'étais fidèle au rendez-vous du mois d'avril. Ou plutôt, une part de moi, âpre et profonde était fidèle, contre moi-même, au rendez-vous de la mémoire et de la mort" (237). Primo Levi's death took place in April 11, 1987. Semprun interrogates such coincidences. Some of these uncanny coincidences manifest themselves in *Mina Tannenbaum*. Martine Dugowson herself found these quite uncanny.[18] She could only interrogate her choice after the facts, once the film was written. Why April? What happened in April? It further reinforces the link between her heroine and history. Is it possible that a collective memory would be stored in all of us that some of us could tap and retrieve at odd points without a conscious effort?

The question that I raised in the introduction concerning the differences between Mina and Ethel can be answered if one looks at the weight of history that they carry on their shoulders along with their cultural heritage. Both friends have overwhelming mothers, albeit different. Ethel's mother is an oppressed and oppressive woman. She is able to articulate her frustration. Mina's mother is "walled in" for the most part until the end, where she voices her own unhappiness with her daughter at a meeting where memory for the Holocaust is supposed to be honored. Mina's character was for a while "in movement" and living as any teenager and young adult. However, because of the unspoken traumatic past, she becomes stuck, unable to proceed and envision a future. Unable to transcend the past, she gives up on life and her talents. Marc-Alain Ouaknin cautions that "il n'y a pas de futur sans passé" (104). Psychoanalytical research has shown that infants need to be told the truth about the (parents') past, even if that truth is difficult to hear. "Sans l'accès à la 'vérité' du passé, il ne peut y avoir de futur" (105). The repressed history of Mina's parents resurfaces and claims her life and her father's sanity.

For Arlette, Kaddish

Notes

1. Mina Tannenbaum, first prize for script (1992), Prix Révélation Georges de Beauregard (Elza Zylberstein) (1994), first prize Festival de Florence (1994), first prize Festival de Femmes de Madrid (1994), Best first work (1995).
2. Elaine Marks, *Marrano as Metaphor*.
3. Steven Unger. Rev. of Elaine Marks. "Marrano as Metaphor: The Jewish Presence in French Writing." *The Journal of the Midwest Modern Language Association.*
4. One of the flashbacks is shot in a traveling shot, taking place in Mina's apartment, moving into different rooms to finally stop in front of a mirror showing Mina as a five year old child. Gilles Penso, "Les effets spéciaux de Mina Tannenbaum" (17).
5. I am borrowing from Alain Finkielkraut's essay *Le juif imaginaire* (53). Finkielkraut evokes two films: *Holocaust* and *Les violons du bal*, as examples of "bad" stereotypical representation: "Les enfants qui regardent la télévision sauront ce qu'était jadis un Juif : quelqu'un qui se balançait en permanence" (53).
6. "Yellow Star": "J'ai gagné la Yellow Star/Et sur cette Yellow Star/Inscrit sur fond jaune vif/Y'a un curieux hiéroglyphe." Elsewhere, he wrote, "Lulu" a song he composed for his son, "Tu es comme moi/comme moi/tié Chinois/mais tu as l'âme sla/ve de papa." Or again, "juif et dieu," Serge Gainsbourg, *Mauvaises nouvelles des étoiles* (109).
7. Ginette Vincendeau (49–50).
8. Martine Dugowson, *Personal Interview*. Many thanks to Martine Dugowson for granting me an interview as she was busy working on her next project.
9. Aldo Nouri. *Interview with Victor*, "Ecoute Israël" France Culture, Paris, 25 Octobre 1998.
10. Claudine Vegh, *I didn't Say Goodbye* (29).
11. Vladimir Jankélévitch, *L'irréversible et la nostalgie* (295).
12. Marie Colmant, "A la limite d'être bêtes" Dugowson is interviewed by Marie Colmant.
13. Alice Y. Kaplan., x.
14. Alain Finkielkraut (52).
15. Walter Benjamin, "The Work of Art in the Age of Mechanical Reproduction."
16. Martine Dugowson, *personal Interview*, "Toute l'ambiguïté du film était de savoir si la marque était vraiment plus forte qu'elle ne l'était vraiment. Si elle était purement objective, mais je crois que la réponse est entre les deux. A la fois, quelque chose d'objectif et de subjectif."
17. Georges Perec, *La boutique obscure*.
18. Martine Dugowson, *Personal Interview*. "En fait, je me suis rendue compte que ça s'était imposé au depart, cette date du 15 avril, et puis en fait c'est toujours le mois d'avril, j'ai pas eu beaucoup de choix et à la fin j'ai fini par me dire mais qu'est-ce qui s'est passé le 15 avril? Et en fin de compte assez étrangement quand j'ai lu le Jorge Semprun, pas le dernier mais l'avant dernier, il parle du mois d'avril comme d'un mois très douloureux, parce qu'en fait, c'est le mois où les camps ont été libérés. Je crois que c'est le 15 avril. SB: Mais c'était inconscient au départ? MD: Oui, j'en suis absolument certaine."

Works Cited

Benjamin, Walter. "The Work of Art in the Age of Mechanical Reproduction." *Illuminations*. New York: Schocken Books, 1969.

Colmant, Marie. "A la limite d'être bêtes," *Libération*, (Mars 5, 1994).

Dugowson, Martine. Personal interview. July 24, 1998.

Finkielkraut, Alain. *Le juif imaginaire*. Paris: Editions du Seuil, 1980.

Gainsbourg, Serge. *Mauvaises nouvelles des étoiles*. Paris: Seuil, 1991.

Gorbman, Claudia. *Unheard Melodies. Narrative Film Music*. Bloomington: Indiana University Press, 1987.

Jankélévitch, Vladimir. *L'irréversible et la nostalgie*. Paris: Flammarion, 1974.

Kaplan, Alice Y. Introduction to Alain Finkielkraut, *Remembering in Vain: The Klaus Barbie Trial and Crimes against Humanity*. New York: Columbia University Press, 1992.

Marks, Elaine. *Marrano as Metaphor*. New York: Columbia University Press, 1996.

Aldo Naouri. Interview with Victor Malka "Ecoute Israël" France Culture, Paris. October 25, 1998.

Marc-Alain Ouaknin. *Bibliothérapie. Lire c'est guérir*. Paris: Seuil, 1994.

Perec, George. *La boutique obscure, 124 rêves*. Paris: Denoël-Gonthier, 1973.

Penso, Gilles. "Les effets spéciaux de Mina Tannenbaum," *Le technicien film & vidéo*, no. 433. (March/April 1994): 17.

Portraits Chinois, Dossier de Presse, 1997.

Semprun, Jorge. *L'écriture ou la vie*. Paris: Gallimard, 1994.

Ungar, Steven. Rev. of Elaine Marks. "Marrano as Metaphor: The Jewish Presence in French Writing". The Journal of the Midwest Modem Language Association, Vol. 3 1, no. 2, (Winter 1998): 104–108.

Vegh, Claudine. *I didn't Say Goodbye*. Trans. Ros Schwartz. New York: E.P. Dutton, 1984.

Vincendeau, Ginette. Rev. *Mina Tannenbaum. Sight and Sound* v. 4. N. 10, Oct. 1994: 49–50.

Three Artists/ Three Women: Orlan, Annette Messager and Sophie Calle

Whitney Chadwick

During the 1980s and 1990s, the work of three contemporary French women artists, all of whom live and work in, or near, Paris, attracted widespread critical and curatorial attention outside France. Annette Messager was the subject of a retrospective exhibition jointly organized by the Los Angeles County Museum of Art and the Museum of Modern Art in New York in 1995. Sophie Calle's first one-person exhibition in North America took place in 1990 at the Institute for Contemporary Art in Boston, and was followed by a succession of New York gallery shows, while Orlan's performance/video/installation pieces received extensive coverage in the pages of *Art in America*, and other publications.

The work of all three women is conceptually based; that is, it is oriented toward ideas, and often displays the traces or results of their investigations into aspects of self and/or the phenomenal world. Moreover all three, each in her own way, has addressed a complex of issues revolving around the tensions between social constructions of femininity and questions of female agency and subjectivity. In accepting postmodernism's embrace of a decentered, unfixed, or fragmented self, these artists have taken up positions within what has become a broadly based and international tendency among contemporary women artists.

It is Orlan whose recent work has been most aggressively situated in relation to contemporary discourses of the female body. In a series of works, called by the artist "chirurgicales-performances" and begun in 1990 in Newcastle, England, she has used her own body to challenge Western culture's aestheticization of female beauty and to expose the fine line between the beautiful and the grotesque. Working collaboratively with a plastic surgeon, she submitted her face and body to a series of plastic surgeries aimed at aligning her features with models of beauty derived from famous paintings in Western art: for example, the smile of Leonardo da Vinci's *Mona Lisa*, or the eyelids of a Raphael madonna.

These surgeries, executed under local anaesthesia, have been simultaneoulsy documented and "broadcast" to distant sites. The most recent of these "chirurgicales-performances" originated in New York, and was transmitted by satellite to the MacLuhan Center in Toronto, the Art Center in Banff, Alberta, and the Centre Georges Pompidou in Paris. Although relying on video and color photographs as tools, Orlan's images go beyond the documentary. Forcing the viewer into an uncomfortably intimate relationship with cosmetic surgery, they expose the artificiality of our notions of beauty and the fine line that separates the beautiful from the monstrous.

Annette Messager's work has also explored the social dimensions of femininity and domesticity. She has employed a wide range of media and technical strategies: from photography and drawing to knitting and embroidery. Her earliest works included 56 "Album Collections" (1972–73), each a compilation of drawings, photographs, handwritten texts or embroidered sentences. A subgroup within the album-collections consisted of images in which women appear as objects of violence. In *Voluntary Tortures (Les tortures volontaires)* (1972), she clipped and assembled illustrations of women submitting themselves to beauty treatments. These ranged from mud baths and facial peels to more radical surgical interventions. The result was an inventory of strange contraptions, exaggerated bodily positions, and reformed body parts that chillingly elaborated the sacrifice of individuality to collective norms of beauty.

In the later series *My Vows (Mes voeux)* (begun 1988) and *The Story of Dresses (Histoire des robes)*, Messager combined tiny photographs of body parts attached to long strings in dense wall arrangements that recall ex-votos or devotional offerings, or installed them in sealed vitrines displaying dresses. Her use of the dress as a surrogate for the female body, and her fragmentation of the body, point toward the traumatic nature of sexuality, the elusiveness of gender, and the multiplicity of identities that Messager established for herself at the outset of her career; among them, Annette Messager Collectionneuse, Annette Messager Artiste, and Annette Messager Truqueuse.[1]

The work of Sophie Calle, like that of Orlan and Messager, also refuses the notion of a coherent and fixed identity (or, in Orlan's case, a fixed corporeality). Calle has used photography and text as tools to "provide evidence of [her] existence," as well as to expose the tension between the public and the private, indifference and desire, the observer and the observed. Since 1979, she has constructed situations, often with unwitting accomplices, in which she tracks, photographs, and records the details of her subjects' lives. In one of her first installations, *The Sleepers* (1979), Calle invited people to sleep in her bed while she watched and photographed them. In *L'homme au carnet* (*The Address Book*) (1983), Calle, using an address book she had found in Paris on the rue des Martyrs, began to construct a picture of its unknown owner by interviewing the people listed in the book; "everyday, through them I will get closer to him." Her written version of these interviews, accompanied by pictures of the interviewees or significant locales described in her conversations with them, were published, one picture a day, in *Libération* over a period of a month. When Calle's "subject" returned to Paris and recognized himself in the newspaper, he demanded an opportunity to respond. He was given half a page and expressed in his "defense," his anger, not at his friends, but at Calle for her invasion of his privacy.

In 1983, Calle and Jean Baudrillard published the book *Suite vénitienne/Please Follow Me*, a collection of photographs and diary-like entries recording the artist's "shadowing" of a man she had met at a party in Paris while he was in Venice for two weeks on holiday.[2] Wearing a wig and disguise, and never making contact with the object of her attentions, she played out an elaborate transference of agency, appropriating the "male gaze" and producing the woman, traditionally the object of others' looks in public, as the viewing subject. As Baudrillard notes, "Nothing [was] to happen, not one event that might establish any contact or relationship between them. That is the price of seduction. The secret must not be broken..."[3]

In *Suite vénitienne*, Calle not only unfixes a gendered history of watching and following, she also refuses her audience the satisfaction that accompanies being able to answer the question "why did this all happen?" Her relationship with Henri B. remains ambiguous. As her attempt to locate him is continually frustrated, her desire grows. "He is consuming me," she admits at one point. This dynamic, which Baudrillard refers to as "not seductive, yet entirely a process of seduction," is similar to the passion that drives the scholar's search through the archives, and the desire to know that motivates the writing (and reading) of crime fiction.[4]

Like Baudelaire's *flâneur*, Calle becomes a recording eye as she waits for Henri B. to possess the social spaces of Venice by marking them with the traces of his presence. Disguised, she situates herself within the spectacle of tourist Venice in ways that enable her to hide from her quarry even as she tracks him; when he recognizes her anyway the game is up. Yet there are few, if any, significant consequences for her. Her pursuit, propelled by a desire, the fulfillment of which is frustrated by a set of predetermined conditions (i,e, that "that nothing was to happen…"), is also defined by the slippage between fact and fiction (the fact that nothing will happen only intensifies her fantasies of what might happen).

The photographs that accompany Calle's narrative have the affectlessness and artlessness of nineteenth-century police photographs of crime scenes. The text that accompanies these images, a chronological recording of the pursuit, alternates between largely uninflected description, and an interior monologue that also records mood and sensory feeling. The form is diaristic, but never confessional:

> Friday, February 15, 1980. 10 A.M. I leave the Locanda Montin as a brunette and don my wig in a tiny alleyway nearby. I'll do it this way every day. I don't want to baffle the proprietors. They are already calling me Sophie.
> I inquire about Henri B. in all the hotels having a first name for a name… at lunch time I look through restaurant windows. I always see the same faces, never his. I've come to find some consolation in knowing he's not where I am looking for him. Henri B. is not.
>
> Sunday, February 17, 1980. 8 A.M. Calle del Traghetto. I wait as I did yesterday. It's Sunday; there are fewer people. It's cold. I resume my comings and goings.

Calle's pursuit, with its unanswered questions and its vague promise that something is about to happen, evokes ambiguous responses. What does this woman hope to gain from her quest? What can she learn? The cool, dispassionate text differentiates Calle's subject from the female stalker, fixated on a male target, fueled by fantasy, lost in a growing obsession. Yet the very decision to follow anonymously puts into play a sort of "cat and mouse" game in which chance encounters direct the narrative. Reading Calle's text late one evening, I am reminded of its relationship to other fictional works in which characters roam city streets in search of elusive targets, as well as its relationship to the crime fiction with its motivated sleuthing.

The Surrealists come immediately to mind: Philippe Soupault's *Last Nights of Paris*, Louis Aragon's *Le paysan de Paris*. And, strangely perhaps, Andre Breton's *Nadja*. I reread *Nadja*, more attentive now to the conditions that shape the narrative.

Breton's pursuit of Nadja is also recorded in the form of a diary that charts his encounters with her, accompanied by photographs of Parisian sites relevant to the quest. There, it would seem, the similarity between Calle and Breton ends. *Nadja*, published in 1927, has attracted a good deal of critical press, much of it from feminists who have (quite rightly) questioned the ethics of making literature out of a man's pursuit of an emotionally disturbed young woman who is denied a subjectivity outside the poet's need for a creative principle and who, once institutionalized, is abandoned by him altogether. Despite this, Breton's pursuit of Nadja is both provocative and unsettling, in part because it also destabilizes (though perhaps in a more limited way) its subject positions:

> November 6. So as not to have too far to walk, I go out about four intending to stop in at the "Nouvelle France," where Nadja is supposed to meet me at five-thirty. This gives me time to take a stroll around the boulevards: not far from the Opera, I have to pick up my pen at a shop where it is being repaired. For a change I decide to take the right sidewalk of the Rue de la Chaussée-d'Antin. One of the first people I meet there is Nadja, looking as she did the first day I saw her.

> October 7. I have suffered from a violent headache which, perhaps mistakenly, I attribute to last night's emotions and also to the effort of attention, of accommodation which I have had to make. The whole morning, too, I have been bothering myself about Nadja; it was a mistake not having made a date with her today. I am annoyed. I suppose I observe her too much, but how can I help it...?[5]

Breton's frustration when he fails to encounter Nadja on his walks anticipates Calle's frustrating search for Henri B. among the pensions and hotels of Venice. Without an object, the searcher becomes aimless, impotent. In order to embrace the Surrealist love of the chance encounter, Breton must relinquish a degree of agency and allow Nadja to direct the narrative. Taking on the coloring of the woman who waits, who is at the mercy of another's unscheduled appearances, he suffers violent headaches.

Calle's *Suite vénitienne*, like Breton's *Nadja*, also absorbs the atmosphere of place into the quest. Detective fiction has long located its psychological resonances in specific geographies: from Sam Spade's San Francisco and Raymond Chandler's Los Angeles to Patricia Cornwell's Richmond and Amanda Cross's New York. In *Nadja* and *Suite vénitienne*, place plays an active role in a narrative in which the line between real people and fictional characters is blurred. Calle has remarked that she first began to follow strangers through the streets of Paris in order to reclaim the city after a long absence. Her passage through unfamiliar streets and into unknown areas produced a new city, one previously hidden from her eyes.

The literary device of making geography an active ingredient in the story, rather than merely a backdrop for the action, has a long tradition in both French literature and detective fiction. Indeed the Surrealists derived much of their knowledge of how geography may compel narrative from detective fiction, and specifically from Allain and Souvestre's series *Fantômas*, first published in 1911. The Fantômas novels, and the movies that grew out of them, left a deep impression on artists and writers, for Fantômas transcends the role of character, becoming a place, an atmosphere, a state of mind.

What Fantômas did for Paris – producing place as psychological ambience rather than visual spectacle – Calle has done for Venice and other sites. In *Suite vénitienne*, she has constructed her own Venice, at first alienating in its unfamiliarity, only gradually to be embraced as its spaces are inflected by her desire, and by the search for Henri B.

In the end, Breton's *Nadja* is motivated by the operations of chance, and by unconscious desire projected into the real world. As the poet comes to realize how deeply disturbed Nadja is, he in turn questions his own desire for her. "Can it be that this desperate pursuit comes to an end here? Pursuit of what I do not know, but pursuit, in order to set working all the artifices of intellectual seduction."[6] Calle offers a perfectly calibrated response to Breton's query. She abandons her pursuit of Henri B. at the train station in Paris precisely because she has no more need of him. In the end, he was somehow incidental to the conditions that motivated her quest.

Like the Surrealists before her, Calle embraces artlessness and purposeless (or unconscious motivation) over the motivated plots of detective fiction. Operating, like the Surrealists, in the gap between art and life, she also operates in the gap between self and other, revealing that in the "disparate space between words and images, vision and knowledge is the camouflage of desire."[7]

Calle's work, about the unseen, unreciprocated act of watching/observing/spying, addresses our own capacity for voyeurism, and our fascination with the lives of strangers. In the end, Calle, like Orlan and Messager, operates in the gap between art and life, self and other. The work of each of these artists elicits a range of discomfiting feelings as we are, in turn, made into reluctant voyeurs, driven to despair by the often grotesque images that result from their investigations, and moved to laughter at their often ironic meditations on femininity and domesticity. While their modes of attack differ, their ability to provoke unease as we vacillate between dread and desire remains constant.

San Francisco, March 1999

Notes

1. See *Annette Messager*. Exh. cat. (Los Angeles: Los Angeles County Museum of Art and New York: The Museum of Modern Art, 1995).
2. *Suite vénitienne* (Paris: Editions de l'Etoile, 1983); English edition (Seattle: Bay Press, 1988).
3. *Suite vénitienne* (Paris: Edition de l'Etoile, 1983); English edition (Seattle: Bay Press, 1988).
4. "Please Follow Me," in Sophie Calle. *Suite vénitienne*.
5. André Breton, *Nadja*, trans. Richard Howard (New York: Grove Press, 1960, originally published in 1928 by Librairie Gallimard, Paris), 90.
6. Ibid., 108.
7. Deborah Irmas, "The Camouflage of Desire," in *Sophie Calle: A Survey* (Santa Monica: Fred Hoffman Gallery, 1989), 11.

"After Nadar". Photographer: Richard Lewis

Calixthe Beyala's "Parisian Novels": an Example of Globalization and Transculturation in French Society

Odile Cazenave

Calixthe Beyala, a Cameroonian woman writer, has become one of the leading voices in the new generation of francophone African writers living in France. In barely a decade, she has achieved spectacular success and has become highly visible at the forefront of the literary scene. With her first three novels[1] Beyala was defined by some critics as "the perfect illustration of a new surge of the African woman today: she wants to conquer other voices, breaking away with traditions and stereotypes."[2] Yet, her works were also considered as an easy popular literature, because of their use of bold images, vernacular language, sex and suffering in settings framed in violence,[3] meant to attract the Western reader. Her choice of publishing houses – Stock, Minerve and Albin Michel – none of which have a particular interest in African literature, has also contributed to make her most visible and out of the norm. Calixthe Beyala is not just known within the small circle of academics and critics, but is also reaching out to the general French readership. She regularly appears on television programs and many radio stations and is frequently asked to comment not necessarily on literary aspects; but rather, on issues concerning African women's status or immigration or questions around minorities in France.

Despite her growing popularity throughout the past decade, she has remained controversial amongst Africans because of her choices in the portrayal of Africa and Africans. In 1996, the controversy came to the center stage of the French literary scene: a few weeks after being awarded the grand prize of the Académie française

119

for best novel of the year for *Les honneurs perdus*, she was accused of plagiarism by Pierre Assouline, the editor of *Lire*, a widely-read magazine devoted to French literature and literary topics.[4]

The object of this article is to reflect on the phenomenon that Beyala represents in herself, as a popular/rized African woman writer in France. Her fame in France and her controversial reputation among Africans serve as a unique case-study of globalization and transculturation.[5] Using her most recent work, I will examine how these novels demonstrate a change in the author's voice. In what are known as her "Parisian" novels,[6] Calixthe Beyala changes the direction of her gaze to focus primarily on the community of Africans in France, in the Belleville neighborhood of Paris. Her early works had centered on Africa and the changes in men and women needed in order to build a better society. In the more recent "Parisian" works, she explores questions of immigration, in terms of its potential and dynamics for African women. These works consider the re-negociation of identities as central to women's experience of migration. They show a progression, from where the female character is part of a family and the community of Malian immigrants (*Le petit prince* and *Mam*)[7] to being single, without family, coming to Paris in order to change and become somebody new (*Assèze* and *Les honneurs*).[8] The author highlights how people's identity becomes closely bound to a geographical condition and entails a transformation of gender roles and a redefinition of power.[9]

Telling about the experience of (im)migrating enables Beyala to give life to the locus of displacement, the Belleville neighborhood. It also allows her to deconstruct the one-dimensional stereotypical representation of African immigrants and non-European immigrants in general. At the same time, through a multiplicity of voices, faces and experiences of immigration, Beyala examines French society from a different angle: her characters, as immigrants, are put in the uncomfortable position of both insider/outsider as the central discourse rejects them to the periphery. *Le petit prince* and *Mam* especially, through their elaborate narrative structures where two alternating narrative voices (the child's and his father's/mother's) address the white Frenchman/woman, succeed in creating an ongoing dialogue with the Other. The perspective has now been inverted; the ex-colonizer has been put in the position of the object and the ex-colonized is now the subject, the I speaking, reflecting, just as an anthropologist would, on the whys and hows of French society.

The author's vivid sensitivity to cultural blending, and her keen awareness of how globalization affects the diaspora in Paris, extends to her portayal of France's transformation and its new profile. French society, willingly or not, is undergoing some major cultural changes: transculturation, as Beyala stresses, does not just go one way. The French too, are absorbing part of the linguistic and cultural inputs of the non-European immigrant communities. Today, there isn't a French supermarket or grocery that does not offer its array of French Caribbean, Maghrebi or Vietnamese dishes. Music, fashion, advertisement, art, all borrow, in one way or another, from African, Maghrebi or Caribbean influences.

The factor of globalization and transculturation can be extended to her painting of characters. One example is particularly striking in that regard. Saïda, the protagonist in *Les honneurs*, changes her ways of being and acting once she has been living in Paris for a while. This is not new. What is new is the extent of her transformation. Unlike the previous novels where the protagonists - M'am, Sorraya, or Assèze – were shown adopting French women's ways and styles, Saïda's change goes in a different way: she now looks more like a woman from the Maghreb. Described as baking middle-eastern pastries for Loulouze, running a bath with rose water for her, she exclaims: "moi, l'Arabe" [I, the Arab woman]; even if Saïda is supposed to be a Muslim, one would expect her to first claim either her nationality or her Africanity. This is a clash with the original textual character, who is a Muslim from Cameroon. One of the possible reasons is that the stereotypical view of immigrant women in France is that of a maghrebin woman, so Beyala might be addressing the French reader. Similar operations of decentering appear elsewhere in Beyala's writing.

Her depiction of Africa, at times, sounds generic and cliché-like: in an interview with Benetta Jules-Rosette,[10] Beyala says that the Africa she describes has nothing to do with pastoralism, tradition, beauty etc. Instead, it is the Africa of the slums, the one she has experienced and that she knows. Yet, these depictions do sound generic as they keep coming back, almost always the same.

Another decentering process appears in the author's historical reconstruction of a period as background to the novel. For instance, some of the expressions and phrases used in *Assèze*, especially some of the ones given as true "cameroonisms" seem anachronistic, they do not necessarily correspond to what was used in the sixties, the period which serves as background in the first part of the novel. More specifically, Sorraya's replies to her father and her behavior toward him appear extremely harsh and strikingly insolent for the time, given the milieu, which is supposed to be the urban middle-class in Douala (Cameroon).

These illustrations of decentering refer to a writing inscribed in a globalized context, incidentally French. The author presents a representation of an Africa that corresponds to her inner Africa, an amalgam of her personal experience while she lived in poor shanty towns in Cameroon in the sixties and seventies, and of current Africa, as she knows it now when she returns to.

Because her status has changed to that of a very successful writer, her experience of the country and of the people now corresponds to a different reality from the one she knew before she left. Her picturing of Africa, of Cameroon, of people's life thus appears decentered, shaped in part by her own experience as an African woman who has been living in France for more than a decade, and who starts seeing Africa with distant eyes. This aspect transpires in the textuality of the narration even though one of her primary objectives, as she still stresses in *Assèze*, is "to tell Africa" [Dire l'Afrique].

In that regard, Béatrice-Rangira Gallimore characterizes Beyala's writing as polymorphic,[11] because of her usage of both the epic and the dialogue, which she blends together in order to evoke the life of underprivileged people in urban environments, for instance, the New-Bell neighborhood in Douala. Gallimore emphasizes the use of idiomatic expressions, words, proverbs and songs in African languages: their combination and insertion into the French language contribute to what she calls an Africanizing of the French language.

> As the author herself has said repeatedly in interviews, her language does not reproduce that of Baudelaire. It is, she says, shaped by the world of the shanty towns where she grew up and where her characters live. (178, my translation)

To this effect, Beyala borrows some words from African languages, bending and blending the French words and adding others in African languages. What is worth noting though, is that the numerous examples are all from Beyala's first three novels. For Gallimore, all these strategies, including the literal translation of African expressions in French and the usage of neologisms, give Beyala's works "a local color" (180) and "betray Beyala's will to africanize and adapt it to the universe of the shanty towns that she described so well in her novels" (181).

I would like to argue this point in a slightly different way. On some levels, Beyala subverts canonical French, by doing what Gallimore rightly defines as giving some local flavor to the French language, mostly by twisting idiomatic expressions. The important point is to see that these idioms refer to stereotypes that are part of the linguistic or cultural French colonial heritage. One obvious example is Loukoum's expression "broyer du nègre" (*Le petit prince*). Here, Beyala uses the fact that her protagonist is a child and may not "remember" the "correct" expression: "broyer du noir." In *Declining the Stereotype. Ethnicity and representation* in *French Cultures* (1998),[12] Mireille Rosello stresses Beyala's subversion of stereotypes: "the text cheats by inserting fake articulations between so-called facts and their stereotypical explanations" (136), substituting words and using the effect of surprise, as in Loukoum's example. In all these techniques, the disruption of syntax and the agrammaticality of the sentence are both made obvious and signal a subversion of stereotypes.

All her "Parisian" works show a strong sense of humor and satire. In the same vein as Cameroonian writers like Mongo Beti, she is bitingly ironic at times, full of euphemisms and innuendoes. Yet, because her readership is primarily French and not necessarily versed or even familiar with African literatures and cultures, she may be misread and misunderstood. There is thus a certain danger where expressions like "la bonne humeur proverbiale des nègres" or "la tribu des nègres" may be taken at face value: not only does the irony get diluted, but instead of subvertion, the stereotypical expression is reinforced. Because of that, part of her writing seems to be feeding into French readers' fantasies about Africa and their quest for a renewed version of exotic literature. Hence the controversy, where African readers may object to a certain artificiality of her representation of African and Africans (and to push it further of the African immigrants as well).

This point brings me to the second part of my analysis: the prevalence of a French readership may have an impact on the interaction writer/text/reader and, eventually, on the writer's work itself, as a complicity is created between the writer and the recipient of this writing. Somehow, part of her metaphors, of images and idiomatic expressions, part of her representation of Africa and African characters, women or men, indicate a gallicizing of her writing. It can be characterized as gallicized in the sense that her images and language refer primarily to a French world and, because of that, seem to be primarily directed at it and to speak to it. For instance, in *Réverbère*, the dreams and language of Tapoussière, the protagonist, refer to a French or European reality, more so than to an African landscape, at a time when the author consciously grounds the story in the realistic mode. It is especially evident in her evocation of a living room, and utilization of le *jeté de table* [table runner] instead of *napperon brodé* [embroidered table mat]. While embroidered mats are common in Cameroonian households, table runners are not, and refer to a different cultural context, that is, French/European. In another example, she has Tapoussière, a young child, dreaming of Goddess Circé's potion, something that is obviously unusual.

Obviously, the immediate response to this statement should be: how can we speak of gallicizing of her writing, when she writes in French and one of her immediate objectives is, on the contrary, to "Africanize" the French language as she has stressed on different occasions. Indeed, there seems to be a striking paradox in such a statement. On the one hand, as is usually the case for Francophone African writers, she uses a number of textual and narrative techniques that help reinforce the idea of a different reality presented to a novice reader.[13] Inserting words from African languages, or African proverbs translated into French, disrupting the usual syntax, using a story-teller or a given reader or audience, are all part of these narrative techniques meant to give the French language a sense of different tension. On the other hand, her writing betrays signs of gallicizing.

My intent is not to take issue with the authenticity of her writing, but rather to reflect on what underlies the author's work on French, that may explain the polarized readers' reactions. To the French reader, the insertion of African words and expressions, or literal translations of proverbs, etc. will appear as truly authentic and evocative of African/Cameroonian environment. But they will appear as such because French readers are not in a position to make an informed judgment. As a result, they adhere to this representation of Africa and Africans. It is thus that the author is celebrated in France as one of the best African voices, as a writer who, in their minds, can communicate and portray current Africa so well. The paradox lies in the fact that she is defined as such by non-Africans, while her compatriots react against her. For Camerooman readers – who are able to discern which expressions are indeed part of their cultural and linguistic background, which ones are neologisms, manufactured by Beyala,[14] and which ones may refer to non Cameroonian idiomatic expressions, thus not directly theirs, but recognizable as African – these same techniques may not be effective. Beyala's characters and environment will appear as artificial, not convincing, something that will not speak to them.[15] Yet, to another African reader, Congolese, Senegalese or Ivorian, the idiomatic African expressions may be more evocative as they will recognize some of these as part of their own linguistic background.[16] What this shows in the end, is a renewed conception of globalization, not strictly synonymous with westernization, but more truly global: by inserting words and expressions from other African languages or French language variations as used in other Francophone African countries, by using characters that are no longer representative strictly of her native country but of other countries and African cultures, including the Maghreb, Beyala manages to globalize the French language and literature in an African way. Her aim at creating a higher-level synthesis of African realities will appear artificial to some and brilliant and unique to others.

Part of this complex process comes from a conscious effort to reach out to a larger audience. Another part may be the result of unconscious decentering in her writing. What I want to suggest is that, while the factor of space is decisive in the transformation of her protagonists, it is even more so when applied to her own space of writing. Living in France has indeed become critical in the evolution of her creation. While her basic vision, that she is still trying to search for alternatives that will allow Africans, men and women, to build a better society, remains unchanged, the direction of her gaze and the tonality of her voice have shifted. France, rather than the African continent, is the space of writing. It therefore contributes to a writing that takes the globalization of the world into consideration, as well as a redefinition of geographic and cultural boundaries for the diaspora living in France. In turn, it suggests a redefinition of the borders of African literary creation. For a writer like Beyala, the direction and quality of her gaze and voice are interrelated with her readership. Hence a protagonist like Saïda, who becomes representative not so much of the African diaspora in particular, but of all the non-European immigrants, of all the visible communities.

As Beyala herself experiences globalization and transculturation, her writing betrays an intricate complex process of "métissage" of the French language. The "métissage" of the language goes both ways: there is indeed a certain gallicizing of her initial writing as the French idiomatic expressions and linguistic stereotypes show. But her voice, too, shows that the author has experimented with africanizing the French language, subverting in turn old French stereotypes, linguistic and ethnic ones. In doing so, Beyala's writing defines her own marks, no longer characteristic of the African novel, but rather of a literature of immigration, and even more so, of the Afro-parisian novel.[17] As such, her voice participates in "dislocat[ing] fixed identities not only of race, ethnicity and nationality, but also of gender, sexuality, class and language."[18] The social and cultural hybridity that is characteristic of her protagonists thus extends, in a most cohesive way, to her voice. Beyond that, she contributes to redefine all literatures in French and eventually French literature.

Notes

1. *C'est le soleil qui m'a brûlée* (1987), *Tu t'appelleras Tanga* (1988), and *Seul le diable savait* (1990); in the rest of the article, we will refer to them as *Le soleil, Tanga* and *Le diable*.

2. See David Ndachi Tagne's review of *Le soleil. Notre librairie* #100 (January-March 1990): pp. 96–97.

3. Tachi Ndagne for instance sees her insistent painting of sex and misery as "the embroideries of an African version of Xaviera Hollander, trying to excite the West with exoticism, misery and sex" (97, my translation).

4. See the following articles that appeared in *Le Monde*: "L'écrivain Calixthe Beyala est de nouveau soupçonnée de plagiat" (11/26/96); "L'écrivain franco-camerounaise Calixthe Beyala accuse à son tour Ben Okri" (11/28/96), Pierre Assouline's article, "L'Affaire de Beyala rebondit", in *Lire*, February 1997, as well as Beyala's response, "Moi, Calixthe Beyala, la plagiaire !" in *Le Figaro*, (26/1/97), page 23.

5. I am referring to the term as used by Françoise Lionnet in her work, *Postcolonial Representations. Women. Literature. Identity* (1995). As the prefix suggests, it is "the act of traversing, of going through existing cultural territories." (13). With the idea of a pattern of cross-cultural movement is associated the idea of "the act of appropriation" (13), which Lionnet remarks, is a more "promising concept than those of acculturation and assimilation" (13). In that regard, French, as the writer's language, is "appropriated, made into a vehicle for expressing a hybrid, heteroglot universe" (13). This act of appropriation goes both ways, borrowing and lending across porous cultural boundaries (Renato Rosaldo), producing in the end "a greater degree of cultural complexity" (13).

6. *Le petit prince de Belleville, Maman a un amant, Assèze l'Africaine* (1994) and *Les honneurs perdus* (1996); we will refer to them in the text as *Petit prince, Mam, Assèze* and *Les Honneurs*.

7. The two novels explore the reconfiguration of power and authority within the community and the family cell, and the resulting new interaction between men and women, between parents and children.

8. The two novels thus illustrate the potential of migrating, but its limitations and risks as well, for most of the female characters converge to the same impasse, where their life seems empty and meaningless, and they can no longer go back to Africa.

9. See Cazenave, Odile. "Roman africain au féminin et immigration: dynamisme du devenir." This article was presented at a conference on *Mondialisation et femmes africaines: transformation des rôles sexués*, Louvain-la-Neuve, Belgium (12–13 December 1997) and will appear in the proceedings, Ed. Chantal Zabus, L'Harmattan, 1999.

10. See Jules-Rosette, Bennetta. *Black Paris: The African Writers Landscape*. Urbana: Illinois University Press, (1998): 201–205.

11. Cf. Béatrice-Rangira Galimore. *L'œuvre romanesque de Calixthe Beyala*. Paris: L'Harmattan, 1997.

12. Rosello, Mireille. *Declining the Stereotype. Ethnicity and representation in French Cultures*. Dartmouth: New England Press, 1998.

13. For an analysis of the characteristics of the new writing in African literature, see Dabla, Sewanou. *Nouvelles écritures africaines*, Paris: L'Harmattan, 1986; Cazenave, Odile. *Femmes rebelles: naissance d'un nouveau roman africain au féminin*, Paris: L'Harmattan, 1996.

14. For example, ils "*se discutaillaient* la place sur le trottoir" (87) [they were discussizing their spots on the pavement]; "sans *attentionner* au train" (105) [without attentioning the train].

15. For instance: "un mauvais payeur, un *ton-fric-pas-connaître*" (63): the expression "un-ton-fric-pas-connaître" sounds inauthentic, as "fric" is not a slang used in Douala. When speaking in that register, people will tend to say something like "dough." On

the other hand, expressions like, "je la *doigtai*" (84) [I fingered at her]; "une *pantaculotte rouge*" (138) [a red pantunderwear] are completely part of the daily language.

16. An expression like "*cela déconfiance* la clientèle" (84) [this detrusts the customers] refers to the Congolese linguistic context, not the Cameroonian.

17. The term refers to the diasporic generation of young authors from Sub-Saharan Africa living in France. Simon Ndjami, Bolya Baenga, Daniel Biyaoula, Alain Mabanckou are all part of this new generation. See my work, *Afrique sur Seine, revue et corrigée: le roman afro-parisien aujourd'hui* (submitted to publisher).

18. Cf. Woodhull, Winnifred. "Ethnicity on the French Frontier." *Writing New Identities. Gender, Nation, and Immigration in Contemporary Europe.* G. Brinker-Gabler and Sidony Smith. UMP (1997): pp. 31–61.

Haïti on Stage: Franco-Caribbean Women Remind

(On Three Plays by Ina Césaire, Maryse Condé and Simone Schwarz-Bart)

Christiane P. Makward

The dramatic texts of women writers from the French Carribean are not well-known. Few critics work in this area and there is not an abundance of texts in print as yet, let alone in translation.[2] The original productions of such plays normally take place at home in the Caribbean; they hardly manage to travel abroad, and if so only for a very limited number of performances in less than highly visible circumstances. For example, it was only after the fact that I heard – although I was based in Paris – that an adaptation by Ina Césaire of Haïtian writer Marie Chauvet's *Madness* (*Folie*) had been performed under the title *Night and Devils* (*La Nuit et les Diables*). This took place late in august 1998 as part of the program "Pigalle-Marron Festival." Similarly, it has proved impossible so far to procure Patrick Chamoiseau's adaptation of *A Woman Named Solitude*, André Schwarz-Bart's masterpiece which we know was inspired, dedicated, and most likely co-written with Simone Schwarz-Bart.

As with the majority of female creative writers in French, writing for the stage and seeing one's work performed are essentially modern phenomema. Of course a Queen of Navarre could see to it that a play she wrote would reach performance in the early sixteenth century. So could a George Sand two centuries later, but the earlier was a queen, the latter an established writer. Ordinarily, female playwrights experience even more difficulty in seing their work performed than women writers in seeing their texts published. That is because performing a play requires faith, instant energies, and hard cash. All of these resources must converge in a highly competitive race for subsidies, overshadowed by equally talented and typically more credible male playwrights. It was only around 1970 (1967 for Anne Hébert, 1968 for Andrée Chedid and Antonine Maillet, 1971 for Hélène Cixous, 1972 for Maryse Condé – who was married at the time to an African actor) that a certain number of adaptations and creations for the stage by the pen of women writers in French came into view. With regards to Franco-Carribean women play-wrights, one notable case in point is the rather obscure status of plays written or created by Aimé Césaire's daughters Ina and Michèle. The Father's name no doubt casts its shadow in their case: their works are essentially ignored by local and Parisian critics, or so believes Ina Césaire, whom I questioned directly on the matter of reception.

The topic of Haïti in Franco-Carribean literature is ubiquitous and noble, it is a noted tradition in dramatic works. This applies to three plays and three prominent women writers I have chosen to discuss here. My title, "Haïti on stage: Franco-Caribbean Women remind," plays with the syntax, signifying that Franco-Caribbean women writers remember and that they want to remind us and the world of Haïti. They invite us to commemorate the history and to be aware of modern Haïti. Theatre work is meant to be – and is nor-mally better off – experienced live. But even in our postmodern age, drama is not always conceived as pure and simple instant "specta-cle." One exemplum might be Mnouchkine's *1789*, another Michèle Césaire's *La nef* or *Bal d'éventails*. What I suggest here is that a play can be devised and conceived as live performance *as well as* leave an-alyzable traces (texts, paratextual documents, press files, less often videos) to serve as a foundation for an acceptable political interpre-tation. It is from such a perspective that I read and watch and teach play-texts. I was fortunate enough to experience two of the three plays discussed here, at the Ubu Repertory Theatre of New York, but I also wish to underline that the reading of play-texts and their pedagogical potential seems to me to be largely ignored. Stage intructions are fundamental in modern play-texts, providing the reader's visual imagination ("the mind's eye") with that fourth di-mension, also labelled "le spectaculaire" by erudites. In fact it is largely at the level of "didascalies/stage-instructions," as an integral part of the readable play-text, that my analysis of Ina Césaire's play is focussed. Had I not read the play-text earlier, had I not been rea-sonably informed of Haïtian history, a lot of "signs" would have been squandered on me as *a bona fide* spectator. These remarks do not so much apply to Schwarz-Bart's play (one only needs to be vaguely aware of modern Caribbean economics), whereas Condé's play stands somewhere in-between: Haïti's history under the Duvaliers is the background needed to follow and appreciate the plot.

Before comparing the plays, I will present each one by chronological order of creation to outline how the question of Haïti is treated through situations and themes. All three were published around 1990. All three were translated and published in American English as publications of Ubu Repertory Theatre of New York (directed by Françoise Kourilky).

Your Handsome Captain (1987) was envisioned and written by Guadeloupean Simone Schwarz-Bart. It contains no reference to the history of slavery nor to Haïtian independence or even the Duvalier years. It is focussed, in an intimate, anti-epic mode, on contemporary Haïtian problems of exile and survival at home, and primarily on the couple, love, child-bearing. A discreet mirror effect pitches Guadeloupe's dependence on France and Haïti's on the USA or the Western World in general. An emblematic Haïtian named Wilnor (no patronym) lives in exile in Guadeloupe where he has secured work. Part of his salary has been saved and buried in a jar under his couch. The spectator will find this out when Wilnor, devastated by news from home and tipsy with rum, undertakes to solemnly burn up his own last resource: private, now derisible, savings. For several years Wilnor has faithfully sent home the best part of his salary to his lovely wife Marie-Ange. It must be noted that – as part of Schwarz-Bart's abstractive techniques – there is no talk of children around her nor of aging parents or any dependent. We will never know whether the two protagonists have never had children before, whether they have a sterility problem, or whether they await Wilnor's return home to reproduce themselves. In any case it has been the situation for years: Wilnor and Marie-Ange (are they both illiterate?) correspond, or rather communicate via audio-tapes four times a year.

What happened, then, that would tie a dramatical situation? A "friend" of Wilnor's was recently charged with remitting gifts and money to his wife. As Wilnor slowly finds out through Marie-Ange's new tape via a number of enchanting rhetorical precautions – that paradoxically reinforce his admiration for his spouse – the "friend" has betrayed Wilnor and seduced the wife. He has demanded sexual favors, but Marie-Ange is not begging for forgiveness or denying her responsibility. She tends to underscore, however, how much the friend "smelled" like[3], felt, sounded and looked like her husband – at least in the trances of desire and on her own boardfloor. At first Wilnor reacts rather predictably: he puts to the flame of a lamp, one after the other, the bills he had secretly saved to build a verandah around their cabin at home. But he cannot help admiring the charm, the strength, the arrogance, the rhetorical confidence, and the biological assurance of his spouse Marie-Ange. Not begging for forgiveness, she is not expecting concessions; she is taking leave of Wilnor. That woman is no ordinary woman. In the end a love chant arises from Wilnor towards life in its primary definition: a human foetus, a fruit of the flesh's weakness and of male artfulness. Marie-Ange has tried to abort (in Schwarz-Bart's delicate, litotic prose "to tire out her belly" but she has failed. She has finally bowed and will give birth. An epilogue shows Wilnor making anxious recommendations to Marie-Ange: she must take great care of herself so the child will be born wholesome and handsome.

Condés' play *Pension les Alizés* (1988, translated as *The Tropical Breeze Hotel*) puts on stage a son of the Duvalierist bourgeoisie. A medical doctor, Ismael has just fled to Paris because, according to his tale for Emma (his seasoned Guadeloupean-French-Parisian, ex-dancer hostess): he has compromised himself with anti-Duvalier revolutionaries. It slowly dawns on the spectator as well as on Emma that he has in fact turned his back on his co-revolutionaries and that he is therefore responsible for the violent death of about thirty persons. The time-frame of the play extends over several months but within a single space: Emma's drawing-room in her Paris home. She has time to "get involved" with Ismael: she pampers him, listens to him, makes excuses for him, supports him within her own standards of dignity and sleeps with him. Indeed she is a superb character and another childless emblem of Caribbean womanhood according to Condé. The play is a tribute to the ageing Caribbean woman, not too far from the reviled mulatta prototype of numerous French language novels and plays.[4] It is also an indictment of collaborationist Haïtian bourgeoisie. The author does not deal directly with the question of the under-class, but social stratification is encoded in Emma's distrust and skepticism. She is of an older generation and from a lower social level: her father's dream was for her to become a medical doctor but she caved under the hardships of exile and became an exotic dancer. So Emma senses – against her own desire to nurture – a master manipulator under the young doctor running for his life.

Now he hears that his beloved (who is of course not his wife) has been arrested and he decides to go back home to retrieve her. Emma's temptation to return home on the arm of a man is short lived. Ismael attempts running out on her and sacks her apartment in search of her savings. That very day, Emma walks in and hands to him a single one-way ticket to the Caribbean. He is terrified and begs her to escort him but she does not waver in her determination to stop dreaming. A few days later one ultimate phone call informs her of his "execution." The spectator is left with Emma at her dressing table, repairing her make-up.

Fire's Daughters (*Rosanie Soleil*) by Ina Césaire was created in 1992 by Ubu Repertory Theatre (New York City). It was directed with utmost precision and high energy by Ntozage Shange, the famed feminist author of *For Colored Girls Who Have Comtemplated Suicide When the Rainbow Is Enuf.* I have analyzed elsewhere[5] certain aspects of this play-text and will only delineate the plot here. Césaire uses an original strategy to put Haïti on stage: her goal is to commemorate the sugar riots of southern Martinique in the 1870s and pay tribute to one of its agents: a fire-carrier, Rosanie Soleil. In order to create this legendary (but historically proven) figure, Césaire constructs a link with Haïtian history and shows her a rebel working within a foursome of females.

The spirit of revolution is grounded in a dual enigma. And here, spectacular and symbolic signs are paramount in developing dramatic tension and spiritual meaning. It is only in the last minutes of the show that the spectator understands the significance of two important details: a round, tall occasional table in a corner which is lovingly adorned with red flowers by Man Soleil "Mama Sun" in Miller's translation): she gesticulates ceremoniously and mumbles in front of it as if it were an altar. Then there is the insistent sound of a ti-bois (a section of bamboo hit with a small stick). It is heard periodically and acknowledged by the women on stage particulary Voisine Fumée ("Sister Smoke") who appears somewhat light-headed from smoking her pipe and cannot help "nosing around." But a demure Mama Sun insists that the noise is made by a "manicou" (a wild animal, the size of a beaver, appreciated for its meat) trapped in the adjoining storage-room. When the neighbor reports the rumor of a wounded man on the run ("un nègre blessé") Man Soleil keeps lending a deaf ear. The dialogue is such, however, that it fosters deciphering. The four characters (Rosanie has a fraternal twin sister) actually have and share secrets. They mainly communicate by metaphors, proverbs and sayings so the spectator is faced with a rather opaque language, another tongue, a creole as it were though it is perfect French (or standard English in Miller's translation). In the end, the twins turn out to have resolved a dangerous situation. A patrol has come to the cabin, searching for the wounded black man but the twins now reveal that they have saved him: he is on his way to a secret meeting to organize a great uprising. The "gros ka" or giant drum (the oratory in a corner) is unveiled and danced to by the four entranced women. This finale, led by Sister Smoke evokes directly voodoo initiation scenes. Césaire uses colored ribbons in the dance to propose what amounts to a Caribbean federation flag: black, red, yellow and green, which combine the Haïtian colors and those of most African flags.

The resolution of the play also suggests that the runaway might have been Man Soleil's only love and that he probably is the twins' father. Hence the jubilation at discovering a hero for a father and the promise of revolution and social justice. The women possessed by the spirit of Revolution mystically see and "follow" the hero on his "lunar" horse, clearly referring to Toussaint Louverture's best-known portrait. They further visualize the new (1870) "Grand Coumbite" ("working party") of Fonds-Gens-Libres in Martinique as a re-enactment of the foundational meeting of the Haïtian Revolution at Bois-Caïman (1791). The reader-spectator is therefore invited to view the invisible but very present hero-father as a forceful, inspiring symbol. Obviously the father-figure has to do with the "absent" but forgiven father of the Caribbean collective unconscious rather than with Ina Césaire's own (and quasi-mythical) father, Aimé, who is well-loved indeed and has always been very "present" to his people, as the world knows.

So the question of Haïti is well-developed in these plays but in completely different modes. All three require a single set and a modest, restricted one at that: the modest schack of the man in Schwarz-Bart's play, Emma's jaded sitting-room in Condé's play and likewise the main room of Mama Sun's cabin, where the women work, talk, wait, and finally dance. Dance, music and singing – all inspired or directly borrowed from Haïtian culture – are common features of the play. Marie-Ange sings on her tape for her husband, who sees her also dancing in his mind (beyond a gauze screen in actual performance) and joins her in the final love dance. Emma and Ismael also indulge and dance to nostalgic tunes in musical interludes; and Césaire's play can be truly spectacular with several songs and complex choreography at work. Both Schwarz-Bart's and Césaire's plays actually require actresses with established singing skills. Through these interludes different levels of symbolic meaning are achieved, the most complex of which is to be found in Césaire's play.

Schwarz-Bart does not refer to Haïtian history but only to daily life, underscoring the island as a country of emigration and hardship but not of despair, a soul-country to which one longs to return and plans to return. The island in this case is an icon of universal poverty as well as a vital and positive space. The fundamental plea is for the fundamentals of life: love and child-bearing, a topic scantily treated by Caribbean women, perhaps because it is only too present in real life. If this sounds trite in my own words, Schwarz-Bart's work of language is magical. It is "creolized" through imagery and largely "litotic" or non-dramatic, and she also relies on humor (through stage instructions in particular, such as Wilnor's mimicks and remarks while he listens to the tape). Here is a sample where Marie-Ange explains, "The first time your good friend came was Wednesday, January second, St-Eustache's Day. I thought of you when I saw him and accepted him in my bed after he threatened not to give me my money. He came back on January 7th, Saturday and again I thought of you. Then I thought of you on Monday, January 9th, on Wednesday, January 11th and again on Tuesday the 17th, and that was it. That day, your image fell off his forehead like a fish-scale and I threw him out, I ordered him never to set foot on my floor again. I've seen nothing since. (*Pause*) I've done all that must be done to tire my belly out (*Pause*). In the end I lost half of my blood and they took me to the hospital. (*Pause*). But the child would not go with my blood, it did not, Wilnor, it didn't. (*Pause*). Goodbye for good, Wilnor." ["Adieu."][6]

With Condé, as one familiar with her work might expect, the language is more straightforward and the intimate does not prevail over the political, although this remains Condé's most "intimate" play, actually written to honor an actress and friend, Sonia Lee. Haïti in the late eighties was a major preoccupation of hers; she also published a text for young readers on the tragic fate of boat people under the title *Haïti chérie* (Bayard, 1987), where she uses the voice of a young girl. In *The Tropical Breeze Hotel* male politics and the violence of the Duvalier regime provide the background: the plot is grounded in recent Haïtian history. But the play must also be viewed within the context of Condé's theatre as part of a "genre" transposable or at least comparable to quite a few historical plays dealing with fascism and politics. Condé has delt with such topics before in her plays and novels, and with the theme of the young revolutionary or the leader with impure motives. In fact Condé's works could be related to Camus' studies on Revolution, raised as she was on existentialist philosophy. A newer generation carries on this impressive political dramatic vein: one can think (in the wake of the foundational *Tragédie du Roi Christophe* by Aimé Césaire) of Sony Labou-Tansi's *Parenthèse de sang* or Michèle Rakotoson's *La maison morte*. Those plays also illustrate (and geographically enrich) a sub-genre of historical drama from around the francophone world (the Congo and Madagascar in the cited examples). To contextualize Condé's play further, I would like to emphasize that it gives exceptional space to the motif of love and feminine psychology: if Emma lets go of Ismael and the desire to go home with a man (as well as visit her mother's grave), it is because she is impressed with the quality of his devotion to his lover. In other words, the emotional prevails over the political for Emma and somehow Ismael's betrayals are redeemed on account of true love. For Condé of course the political had to be upheld and Ismael must not survive.

While Condé inscribes the political dimension more forcefully among the three plays treated here, it is Ina Césaire who gives Haïtian history a mythical dimension in hers, a play about an obscure Martinican female rebel. Césaire posits the Haïtian model of revolution as the spiritual force behind Martinican struggles. Although the same ideal of love and the monogamous couple appears in *Fire's Daughters*, it is definitely a marginal theme, overshadowed by the women's commitment to social change, be it through fire. Their rescue and protection of the male hero is a situational outcome of their spirit of freedom, inherited from and rooted in Haïti's history.

Finally, in the plays discussed, the stake is not heroism but a specified struggle: a revolution – small or large – must happen. The man need not die as hero or martyr, but he needs to start a new existence where human love and life values can be central. Condé "executes" her male protagonist but her heroine, Emma, survives and remains pure at heart. Wilnor wins in that he recovers his love and admiration for his wife despite the crisis of her sexual betrayal; meanwhile Marie-Ange has retained her integrity through her confession, and she has grown in stature as well as in her belly (remember that we are not told that she has had children by Wilnor). Mama Sun and Rosanie (as well as Einasor[7] and Sister Smoke) all come through the crisis empowered and jubilant. Clearly these are modern women's discourses, assertive of life and femaleness. I would venture that "Haïti," with its multifarious connotations in Caribbean and world history, holds the place of the African spirit, working as the prime source of inspiration and model of liberation in these plays and probably in all Black works referring to Haïti. "Haïti" is the heroic shepherd (not just Toussaint, or the other founding fathers) of Caribbean creative imagination. The icon cannot be blamed for women's troubles but it is clearly presented by several Franco-Caribbean women playwrights as an icon in need of re-visitation/revision.

Notes

1. A preliminary version of this article was delivered at the haïtian studies conference of october 28–31, 1998 in Port-au-Prince, Haïti. A travel grant from the penn state glo-

bal fund, the french dept and the dept of comparative literature enabled me to attend this conference, organized by Alix Cantave.
2.   See Texts Cited for my own articles on Condé, Ina Césaire and Michèle Césaire.
3.   Psychiatrist have told us that the olfactory function was the most archaic of the five sensory functions.
4.   The exemplum of the reviled mulatta is Mayotte Capécia. See my book, *Mayotte Capécia ou l'aliénation selon Fanon* (Paris: Karthala, 1999. ISBN : 2–86537–860–8).
5.   See Makward, 1997.
6.   My translation from p. 36.
7.   I have shown how Ina Césaire affiliates herself through onomastics with Rosanie (cf. Makward, 1996).

Texts cited

Césaire, Ina. *Rosanie Soleil*. 1992 [unpublished in French]. Translated by Judith G. Miller as *Fire's Daughters*. New York: Ubu Repertory Theatre, 1993.

Condé, Maryse. *Pension les Alizés* (Paris: Mercure de France, 1988). Translated as *The Tropical Breeze Hotel*. New York: Ubu Repertory Theatre, 1994.

Makward, C. "Reading Maryse Condé's Theatre," *Callaloo* 1995. 18, 3: 681–689.

"De Bouche à Oreille à Bouche : Ethno-dramaturgie d'Ina Césaire," *L'Héritage de Caliban*, Maryse Condé, ed. (Guadeloupe: Jasor): 132–146.

"Filles du soleil noir; sur deux pièces d'Ina Césaire et Michèle Césaire" in *Elles écrivent des Antilles*, Suzanne Rinne and Joëlle Vitiello. Paris: L'Harmattan: 335–347.

Schwarz-Bart, Simone. *Ton beau capitaine*. Paris: Seuil, 1987. Translated as *Your Handsome Captain*. New York: Ubu Repertory Theatre.

Chantal Chawaf's Mourning Child

Michèle Respaut

Chantal Chawaf's *Le manteau noir*, published in 1998 by Flammarion, has received glowing notices in the press, to a large extent as a "breakthrough" work that recapitulates and transcends the oppressive themes that have always characterized her writing. Indeed, it is a book filled with long, repetitive, and painful passages about lost parents, dead children, dismembered bodies. Called a "novel" on the title page and an "autofiction" on the back cover, it is also said there to shatter "certains tabous sur une époque obscure (certain taboos regarding a dark period)," namely the horrors of the Second World War. Much of its resonance for reviewers indeed would seem to come from its participation in a national vogue of writing, previously explored in Blanchot's *Ecriture du désastre* (1980) and Duras' *La douleur* (1985), about the unspeakable events of half a century ago, in forms that fluctuate between novelistic creation and personal memoir.

As the reader gradually learns, *Le manteau noir* recounts the struggle of a woman, called Marie-Antoinette, through her childhood, adolescence, and adult years, to discover her true origins. Haunted from her earliest memories by images of a maternal body among visions of destruction and myriad shattered forms, she learns that she was born by caesarian section to a couple killed during the Allies' bombings of Paris suburbs, her mother having expired just after her birth. Scenes of herself as a death-marked child in a sterile nursery mingle with glimpses of her adoptive mother (Dadou) and father, who, she later discovers, acquired her illegally. While her birth mother is imagined as refined, and indeed noble, Dadou, who worships the protagonist, speaks the language of the lower classes. Dady, as she calls her adoptive father, was a collaborator during the Occupation and subsequently experiences business failure.

This information comes to the protagonist and the reader in sporadic, intermittent fashion, in a text heavily laden with Chawaf's recurrent thematic concerns and stylistic modes. A firm armature is however supplied in the book's division into a Première Epoque, "La guerre et après la guerre," (The First Part: "War and after the war") with chapter titles that carry the protagonist from infancy to adolescence (and to an explosive confession by Dadou and Dady that she is in fact adopted). Then in the Deuxième Epoque, "Le voyage de retour," (The Second Part: The Return Trip) her extensive investigations and archival research, to which are joined "témoignages" (eye-witness accounts) from presumably real individuals, produce much information on the bombings and deaths, but not the identity of the birth parents. Nonetheless, at the end of the work, Marie-Antoinette attains serenity in her dedication to the mission of becoming a writer.

The division into temporal periods and the chapter titles do not of course make the reading of this work linear in any simple way. On the contrary, *Le manteau noir* might be thought to illustrate the proposition that Freud was on target in his arguments about compulsive repetition, the illusoriness of "memory," and the sexual dynamic relating parents and children. (And/or that Chawaf, like many other writers, knows a good deal about Freud). Indeed, reading *Le manteau noir* gives the reader a not altogether pleasurable and overly long sense of déjà vu, extending back through *Maternité* and *Rougeâtre*, to Chawaf's first book, *Rétable la rêverie*. This short work, published in 1974, is based on the identical scenario as the author's latest, 400-plus page "autofiction" which, according to the dates given on the last page, was five years in the making.

Certainly the sense of being foreign experienced by the book's protagonist in the long opening sequence is that of an orphan. Much else is understandable in terms of the Freudian mechanisms suggested above, and specifically as deriving from the later revelations about the true circumstances of her birth. Hence we repeatedly encounter intense images of the mother's stomach and womb, of the birth trauma, as well as virtually apocalyptic scenes of bombings, destruction and mutilated bodies. In this vividly red initial sequence (red for birth, red for violent death), it is the birth mother, the "virtual" mother, the "mère matricielle," who in her death is compulsively imagined – as invincible, all-powerful, perfect.

A deathly white sequence follows, conveying the experience of the very young child in a nursery which, she later learns, was directed by a Nazi sympathizer under the Pétain regime. She understands there that only one nurse can bear looking at her, because she smells of death and provokes fear. Again and again the scenes of bombing and of horribly fragmented bodies intrude. Recurrently, too, her parents appear in ghostly fashion, as "fantômes" and "revenants," as ghosts.

Subsequent passages involve a complex dialectic in the protagonist's experience and imagination of adoptive and birth parents, with emphasis on the mothers – Dadou and the "mère matricielle." As already mentioned, Dadou speaks a racy, almost gutter French, which contrasts with the reserve, dignity, sense of superiority of the protagonist and therefore of her imagined birth mother. Nonetheless Dadou is seen as a worshipful maternal figure, and the protagonist conveys her own sensuous pleasure and wonder at the way in which she is looked upon, caressed, fed. Mingled with her sense of strangeness and her hostility, there is gratitude. But, while she constantly fantasizes about her dead mother, Marie-Antoinette cannot imagine a similar process as occurring in the mind of Dadou. Instead, what happens may be conceived as a transfer of a sense of abandonment by the dead mother onto the figure of Dadou, and a simultaneous appropriation by Marie-Antoinette of the best of the real and imagined qualities of both of her mothers. Although constantly seeing herself as an orphan, the protagonist is mentally surrounded by multiple maternal figures.

Marie-Antoinette's adoptive father, Dady, is given less emphasis, with the exception of the child's happy memories of her experience at the country estate in Vaucresson which he later loses in his financial decline. There she played among the trees, echoing another motif, that of tree trunks shattered by bomb blasts, but instantaneously replanted. In the protagonist's mind personal symbolism is generated - her genealogical tree has been destroyed, and she has been replanted in another. Curiously, in this mother-haunted work, the phallic and paternal motif emerges strongly in the positive concluding pages. Clothed in a pink dress, evidently a fusion of the earlier red and white patterns, Marie-Antoinette begins to write among trees recalling the trees of Dady's lost country estate.

But this resolution cannot occur until after the long second "Epoque," a two-year period following the death of the adoptive parents, in which Marie Antoinette constantly wears the black coat that provides the title of the book. Ill-fitting, with sleeves too long, and shapeless so as to hide her developing self, the coat represents at once her mourning and the chrysalis from which she will later emerge, reborn. Clothed in black, for two years she pursues her past, alternating between the blackness of the archives and the stifling outer air, questioning witnesses and librarians, consulting documents. A further kind of reiterative writing is encountered here, and we realize that her hands, themselves ink-stained from handling ancient documents, are creating another overblown text destined to replace the simple formulas of the absent birth certificate (destroyed as part of the illegal adoption).

Marie-Antoinette's search for her name, for her true identity, therefore proves fruitless, yet finally produces a liberating experience (409–411). Forever separated from "l'autre monde" ("the other world") inhabited by her birth parents, for the last time she sees "les ombres des deux fantômes se profiler au-dessus des arbres" ("the shadows of two ghosts above the trees"). Begging forgiveness for being alive herself, she is reduced to listing the scores and scores of Allied bombings of Parisian suburbs from 1942 to 1944, concluding, "En 1944, en cinq mois, d'avril à août, les bombardements avaient tué sept mille personnes et en avaient blessé neuf mille" ("In 1944, in five months, from April to August, the bombings had killed seven thousand people and wounded nine thousand"). Personal loss and national mourning, a half century after the unspeakable events, come together, in a radically reduced form of writing, that of the list.

Immediately there follow the questions: "Comment témoignera-t-elle? Pour dire l'indicible? ("How will she bear witness? Say the unsayable?") The answer comes quickly: "Elle a été foetus, petite fille, femme quinquagénaire. Elle n'a plus qu'à être écrivain, qu'à tenter d'écrire la constance cruelle d'un souvenir à travers tous ces ages [...]" ; "C'est l'écriture qui saura, qui pourra dire. C'est par l'écriture que la parole reviendra [...]" ; "Ses parents le lui disent : 'Sois écrivain !' Il faut témoigner contre la guerre, défendre toutes ces pauvres multitudes de civils tués [...]" "She has been a foetus, a litlle girl, a woman in her fifties. It only remains for her to be a writer, to attempt to write the cruel constency of a memory throughout all these ages [...]; writing will know, will be able to say. It is through writing that speech will come back [...]. Her parents say it to her: 'Become a writer !' You must bear witness against the war, defend all these poor multitudes of killed civilians [...]"

Just as quickly, there follows the concluding segment of the book (415–417), which is intended to establish a lightened and liberated tone. A woman clothed in a pink cotton dress begins to write her life story in the garden of a hotel with a view of the sea that she has rented for two weeks ! Here the lightness and the sudden acceleration of time verge on unintentional self-parody. The reader of Chawaf's corpus in the "post-apocalyptic" setting announced by Blanchot may also find what follows, in this positive coda, to be overly familiar, even banal. The trees reappear, with an exhilarating symbolism of ascension, air, light, and the fullness of animals and birds in universal nature – "La vie est partout [...]" For the first time, too, the narrator, heretofore referred to as "elle" or "tu," speaks in the first person, as she feels the wind "sur ma peau nue" ("on my naked skin"). Quickly this nakedness expands into a familiar Chawaf version of body oriented "écriture féminine": "Mon corps s'ouvrait, ma peau nue, sous mes vêtements s'excitait, humait le terreau, je sentais les émanations des esprits des bois passer entre ma chair et ma joie, entrer, circuler, courir, affluer aux battements de mon coeur en liesse dans ma poitrine gonflée de parfums comestibles [...]" ("My body opened up, became excited beneath my clothes, smelled the compost, I felt the emanations of the spirits of the forest pass between my flesh and my happiness, enter, circulate, run, flow into the beatings of my exultant heart into my chest swelling with edible smells"). A page of this kind of writing reinvests the trees with the maternal and familial presence, which however does not prevent a solitary sense of self: "Au sein du silence, je me reconstituais, à l'écart" ("In the heart of silence, I was reconstituting myself, apart").

I presume and hope that I am not the only reader to see this last as the dominant note in a work and a mode of writing that is ultimately narcissistic and invasive. Orphaned and obsessively in search of her mother, Marie-Antoinette/Chawaf produces a text that itself is womb-like, constantly containing and producing a mother and a father, but most of all herself. The book's last paragraph, a single, long, open-ended sentence, is a particularly lame and revealing example of this kind of writing. Again the trees are there, identified both with the mother and with the "immémorial arbre généalogique des lignées de la terre archaïque dont je descendais et dont je ne pourrais jamais trahir l'amour [...]" ("The immemorial genealogical tree of the lines of the archaïc earth from which I issued and whose love I would never be able to betray"). Once more the protagonist merges with nature, becoming both tree and squirrel. And once again, as throughout her production, Chawaf's body writing comes to the fore, as Marie-Antoinette evokes "cette vitalité qui bouillonnait, crachait comme de la lave dans l'éveil de ma chair [...]" ("this vitality that seethed, spat like lava in the awakening of my flesh"). But the final words express the writer's noble mission to remember and to defend – "la défense de la vie partout où elle était agressée, méconnue. L'important avait été de me souvenir..." ("the defense of life wherever it is attacked, ignored. The important thing was to remember ..."). Evoking great personal suffering as well as the past of a nation striving to remember while also striving to forget, *Le manteau noir* may be seen as a courageous endeavor, but also as banal repetition, and ultimately as a kind of post-apocalyptic commonplace.

Translated by Dawn M. Cornelio

Big Bad Wolf: A Short Chapter in the Long Story of Franco-American Relations

Susan Rubin Suleiman

In 1995, France's conservative daily *Le Figaro* was found guilty of libel and condemned to pay damages, after a suit brought by my colleague Alice Jardine and me. What follows is my highly subjective account of the story, with a few speculations about its current cultural and political significance.

The news arrived on a sunny day in April 1994, when my friend Denis Hollier called me from New Haven: "As-tu lu Le *Figaro Mag*? Que vas-tu faire?" he asked. No, I hadn't read *Le Figaro Mag* – neither had he, until someone called him from Paris. He was mentioned in the article, and he was furious. I was mentioned too, he said – in fact, the Harvard French department was featured. I had better go and read the thing; I wouldn't be pleased, he predicted.

A quick trip to the kiosk in Harvard Square, and I held the glossy magazine, weekly supplement to *Le Figaro*, in my hands. April 16, 1994: we were not quite the lead story, that role was reserved for "SOS Rwanda." But we were next: "Enquête sur les campus américains: cette drôle de France, *Made in USA*," by one Victor Loupan, with cartoons by Calvi to liven up the prose. A man in stocks, his feet in chains, walks painfully on what appears to be a "typical American campus" lawn while three women students – one very tall, one wide, all wearing "sensible shoes" – look on: "He wanted to teach us a reactionary author, white, antifeminist, a certain Molière," one woman says, while another adds: "And French to boot."

What was going on here? And what did it have to do with Harvard, where the canon of French authors, classical and modern, has been taught uninterruptedly for decades?

It didn't take long to figure it out. Victor Loupan had come not to "survey" but to bury all those American academics he could associate, from near or far, with "le politiquement correct." But especially, women. Armed with stereotypes and a well-thumbed copy of Dinesh D'Souza's *Illiberal Education* (remember that bestselling 1991 diatribe against feminismdeconstructionmulticulturalism? A flag of the conservative backlash in the U.S.), Loupan had spent a day in Cambridge and spoken to one or two male colleagues at Harvard. He had made no attempt to contact us "feminists," his targets. Guerilla warfare, I mused (or did he think we bacchae would tear him limb from limb?).

"Harvard est le temple du *politically correct*. C'est-à-dire de la nouvelle police de la pensée. Un auteur ancien y est un auteur suspect. Voire proscrit. Une oeuvre contemporaine y sera enseignée si son auteur est femme (au minimum), de couleur (si possible), et homosexuel (c'est parfait)."[1] In short, we women of Harvard were destroying French literature as well as ruining American education: Loupan had seen us with his own eyes, Alice Jardine, Nadine Bérenguier and me, dispensing our poison to poor brainwashed students in the classrooms of Boylston Hall.

Oh, the powers of fantasy ! Nadine, a junior colleague specializing in 18th century French literature, was on leave in Berlin that spring; and I was not teaching my course on 20th century realist fiction, in which M. Loupan claimed he heard me lecture (on "the ideology of the white heterosexual man, of course: the thought of the enemy" – p. 10). As for Alice, she hadn't had any visitors in her classes lately.[2] Our brave journalist had simply read the course catalog or rather, misread it – and let his imagination do the rest. Feminists, especially American feminists, are man-hating lesbian ideologues, everybody knows that. At least, everybody that Victor Loupan was writing for knew that. Why, then, bother to seek out the facts? They would only cloud his clear certainties – about American women and American universities, indeed about the cultural evolution of this whole big country he had come to analyze on a two-day trip.

Tocqueville, he wasn't.

Was I laughing yet? Well, almost, it was so ludicrous: Monsieur Loupan obviously took himself for a Big Bad Wolf, Grand Méchant Loup, baring his fangs at us poor piglettes. But so far, he had shown himself to be merely a little man ("not a *loup* but a *loupan*," I murmured) with a poison pen and a hyperactive fantasy life.

Then my eye fell on a paragraph I found not funny at all: "Il fut un temps pourtant, où la faculté de français de Harvard était l'un des pôles intellectuels de l'Université. Elle avait en son sein des sommités telles que Paul Bénichou..., ou Jean Bruneau... Parmi les femmes qui ont succédé à ces grands professeurs, seule Alice Jardine peut présenter un semblant de bagage universitaire. Et lequel? Une traduction du français en anglais. De quelle oeuvre? D'un livre de Julia Kristeva."[3] In other words, we were not only feminazis but incompetent females, without the slightest academic accomplishment – oh yes, Alice had a tiny claim to "baggage" as a translator, but as for Nadine and me: zero.[4]

Now I am a fairly even-tempered person; my years spent as the mother of two teenage sons have trained me in diplomatic skills. But after reading those lines, I was mad as hell. The would-be Méchant Loup had crossed a line: malicious fantasy is one thing, but malicious incompetence is another. A right-wing French journalist out to "get" American feminists had, one might argue, the right to spin fantasies about those he considered his enemies. But did he have the right not to do his job? The most inexperienced rookie would have known to at least check a library or bookstore before making sweeping claims about a Harvard professor's academic qualifications or accomplishments. Loupan had not even bothered to do that, but jauntily proclaimed that we had none. No baggage, only the semblance of baggage and very little of that... Would he have dared to treat a male Harvard professor, even one he called his enemy, with such nonchalant disregard, such casual irresponsibility, I wondered.

I called Alice Jardine, my good friend and colleague; her reaction to the article was similar to mine, as was Nadine's. Our students and other colleagues were outraged too. The question was, as Denis had asked: what would we do about it? I called friends in France, who gave me the name of a lawyer specializing in libel, Maître Hervé Cren. After he read the article, he faxed me to say he thought we had a case against the *Figaro*: our reputation and honor had been "touched" by that paragraph about academic baggage. The *Figaro* was evidently worried, for it devoted a whole page of *Le Figaro Magazine* to the angry letters several of us – including Nadine Bérenguier and Denis Hollier – sent to the Editor in reply to Loupan's article (May 20, 1994). Our letters were prefaced by a dismissive Editor's note, but the fact that they were published *en masse*, uncut, indicated a certain anxiety.

After several more weeks of consultation and soul-searching (neither of us had ever sued anyone), Alice and I decided to sue the *Figaro* for libel, "atteinte à l'honneur et à la considération." We were

encouraged by the fact that French libel laws are generally more favorable to the plaintiff than American ones: it is enough to show that
the libelous statements were not made in good faith, and that they
are such as to harm one's honor and reputation (in the U.S., one has
to show actual harm done). Even more important, perhaps, the
French legal fees would not become uncontrollably high (in the
U.S., the fees are truly daunting). There was a risk, of course, that
we might lose, and in either case the expenditure in time and energy
would be huge. But we felt we had to do it: the insult had been at
once too casual and too grave, the lack of journalistic integrity too
glaring to be passed over in silence. We hoped that our case would,
if nothing else, make the *Figaro* and other French papers pay more
attention to elementary fact-checking before they let loose their
venom on things "made in USA."

Close to three years and several unexpected twists later, the legal saga came to a happy conclusion (for us). The French courts
considered the statement about "no baggage" libelous, and specifically dismissed any defense based on the "good faith" argument:
"faute de s'être livré à une enquête sérieuse... lors de la préparation
de son article, M. Loupan ne saurait se prévaloir du bénéfice de la
bonne foi" ("Since he did not conduct a serious inquiry... in preparing his article, M. Loupan could not claim the benefit of good
faith"). In what must surely be a rare occurrence in legal history,
journalistic laziness and incompetence were juridically recognized
and punished: both Alice Jardine and I were awarded damages.[5]

Aside from the very real, not to be underestimated, sense of
personal satisfaction we derived from our victory, is there any edify-
ing lesson to be drawn from this tale? Perhaps not (though Alice and
I are sometimes tempted to sing the praises of the French legal system, which acted with admirable impartiality, "above the fray"). But
the story suggests at least two questions worth pondering, one concerning women, the other concerning current Franco-American relations.

First question: Is it more "permissible" in our culture to attack
women – including, or perhaps especially, women who are perceived
as powerful – than men? I ask this because of the grossly disrespect-
ful way in which Loupan did his hatchet job on "the women of Harvard." Curiously, it is the very incompetence that led to our legal
victory that rankles: he did not even take the trouble to attack us
properly, for example by reading our work and then dismissing it as
"worthless." Had he done that, we couldn't have brought a suit
against him: a critic is entitled to his opinion. But he was so sure of
his right to insult us, and of our own "lack of baggage," that he

thought he could get away without doing even a minimum of work. That fact itself is perhaps the clearest indication of a cultural prejudice – one that is as prevalent in France as in the U.S., and probably elsewhere. What exactly is the "baggage" one can be so certain women lack that it needs no verification? The cultural assumption about phallic privilege can hardly find a better illustration.

It should be emphasized, furthermore, that our kind of victory is rare. In many cases, the verbal attack – on a woman's scholarship, teaching, ideas, even her physical attributes – is more clever, if not less mendacious, than Loupan's botched job; and more often than not, those who are targeted simply cannot afford the time, energy, and money needed to fight back.

Second question: Is it more "permissible" in France to attack the United States today than, say, twenty years ago – and if so, of what is that permissiveness the symptom? It seems clear that the French attacks on American "political correctness," many of them astonishingly ill-informed and ill-intentioned, which have been launched since the mid-1990's have little to do with American politics (where similar attacks have a quite different ideological valence) and everything to do with current French debates and anxieties: over "le consensus républicain" and whatever might threaten it; over immigration and the role of minorities in "diluting" French "identity"; over the humiliating memories of less than glorious epochs in recent French history, uncovered by the trials of Paul Touvier and Maurice Papon; over the increasing role of English as a global *lingua franca* and the decreasing role of French; over the increasing cultural hegemony of American film and American rock music even in France; finally, over all the challenges France will have to face as it moves into a less prominent role in global culture and politics.

Not since De Gaulle's diatribes against "l'Amérique" in the 1960's (caused, incidentally, by similar anxieties about France's role in the world) have we seen so many French verbal rockets aimed at the United States. In such a climate, one encounters the surprising phenomenon of agreement between right-wing hacks like Victor Loupan and respectable liberal intellectuals like Alain Finkielkraut, both of them bent on whipping what they see as their enemy – perhaps not so much the "politiquement correct" (although that is how they may see it) as the *made* in *USA*. Is it not a telling coincidence that Loupan's "bible" when he walked the halls at Harvard was published in French in a series edited by Finkielkraut?[6] Like the proverb, these two men can affirm: "The enemy of my enemy is my friend."

Rarely has the misunderstanding between France and the U.S. been greater, it would seem, than today. A full unpacking of this statement would require another essay, for I have not dealt here with the American side of this misunderstanding. As the *Figaro* story shows, however, one of the shared conflictual terrains is that of cultural politics. If French intellectuals often allow national anxieties and a certain anti-Americanism to cloud their view of American reality, Americans don't always fully appreciate the political and intellectual tradition that makes French intellectuals, especially those on the Left, suspicious of every kind of particularism.[7]

Yet, the picture is not all bleak. The young French scholars we welcome at Harvard each year, from the Ecole Normale Supérieure and other institutions of higher learning, show a far more open attitude, both toward the U.S. and toward French identity, than do their elders, the generation of Loupan and Finkielkraut. Similarly, the American students we send to France each year manage to maintain their love of things French (Francophilia is still alive and well on these shores) along with a clearheaded view of France's failings, past and present.

It will be more mutual study and intellectual inquiry (genuine "enquêtes," not yellow journalism) that will produce new, positive chapters in the ongoing story of Franco-American relations.[8]

Notes

1   Harvard is the temple of the *politically correct*. That is, of the new thought police. There an ancient author is suspect, banished even. A contemporary work will be taught if its author is a woman (at the minimum), of color (if possible), and homosexual (it's perfect)." *Le Figaro Magazine*, April 16, 1994, p. 10; my translation.

2   But she had had the visit of Dinesh D'Souza a few years back, and he published a caricatural account in *Illiberal Education*. Loupan merely parroted D'Souza, another corner-cutting measure no doubt.

3   Yet there was a time when the French faculty at Harvard was one of the intellectuals poles of the University. It harbored in its midst such towering intellects as Paul Bénichou..., or Jean Bruneau... Among the women who succeeded these great professors, only Alice Jardine can present a semblance of academic qualifications. What? A translation from French to English. Of which work? A book by Julia Kristeva." (pp. 16–17)

4   At the time Loupan wrote those words, Alice Jardine had published, among other works, her acclaimed book *Gynesis: Configurations of Woman and Modernity*, several co-edited volumes including *Men in Feminism* and *Shifting Scenes: Interviews on Women, Writing, and Politics in Post-1968 France*, and numerous articles. My publications included *Authoritariam Fictions: The Ideological Novel as a Literary Genre, Subversive Intent: Gender, Politics, and the Avant-Garde*, the edited volumes *The Reader in the Text* and *The Female Body in Western Culture*, and dozens of articles. Full professors at Harvard, we had both held prestigious fellowships, received significant awards, directed NEH Summer Institutes. As for Nadine Bérenguier, she had diplomas from France as well as a Ph.D. from Stanford, and was working on her first book after publishing several articles.

5   The legal twists in this case were quite fascinating, baroque even. Due to a technicality involving the date when the affidavits were delivered to the *Figaro* (we were filing se-

parate suits), my original suit was thrown out by the court: my affidavit had been mistakenly delivered two days after the deadline by the *huissier*, the official to whom it had to be submitted by our lawyer for delivery. (In libel cases in France, there is a three-month statute of limitations for suing, and we had waited until the last minute to bring our suits). After Alice won her case, I was able to bring – and win – a suit against the *huissier* for depriving me of the compensation I would certainly have won against the *Figaro*. But before that, we had to wait until a second judgment was handed down in Alice's case, for the *Figaro* appealed the original judgment – and lost again. Our lawyer, Maître Cren, handled all the cases with practiced calm, efficiency, and humor: at the first trial, he arrived with a small suitcase full of our publications, our "baggage."

6   Dinesh D'Souza, *L'éducation contre les libertés*. Paris: Gallimard, 1994.

7   The current debate, in France, over the kind of information reportable on the census (should ethnic origin be indicated? For what purposes?) shows just how complicated this question is. See *Le Monde*, November 6, 1998, p. 10.

8   I wish to thank Alice Jardine, Daniel Suleiman, and Michael Suleiman for their very helpful comments on an earlier version of this essay.

A Conversation with Marguerite Yourcenar[1]

Assia Djebar

1. Rather than thanking you directly for the 1997 "Marguerite Yourcenar" prize for my stories in the collection *Oran, langue morte*, I ask if you will instead allow me to hold an imaginary conversation with Madame Yourcenar.

The idea came to me when I discovered that Marguerite Yourcenar, the young translator of Virginia Woolf's *The Waves*, had met her great English elder sister in London. Whenever Yourcenar mentions this interview, we are all – we women writers at the end of this century – inclined to tremble with emotion at the thought of this tête-a-tête, some sixty years ago, between these two extraordinary women, the one thirty years older than the other. Yet it seems that nothing was really said: of course, Madame Yourcenar was merely a translator in the eyes of Virginia Woolf who, nearing the end of her life, was doubtless the more vulnerable of the two.

Yes, their meeting seems to have been purely symbolic, since Woolf was allowing the young Franco-Belgian woman complete freedom in her translation. Thus, there would not have been an actual "conversation": no current passed between these two sensitive, good-hearted women, there was not even a literary exchange since Yourcenar most likely didn't dare refer to her own writings in front of the "grande dame" of English letters…

In fact, it seems to me that the opposite of what one would have expected must have occurred: the older, more famous woman turning out to be more fearful, penetrating more deeply into those anxieties that would, in the end, get the better of her and eventually lead her to commit suicide (I have seen that house with that garden, and especially that river in which she drowned herself, large pebbles in her pockets).

So it was: the younger woman, the one who was almost just starting out who, sitting before Virginia – who seemed frozen by timidity or propriety – was already stronger; disappointed only when she left that Virginia Woolf had demonstrated a merely courteous and tolerant good will toward her French translator.

There was no true conversation-made up of exchanges, questions, comments, intersecting doubts – like those that might have taken place at times between women writers of different languages and different countries, at least, let's say, in the last two or three decades.

Why, then, have I sketched this hollow meeting between Madame Yourcenar and Virginia (and you see that, even for us today, Yourcenar remains Madame Yourcenar and the great, the disconcerting Virginia Woolf becomes, more often than not, "Virginia")?

I have done so in order to confirm for myself that all encounters between writers separated by 20, 30, or 40 years are, more often than not, symbolic. I console myself in this way for never having met – I, anonymous in a conference room, up close or from a distance – Madame Yourcenar ! What remains, then, is convention, the literary exercise of the imaginary conversation.

2. "Madame Yourcenar," I would say first, "when faced with the two masterpieces that established your international reputation – *The Memoirs of Hadrian* and *L'oeuvre au noir* (both written in the United States and separated, it may help to recall, by 17 years of work) – I, your reader, who have kept these novels on my bookshelves (despite moving several times from country to country, and now from one continent to another) – I, the reader and the author who began to approach the genre of the "historical novel" only some fifteen years ago and, let's say, in the second half of my life, when confronted with these two works swarming with characters, actions, ideas, I always begin at the end, that is, by the author's notes.

For I thank you for proceeding, at the moment of publication – and I would say as a woman 'in her kitchen,' or as an apothecary, or a chemist – to give the details of your compositions, your recipes, let's say simply your sources. First I would like to hail the author, or the artisan, with her meticulous and scrupulous honesty for enumerating, for both the book that takes place in antiquity and the one that takes place in the 16th century, their erudite sources: the literary reminiscences, the images and statues of ancient art, the drawings, the bas-reliefs. Zeno (born ca. 1510) you remind us, would have been a contemporary of the great surgeon Ambroise Paré, of Giordano Bruno who was burned at the stake (Zeno, on the other hand, killed himself); you tell us that several episodes of his life were borrowed from the life of Erasmus (the illegitimate birth, for example). You inform us that a surgical operation was based on Ambroise Paré's narrative of it in his memoirs. Several passages of dialogue where Zeno speaks are, you acknowledge, from Leonard de Vinci. And as for the alchemical formulas in Latin, you took them directly from learned works on alchemy whose references you give.

In sum, Madame Yourcenar, you turn the cards face-up, you unfold the secrets of your creation… You point out quite proudly that you created false things (the imaginary Zeno) with scattered bits of realia found, read, or seen, and that the alchemy of writing produces vivid life that dances dazzlingly before our eyes.

You allow us to be the judge. And, as you remark at the end of *Hadrian* (your notes were published six or seven years after the original edition that appeared in 1951): "One foot in erudition, the other in magic, or, more precisely, and without metaphor, in that kind of magic that consists of transporting oneself in thought inside someone else." And, just a little further on, you add (alternating in your inimitable way skepticism with serenity and the confidence of someone who is ending her work as it should be ended): "Everything escapes us, and everyone, and we ourselves. My father's life is more unfamiliar to me than Hadrian's !"

3. The statement "everything escapes us" can seem surprising coming from a woman like you who no doubt has been too quickly idolized by others for her mastery of character and style. I am coming back to this statement, this time to tell you: the words "everything escapes us" remind me of how your author's notes at the end of those two "power-novels" that I would define above all as "European" (the one set in the West of the Roman Empire, the other set in the 16th century, during a time of religious schisms and French-Spanish rivalries), reveal to us that these works, constructed on the foundation of a broad vision of the world and on the supreme will of woman, nonetheless might never have seen the light of day.

Yes, you tell us so yourself. With a slight smile, almost in passing. In these two long post-scriptums, you have, more than anything, retraced for us the genesis of your writing.

You resuscitated the Emperor Hadrian, and seventeen years later you invented Zeno. Both Zeno and Hadrian were men of peace, struggling to maintain it, bent on healing, on avoiding persecution, and on providing a lucid view of the tumultuousness of their eras…

But it was by a hair's breadth that you were able to deliver unto us the almost miraculous accident (and there is a shadow of a novel behind each novel) of the definitive birth of characters that had haunted you since your youth.

Let us recall, following in your footsteps, that you conceived this book that brings Hadrian back to life between 1924 and 1929, between your twentieth and twenty-fifth birthdays. These abandoned pages were taken up again between 1934 and 1937; only a single sentence from that 1934 text, itself abandoned, remains in the present text. Thus, you had abandoned this project between 1939 and 1948, and here you add this revealing commentary: "...sinking into the despair of a writer who does not write."

Then a miracle occurs: in December 1948, you receive a trunk filled with 10-year-old papers from Switzerland. In one night, you sort, toss, burn... Then, on five typewritten sheets that you are about to destroy, you read what begins "My dear Marc,": "Marc," you say to yourself. "What friend, lover, distant relative is he?" You don't recall any Marc. You read a few more lines.

It turns out to be Marc(us) Aurelius, and the pages are a fragment of the 1939 manuscript... that you thought had been lost ! ... That night, you reread Dom Cassius, and a History of Augustus. That night, you make the decision to go back to the Emperor...

"I was leaving for Taos, in New Mexico !"

In a sleeping car between New York and Chicago, you write. The next day, in the station in Chicago (the train is blocked by snow), you write. And you write in the train to Santa Fe... You add: "I can hardly recall a more ardent day, nor more lucid nights !..."

Then... then, on 26 December 1950, that is, exactly two years later, on Mount Desert Island, you write the final pages of *The Death of Hadrian*, which ends with his last thought: "Let us try to enter into death with our eyes open !"

You also remind us that the source for *L'oeuvre au noir* was a 50-page narrative entitled "D'après Dürer" published in 1934. This text is itself merely a remnant saved from what you call "a too ambitious novel," conceived between 1921 and 1925.

Here again, renunciation casts a black shadow at the start: the young woman of vast vision must admit that she does not (that she will never) have the means to express what exists in her imagination-I was about to say her "visitation."

In 1955, 21 years after the fifty-page narrative, the remains of that novel dreamed of 10 years earlier, the book is nonetheless, finally, begun. Of the first original outline there only remain, you tell us, a few fragments in the chapter entitled "Conversation at Insbruk." The present *Oeuvre au noir* was in the main composed between 1962 and 1965.

In an interview you give later, you mention the day you finished your novel in your house on Mount Desert Island: once again it ends with the hero's death; this time, a voluntary death. You say you repeated the name Zeno three hundred times – as if to fill yourself with it, to become drunk on it. "Zeno exists at last !" you thought. Exhaustion or victory? In any event, here also, after abandonment, renunciation, distance, you return to the task and, in a final, long, slow movement, the book is born at long last.

Perhaps it was necessary [I am returning to your notes to *Hadrian]* to find this solution of continuity, this rupture, this night of the soul that so many of us have experienced, each in her own way, and so often in a way much more tragic than I ... to force me to try to overcome, not only the distance separating me from Hadrian, but above all the one that separated me from myself !"

And there we are. I am illuminating here a sensitive – I was about to say vulnerable – spot.

For you are vulnerable, Madame Marguerite Yourcenar; or, in any case, you often have been ... In your labor, on your path to writing, and in spite of all your travels, your pleasures, your freedoms, and your amazement at being alive.

To conclude, I must return to that encounter I mentioned at the beginning: you, the secretive young person, seemingly timid as you sit before Virginia Woolf to ask for *licence de traduction française* !

It was easy for me to imagine Virginia in pain, suffering, weakened, and because of this, already distant. Whereas I sketched you strong too quickly. The stronger of the two. Young, proud, and merely disappointed by the non-exchange, by the convention that did not allow for real dialogue. But now, having followed you a bit today in the shadow of your two greatest books, I discover you to be fragile, doubting, in despair, then, miraculously, finally taking off, and, as you say almost lovingly, knowing at last, in creation brought to its end, "ardent days and lucid nights !"

As for me – made vulnerable by my present expatriation, by the shadow that follows me or penetrates me, by my Muslim culture in the feminine – it is in your hidden weakness, so rarely revealed, but which you yourself acknowledge, and in the tenacity of your creative effort that I feel myself somewhat reassured: thanks to you, in your presence. Following your example – on American soil, and so far from the land of my birth – still and forever in tumult – I am brought back, in my turn, to this sole movement of writing. I write in displacement, but this writing reinvents its anchors.

Madame Yourcenar, in this you remain exemplary. Ten years after your death on American soil, your French language transported here, I will sum up your life as "a wandering life" joined to "an immobile life."

Thanking you for your stoic example,

Assia Djebar
Boston
9 December 1997

Translated by Alyson Waters

Notes

1   This text is Assia Djebar's acceptance speech for the Prix Yourcenar awarded in December 1997 at Harvard University, Cambridge, MA.

Mid-Life Memoirs and the Bicultural Dilemma

Isabelle de Courtivron

I. Living My Life Through Texts:

George Sand was one of my earliest models.

As I emerged from my "jeune fille rangée" upbringing, Sand represented the free spirit, the androgynous, liberated woman, the energetic revolutionary, the indefatigable *provocatrice* of her milieu, the productive and socially-defiant figure whom I could admire, and perhaps eventually emulate, at a time when intellectual and sexual challenges dovetailed with the energy of the Sixties. I became less enthusiastic when I delved into *Lélia*. I read the novel as a cautionary tale, a concession by Sand that autonomy and intellectual endeavors could render a woman frigid, as if it were the inevitable punishment for usurping the masculine freedom to love and to write.

Nevertheless, I went on to graduate school where I resolutely moved into my Anglo-American feminist phase. These were my Kate Millett and Doris Lessing years. *Sexual Politics* provided the analysis; *The Golden Notebook* provided the narrative. Anna and Molly sitting in their London flat, referring to themselves as "free women" represented a completely new category, no longer defined by their relationship to men but observing the institution of marriage from "the safety of the sidelines." Doris Lessing had created the first contemporary women characters to whom I could fully relate. Like Sand, she was unafraid to show the high price to pay for this freedom. She chronicled the uncompromising, neurotic hyper-consciousness of her heroines, the fragmentation of their lives symbolized by Anna's four notebooks, their insecurity, the raw, tentative, unfinished nature of their "pioneering" existence, their tense and conflicted relationship with men and, most of all, their loneliness. But she also focused on friendships between women in ways that I had never found in any other book, friendships based not just on common rebellion but on boundless discussions, on the incessant exchange of words and ideas. In their conversations I saw the reflection of those I held daily with my own friends. For years, I would follow Martha Quest, then Anna Wulf, and finally Kate Brown, through various stages, crises, and epiphanies. But although they never ceased to reassure me that I was not alone, their frightening experience of mental disintegration (and ultimately, that of Kate Millett's heroines as well) often seemed as discouraging as Lélia's fate.

As I neared the age of thirty and reluctantly decided on an academic career, mostly because I could not imagine myself living outside the world of books, Simone de Beauvoir began to prevail. I admired her cerebral commitments, her political principles, her sound feminist analysis, her refusal of marriage and motherhood, the way she lived out her ideal of balancing freedom and companionship in her relationship with Sartre. My rebellion against my milieu, my education, and my family; my belief in the intellect, in "projects" and in transcendence; and my scorn for tepid compromises in any domain, closely resembled hers. Only gradually did I begin to read between the lines and to balk at her distrust of the female body and at her adherence to a reductive version of the intellectual. Having been an inspiration for me during the glorious and manichean years of my more youthful rebellions, Beauvoir's inflexibility eventually began to appear as a denial. As I gradually acknowledged the inevitable complexities and ambivalences which dominated so many aspects of my own life, intellectual as well as emotional, I hungered for ways to deal with these, not to repress them as I felt Beauvoir had.

So, in my forties, I turned to Colette. Her need for passion and the resulting temptation of submitting to a lover's will initially made me wary; yet I began to recognize that what drew me to her was her lucid acceptance of contradictions. As I read and re-read her books, I understood that they were all about negotiating solitude. That although her writings were inhabited by dogs, cats, lovers, fellow artists, a daughter, she was constantly in search of a delicate equilibrium between the self's need for solitude and the self's need for others, between the enslavement of passion and the reconciliation with the autonomous self. I admired Colette for being unafraid to reveal her vulnerabilities and her fragilities, and at the same time for refusing to capitulate to them. It seemed to me that she embraced rhythms, emotions, and forces she could not control, that she accepted love, desire, need, loss, and the inevitable changes they wrought; but that she always deftly guided such changes into forces of self-renewal.

Yet the cultural duality of my own life made Colette's model only partially acceptable. The French side in me resonated. But the American side resisted turning love and desire, or the loss thereof, into the only markers of a woman's life. By the time I turned 50, I was once again facing what Eva Hoffman calls the Great Divide and turning to a new set of writers for inspiration and guidance.[1]

II. As Gilbert Bécaud would say: "Et maintenant, que vais-je faire?"

Virtually all personal narratives which deal with aging, whether written in French or in English, exhibit similar patterns. They begin with the shock (Beauvoir would say "le scandale") of turning fifty – which, in previous generations, would probably have been 30, then 40. It is a marker which brings with it the twin realizations of invisibility and mortality or, as Phyllis Rose puts it "the fear of the unlived life."[2] What follows this jarring realization is often described by women writers as a "pause." The narrator reaches a summit (sometimes a plateau) from which she can look both backwards and forwards, gauging how far she has climbed and with what difficulties, and from which she can scrutinize with lucidity what lies ahead. Some narrators focus on the horizons ahead, eventually referring to the rest of their life as "the second act," or as "a new beginning." In their case, the "pause" serves to free them from social expectations and to harness their new-found energy toward the future and toward the world. Others, looking inward, linger nostalgically on the paths already traveled: for these writers the "pause" is a first step on "the road back," as they prepare themselves for detachment and poetic serenity. This, I found, is where cultural differences clearly appeared: the particular theme of "le retour" was more pronounced in French texts, (after all, isn't menopause referred to as the "retour d'âge"?), whereas the "new beginning" version tended to occur more often in English and American texts."[3]

Here is Beauvoir at 50: "To grow old is to set limits on oneself, to shrink (....) I have lived out stretched toward the future, and now I am recapitulating, looking back over the past."[4] And Colette: "Everything is much as it was in the first years of my life, and little by little I recognize the road back[5]." On the contrary, Gloria Steinem asserts: "From this new vantage point, I see that my notion

of age bringing detachment was probably just one more bias de-
signed to move some groups out of the way," and adds: "the older I
get the more intensely I feel about the world around me".[6] Carolyn
Heilbrun, who considers that "aging set me free,"[7] writes: "The
turning point of fifty, I had become convinced, ought to form as vital a milestone in a woman's life as graduation, promotion, marriage, or the birth or adoption of a child (...) I wanted to urge
women to see this new life as different, as a beginning, as a time re-
quiring the questioning of all previous habits and activities, as, inevitably, a time of profound change."[8]

The narrator's confrontation with her mirror is a recurring to-
pos in mid-life memoirs, regardless of which side of the Atlantic
these are written. But the reaction to being or, more accurately, to
no longer being an object of desire, and the awareness of new social
and sexual invisibility, are construed either as cruel or as liberatory
phenomena depending on cultural parameters. In other words, it
depends both on the construction of femininity of a particular society and the degree to which a woman's identity has been invested in
the latter. In this respect as well, two distinct patterns tend to pre-
dominate, neither of which is particularly reassuring to this middle-
aged Franco-American reader of women's texts.

In Doris Lessing's classic text, *The Summer Before the Dark*,
Kate Brown, a 45 year-old wife and mother who is left on her own
for the first time during one summer in London, undergoes a major
physical and mental breakdown. This crisis has to do with her loss of
identity when she realizes that her own image has always been fash-
ioned by others's expectations; her growing rage is primarily generated by what she understands to be the artificial constructs of femininity which have defined and alienated her. She realizes that when
she loses a great deal of weight, dresses carelessly, and stops dying
her hair, she becomes invisible to men: "A woman walking in a sag-
ging dress, with a heavy walk, and her hair – this above all – not conforming to the prints made by fashion, is not 'set' to attract men's
sex. The same woman in a dress cut in this or that way, walking with
her inner thermostat set just so – and click, she's fitting the pattern.

Men's attention is stimulated by signals no more complicated
than what leads the gosling; and for all her adult life, her sexual life,
let's say from twelve onwards, she has been conforming, twitching
like a puppet to those strings..."[9]

Although Kate Brown has an affair with a younger lover during
this crisis, it serves only to fuel her hostility toward men in general.
Her anger echoes that expressed by a number of contemporary
American and British writers who focus on the subject of meno-

pause, not always literally (though a great deal of ink has been spent on the pros and cons of HRT) but as a metaphor. Only after this stage, they suggest, can a woman be Free At Last (including from what British writer Eva Figes calls "foolish longings"). Germaine Greer sees in menopause the revenge of the female eunuch: "Many women realize during the climacteric the extent to which their lives have been a matter of capitulation and how little of what has happened to them has actually been in their interest... to be unwanted is also to be free."[10] This liberation ushers Greer and her cohort into what Margaret Mead once described as "post-menopausal zest." Gloria Steinem embraces this point of view: "I am also finding a new perspective that comes from leaving the central plateau of my life, and seeing more clearly the tyrannies of social expectations (...) Though this growing neglect and invisibility may shock and grieve us greatly at first and feel like 'a period of free fall' to use Germaine Greer's phase, it also creates a new freedom to be ourselves (...)"[11]

I, for one, am suspicious of even the most self-assured of these calls to celebrate "cronehood," for they simultaneously condemn the unfair social phenomenon which dictates that women become "unwanted" after a certain age *and* glorify this invisibility because it means we are no longer subject to men's objectifying gaze. The implication is that women have been so sexually victimized that we should celebrate when we reach the age where we become sexually retired; *but* at the same time, that we should continue to condemn this retirement as yet another unfair social conspiracy on the part of a sexist society. I'm not sure that I can wholeheartedly agree with either of these claims.

While exasperation and anger at having been objectified for decades, then suddenly discarded, propels a number of American and English feminists toward the next activist phase in their lives, French texts tend to negotiate this transition in a very different manner. In their case, the emphasis on elusive and delicate issues connected to the waning of desire, pleasure, and seduction leads to a combat against the self rather than against the world, and tends to result in the passive acceptance of feminine "destiny."

The classic model of the "no-longer-young" woman remains Léa in Colette's *Chéri*. The end of Léa's love affair with her young lover precipitates the painful renunciation of sexuality, but it also makes way for a resolute peace of mind in the sequel, *La fin de Chéri*.

"I haven't taken too long to understand that an age comes for a woman when, instead of clinging to beautiful feet that are impatient to roam the world, expressing herself in soothing words, boring tears and burning, ever-shorter sights – an age comes when the only thing that is left for her is to enrich her own self," writes Colette in *Break of Day*.[12] Very much the French woman steeped in a culture of seduction, she saw the waning of romantic obsessions (even if this was an unwelcome process) as a signal to cross over the threshold into another, more peaceful, life. From hereon she intended to stop concentrating on "those pleasures we lightly call physical" and to focus on earthly pleasures of a different sort. This solution may have seemed plausible, and even admirable, at the beginning of the century: women had fewer options and a shorter life expectancy. Yet the French daughters and granddaughters of Colette continue to accept as a "natural" phase, albeit with considerable chagrin but with similar serenity, the waning of their desirability. Indeed, one continues to find echoes of the traditional Colette model in texts published throughout the 1990's in France, for example, in Claire Gallois' *Les heures dangereuses* or Noëlle Chatelet's *La dame en bleu*.

Gallois' narrator, who has just turned 50, bemoans the unfair situation which dictates that women at her age are no longer desirable even though they still desire. A divorced woman with a grown son, she is involved simultaneously in two passionate love affairs, both with married men. One of her lovers is ten years younger than she, handsome, intelligent and, for all intents and purposes, unable to stay away from her, physically or emotionally. Most of the narrative revolves around a familiar Colettian dilemma: To be acutely aware of the approaching if unjust social destiny but to squeeze pleasure until the last drop; to remain lucid about this unavoidable situation and attentive to its compensations; to love and understand men enough not to begrudge their own limiting realities; to build up plenitude so that when the moment to step back has arrived it brings with it the challenge of elegantly negotiating this turn rather than bitterly decrying it, or shrilly proclaiming it. She ends this feminine swan song with a very Colettian spin: "I remain *poétique*, that is to say, preoccupied with the beauties of existence."[13] Very well; but the obvious point begs to be made: if and when the younger lover finally does go away, what will Gallois' narrator do with the rest of her long life?

Noëlle Chatelet's *La dame en bleu* attempts a symbolic answer to this very question. Solange, an attractive, divorced, 52-year old Parisian, has an exciting job, a supportive daughter, many friends and, of course, a skilled and passionate lover. One day, after a quasi-mystical encounter with an old woman in the street, she decides to anticipate old age before she is forced into it. Gradually, she discovers the joys of slowing down, frees herself from her enslavement to the world of appearances, to the fast social and professional track, stops wearing make-up, throws away her fashionable clothes (which, in true *Liaisons dangereuses* style, she defines as her "battle gear"), pins her hair back and stops dying it. She gently turns away from her un-comprehending lover: "Feeling melancholy, Solange? Absolutely not. She is pleased that all this madness of love has existed in her life – she is even proud of it – but she is much happier now that it is over, finally over."[14] Soon thereafter, she enters an idyllic retirement home where she gives herself peacefully over to the comfortable, amused, and detached observation of minute daily events.

The loss of social and sexual "visibility" is thus interpreted and resolved in different ways, depending on a particular woman's culture (and there are, of course, as many interpretations as there are cultures; but I am trying to focus here on the comparison between a group of French and Anglo-American writers of my generation). Colette-like, Chatelet's narrator fantasizes over creamy hot choco-late and buttered toast in the cocoon of an esthetic and sensual (if to-tally unrealistic) old-age residence, while Alix Kates-Shulman, who spends her 50th year on an island in Maine, proudly survives on a diet of beach plants, reads at the light of a kerosene lamp in a sleep-ing bag, takes sponge baths, does without septic tank, electricity, or telephone, has a baseball bat ready to ward off potential aggressors, and weathers hurricanes fearlessly.[15] In both cases, these rituals usher the narrators into their middle years and ultimately toward a new form of independence. But they do so in very different modes.

Indeed, French women tend to wax poetic, fatalistic, and serene; Anglo-Saxon women tend to wax angry, energetic, and po-litical. The Americans turn the phenomenon into a lesson for a col-lective "we." Deconstructing the mechanisms of this latest patriarchal plot, they get mad, then get busy. French women, mean-while, tend to philosophically acknowledge their "destiny," resist it as long as they can (which means remaining desirable for as long as possible), then set about searching for new forms of affective and sybaritic stability.

While Colette asks man to be her friend now that her "militant" life is over and to co-exist with her side by side into old age, Erica Jong writes: "At fifty, the madwoman in the attic breaks loose, stomps down the stairs, and sets fire to the house."[16] Gail Sheehy, during a mystical journey up the proverbial mountain where she meditates as the sun rises, suddenly feels a surge of energy: "I couldn't wait to get back to my laptop, my writings... my passion."[17] To Simone de Beauvoir's long list of "never agains," to her lamen-tation at the age of 52 that "I shall live for a long time in this little landscape," to Gallois's protest that "No one will ever fall in love with me again. I know it all too well, from here on everything will lead to farewells," Leslie Cottin Pogrebin responds: "I want that passion. The fire in the belly that makes a person ignore all the reasons to do something. The energy that keeps one barreling toward the goal. The wild, sure sense of what has to happen next. The strength to stay up all night and get it finished. The talent to persuade. If I cannot add years to my life I can add life to my years...If I can stuff my days with meaning and mindfulness, I should be able to keep my eyes on the prize and off the hourglass."[18] Maya Angelou, in *Even the Stars Get Lonesome*, sums it up with the most familiar of American slogans: "Mostly, what I have learned so far about aging, despite the creakiness of one's bones and the cragginess of one's once-silkened skin, is this: do it. By all means, do it." [19]

III. Mature Mistresses vs. Midlife Militants

I can not identify with either of these models. I am neither eager to become an agitator on the Crone Circuit – no matter how celebratory; nor to retire gracefully to the convent – no matter how good the food is there. In the absence of any creative alternative, I have been trying to understand the cultural basis for such differing approaches to aging. It is tempting, of course, to fall back on the familiar explanatory dichotomies and to suggest that if "Anglo-Saxon" women seem quick to erase the body and the flesh with which they were never wholly comfortable, to turn away from desire and invest their newly-released energy into fresh battles (as Francine du Plessix Gray writes, "free from being seen, they now are free to be heard"[20]), it is because they share the legacy of Puritanism. And to conclude, on the other hand, that French women who are the inheritors of a long tradition of *libertinage* and have been historically locked in the prison of *féminité* and the myth of *séduction*, become resigned to putting down their weapons when they are no longer considered "women" and to seek solace in lyrical passivity.[21]

More enlightening, I think, have been the debates surrounding Mona Ozouf's book on "la singularité française."[22] Ozouf makes a claim for the exceptional harmony between the sexes in France, a claim which is avidly defended by many French men and women alike and is often, and predictably so, opposed to the specter of the "war of the sexes" which allegedly rages in the US. But it is not so much Ozouf's shaky polemical stance which interests me here. What I find revealing is that despite her opposition to the dreaded gender "differentialism" of American feminists, Ozouf systematically weaves through her ten portraits of famous French women the suggestion that women's relationship to time is gender-specific. As

Lynn Hunt points out, Ozouf's biographical sketches demonstrate that women do not "master" time but rather "accept it by knowing it in intimate ways." This position, which Eric Fassin correctly identifies as the "naturalization of feminine destiny," provides me with an important clue as to why French women find it more noble to "renounce" and American women to "resist." [23]

In her discussion of Ozouf's controversial book, Hunt unpacks the cultural differences at work in the opposition between French and American historical attitudes toward the self. The widely-shared American mentality, she writes, is "deeply anti-historical, voluntarist, and self-obsessed" and inevitably results in the opposition between control and victimization, between autonomy and constraints.[24] If one takes this argument further, it stands to reason that, like gender, aging would be considered by American feminists as a predominantly social construction to be exposed and opposed. This would explain why so many recent mid-life writings, be they autobiographical, fictional or scholarly, espouse pedagogical and political goals. Morganroth-Gullette's call to arms, in *Declining to Decline*, is the latest and perhaps most extreme example of this approach: "Age Studies names the interdisciplinary movement that wants to disrupt the current age system in theory and practice... I envision the anti-middle-ageist movement crossing boundaries – racial-ethnic, male/female, gay/straight, privileged/immiserated, left/right – uniting people by presenting them with credibly self-interested causes for forming coalitions."[25]

At the same time, these historical differences in mentalities would also account for the much vaunted "exception française." After all, if French women elegantly accept inevitable "natural" renunciation at the age when they "cease to be women," then there is no reason to become angry at the other sex. Nor to gather in interest groups or classrooms or courtrooms in order to critique and protest arbitrary social dictates. If French women accept unquestioningly "l'ordre des choses," even when it benefits men primarily, then it is no surprise that harmony between the sexes should reign in their society.

Nineteenth-century French literature has bequeathed a gallery of memorable, self-sacrificing, mature mistresses who release their young lovers after having educated them, at which point their own life ends – oftentimes literally. In Radiguet's *Le diable au corps* (1923), the 18-year old heroine, who has been seduced by the 16-year old narrator, suddenly turns away from him in despair because she is "too old for him". She explains that 15 years hence, her youth will be ending while his will be in full flower (in fact, she conveniently dies way before this dire prophesy can come true). To a large degree this masculinist paradigm, and its attendant consequence, that men remain men when women are no longer women and will therefore necessarily be unfaithful, continues to be profoundly internalized by both sexes in Gallic society (see, for example, this past summer's masochistic best-seller, Francoise Chandernagor's *La première épouse*). Meanwhile, in the United States, feminist writers continue to impute life cycles to patriarchal conspiracies and to define themselves as "victims of age ideology," as if physiology, desire, mortality, and Time played a peripheral role in our life trajectories.[26]

My mother was raised during a time, in a culture and in a milieu, where the only alternatives to becoming a full-time wife were either the nunnery or prostitution. During my childhood, I cannot remember encountering a single woman doctor, dentist, lawyer, publisher, architect, politician, or journalist. I did not have any women teachers after grammar school, which strikes me as sadly symptomatic since I practically never studied anything but "girls'" subject matters. Thus, as long as I wanted to become a ballet dancer when I grew up, I had models; after that point, I was painfully bereft of alternatives. So I turned to literature. Over the years, fictional characters and their authors became my faithful companions; I owe much of my growing to the ways in which I successively embraced or rejected many of them. And since I was never able to fully define myself as either French or American, I navigated between the two cultures in pursuit of idealizations or repudiations which would help me take the next step. Now, once again, I find myself confronting the assault of parallel visions without helpful signposts on either side of the Atlantic. But I take comfort in the knowledge that I am not alone in this situation, that many of my friends, with whom I still have those Doris Lessing conversations, are asking the same questions about this most uncertain of ages. And that, absent the guidance of literary texts or cultural exemplars, we are nevertheless pursuing this unchartered journey with a resolutely bicultural imagination.

Notes

1. Eva Hoffman, *Lost in Translation: A Life in a New Language* (N.Y.: Penguin Books, 1987), p. 272.

2. Phyllis Rose, *The Year of Reading Proust: A Memoir in Real Time* (N.Y.: Scribner, 1997), p. 33.

3. I am aware that I will be making broad generalizations about "French women" and "Anglo-Saxon women" when in fact I am limiting myself to a handful of mostly white, heterosexual women from France, the US, England, and Australia. However, since this essay is autobiographical, I have chosen to discuss authors with whom I identified, and thus whose work had the most impact on me.

4. Simone de Beauvoir, *Force of Circumstance* (trans, Richard Howard, N.Y.: Harper & Rowe, 1977), p. 655.
5. Colette, *Break of Day* (trans. Enid McLeod, N.Y.: Farrar, Straus & Giroux, 1961), p.9.
6. Gloria Steinem, *Moving Beyond Words* (N.Y.: Simon & Schuster, 1994), p. 249.
7. Carolyn Heilbrun, introduction to *Reflecting on Menopause* (ed. by Joanna Goldsworthy, N.Y.: Columbia University Press, 1994), p. xvi.
8. Carolyn Heilbrun, *The Last Gift of Time: Life Beyond Sixty* (N.Y. The Dial Press, 1997), p.1.
9. Doris Lessing, *The Summer Before The Dark*, (N.Y.: Vintage Books, 1973), p. 186.
10. Germaine Greer, *The Change: Women, Aging and Menopause* (N.Y.: Knopf, 1992), p. 254.
11. Gloria Steinem. *Moving beyond Words*, op. cit., p. 250.
12. Colette, *Break of Day*, op. cit., p. 34.
13. Claire Gallois, *Les heures dangereuses* (Paris: Grasset, 1992), p. 242 (trans. mine).
14. Noelle Chatelet, *La dame en bleu*, (Paris: Stock, 1996) p. 41 (trans. mine).
15. Alix Kates-Shulman, *Drinking the Rain* (Farrar, Straus & Giroux, 1995).
16. Erica Jong, *Fear of Fifty* (N.Y.: Harper Collins, 1994), p. xxiv.
17. Gail Sheehy, *The Silent Passage* (N.Y.: Pocketbooks, 1993), p. 253.
18. Leslie Cottin Pogrebin, *Getting Over Getting Older* (N.Y.: Little, Brown, 1996), p. 311.
19. Maya Angelou, *Even The Stars Get Lonesome* (N.Y.: Random house, 1997), p. 24.
20. Francine Duplessix Gray, *The New Yorker* (Feb/March 1996).
21. For one of the more chilling examples of this, see Francoise Giroud's acknowledgment to the much younger Bernard-Henri Levy that women who are no longer desired should be able to become men rather than continuing to live for so long like zombies ! *Les hommes et les femmes* (Paris: Olivier Orban, 1993).
22. Mona Ozouf, *Les mots des femmes: Essai sur la singularité française* (Paris: Fayard, 1995)
23. Eric Fassin, "The Purloined gender: American Feminism in a french Mirror" in *French Historical Studies*, Winter 1999.
24. Lynn Hunt, "Time, Constraint, and the Lives of Women" quoted in English by permission of the author, trans. into French in *Le débat* no. 87, Nov/Dec 1995, pp. 126–130.
25. Margaret Morganroth-Gulette, *Declining to Decline: Cultural Combat and the Politics of the Midlife* (Charlottesville & London: University Press of Virginia, 1997), p. 17.
26. Gulette, op. cit., p. 15.

Defense: a Path in an Era

Geneviève Fraisse

For those who come out the Sorbonne, whether as student or professor, we know that several paths are open. Specifically, there are two opposing ones, as Georges Canguilhem said about of psychology: one descending toward the Seine, and the police headquarters, and the other climbing toward the Pantheon.

However, if there were two paths for me in Autumn 1973, they were not opposing ones; instead, they formed a perpendicular line. Delivered from the constraints of academic competition, I immediately took the path of the archives: specifically, the feminist archives preserved at the Bibliothèque Marguerite Durand, in the mayoralty of the fifth *arrondissement*, exactly opposite the Pantheon. The existence of this antiquated library had been revealed to me by a young American feminist magazine, *MS*, under the heading "Lost Women." These lost, forgotten women were nonetheless absolutely remarkable, as perusal of their archives made evident.

At this same time, I took the path of the University of Vincennes, where the noise of philosophers, psychoanalysts and militants attracted me less than the presence there of a few young Althusserians or former Althusserians, who after 1968 offered a thought that I supposed to be less academic than that imposed upon the female student at that time. It was there that I found what I was looking for: the renewed attempt at a political thought.

The library of feminist archives moved to an anonymous intersection in the thirteenth arrondissement; the University of Vincennes, henceforth called simply Paris VIII, was also displaced to the northern suburbs of Paris. Thus the geography of my interests was undone and then recomposed. It did not blur, for the history of these interests continued, between feminist texts and political philosophy. If the paths were perpendicular, it was because they share a common point of origin: the political question of the equality of the sexes. This perpendicular tension is today the same as at its point of departure. That is what I would like to discuss here, in four themes: the difference of the sexes, the form of knowledge (*connaissance*), historicity, and the rupture of the 1800s.

1.

"The difference of the sexes," the title of a book which appeared in 1996 and title of the body of work that I propose to the jury, is an expression which is both dear and enigmatic. Is it the fact of difference, the fact of the existence of two sexes, men and women? Is it the principle of difference, with its necessary definition, or rather its definitions, of the masculine and the feminine? Neither the facts, nor the norms, which cross and uncross throughout history, nor the play of distance and proximity between woman and feminine, man and masculine, gives a satisfactory solution to this obvious enigma.

The obvious enigma: everyone has an opinion on this subject; everyone believes in the truth of her or his opinion and hopes to draw nearer to science. I have no opinion and I prefer to defer the opinions of others. First, I retain simply that humans, men and women, are one thing, and qualities, masculine and feminine, are another.

Caught between the political question of the relation of equality between the sexes, and the philosophical and extra-philosophical triviality of the definitions of sexual difference, the conceptual difficulty is posed from the start. There is no definition of the difference of the sexes. And I have not presumed to look for this definition; I have chosen to find the spaces in which this difference is thought and in which it is conducive to thought. An important distinction: the difference of the sexes, in discourse, is always there for itself and for something else. In that sense as when, it is elusive.

As a consequence, "the difference of the sexes" cannot be substituted for "sexual difference," genre, or gender, Masculine-Feminine. Sexual difference and Masculine-Feminine necessarily encounter the question of essence, the exigency of the content of Being. Though this content may undergo variations, it is nonetheless still assumed that the equation can be given, its character affirmed. And the fact that today women intervene with force to give

to "woman" and "feminine" a less archaic version than before, reinforces the stakes of the definition.

Genre, or *gender*,[1] is a concept from across the Atlantic, the
epistemological ambition of which overcomes it absolutely in terms
of definition. The declared stake at the outset was to mark the social
and historic dimension of the difference of the sexes outside of biological reference. But this concept, *a priori* an empty shell, brings
along with it that which presided over its fabrication, namely, this
rupture with biological difference, with sex: the sex of the body, or
sexuality; it matters little here. Despite its semantic evolution, it has
the flaw, in my eyes, of having maintained the classic opposition between nature and culture. Moreover, I think that we must foil this
binary game, and that one of the essential traps of a way of thinking
the difference of the sexes is there. The concept of gender (*genre*) is
therefore already an epistemological position, in spite of its epistemological aim. Let us note with amusement that on this side of the
Atlantic we now talk about gender (*genre*), coming back to the correct grammatical use of masculine and feminine genders. And I subscribe to this new use of the word. The need for conceptual clarity,
therefore, does not escape the confusion of uses or of their evolution. Grammar seems to me to be a rich intersection of possible
analyses.

And this is a good thing. *Geschlecht*, in German, means both sex
and gender. *Geschlechtdifferenz*, says Hegel: differences of the sexes.
I stand firm on this.

What will I then place in this name "difference of the sexes" if I
presuppose nothing? First, the cognizance (*connaissance*) or the recognition (*reconnaissance*) that it is an object of thought which does
not exist in philosophy. And nonetheless, it intervenes ceaselessly in
the space of thought. It is at the point of origin, the first difference
beginning from which humanity thinks itself; and it is a space of me-
diation of discourse, a means of exchange for treating philosophical
matters. As I will show, that is why the difference of the sexes is a
form of knowledge (*savoir*).

That is why it was necessary also to affirm that there is no feminist philosophy, and no feminist research. No philosophy which
would give a positive essence to difference, no research work that
would be sure of its epistemological presupposition. Neither the object, nor the subject of reflection are given from the outset. If the
difference of the sexes is an aporia, in the sense that it is not a question of choosing between the similar and the different in men and
women, then this aporia is not an impasse but an infinite and un-
heard-of overture.

I propose therefore that epistemology – the construction of a field, the discovery of a method – is what conditions the gaze on the difference of the sexes.

2.

Because there is no definition of the difference of the sexes, there is no theory of the knowledge of this difference. At most there is a form of cognizance (*connaissance*). This is my sub-title. If there is a form to the cognizance, the object and the subject of cognizance are given in one single movement. It was necessary for me to begin from this discomfort of having to identify, within what is called the "exercise of knowledge" (*savoir*), both the thinking subject, a *sexually marked being* (*être sexué*), and the object to be thought: this relation between the sexes which in the modern period can no longer go without a reflection on their equality. At times I have privileged a reflection on the subjects – subject of reason, subject of knowledge, citizen-subject, subject in love; at times I have looked for the incidences, opportunities, political conflicts or mythical reshufflings, where the difference of the sexes gives itself to be read as a stake of political history and of philosophical thought. Henceforth, the work of bringing to light a difference as invisible as it is present resembles a phenomenology, an unveiling of spaces and stakes, I without an ontological support. Here again, I distance myself from certain feminist readings of repression, of the foreclosure of the difference of the sexes. Following Michel Foucault, but differently, I see difference everywhere, where one must think the equal or the unequal, where one must think something philosophically new.

Thus my commitment to inventing nothing, to recovering everything that has already been given to me: the philosophical tradition as a whole, as a history of feminist achievements and thought during these two last centuries in particular.

But why this insistence on disengaging myself from contemporary tendencies in works which are close to mine in thematics and objectives? Because, what is at stake, as I see it, is a possible way of thinking, the construction of thought. An example of discordancy. I refuse to debate the opposition between equality and difference, a feminist debate at once classic and degraded. Since the infancy of philosophy, we know that difference is the opposite of identity; since Hegel we know that equality plays the role of a third, comparing term (*terme comparant*). If we contract three terms into two, it is because we combine two registers: the political, which places equality opposite difference; and the ontological, which knows that equality can intervene only in a relation between the similar and the different, that in this aporetic situation in which men and women are at once identical *and* different.

If my research deals with the form of cognizance (*connaissance*) it signals this dynamic circularity between the subject and the object of knowledge, this form of knowledge also imposes the multiplicity of spaces of knowledge. It appears that that knowledge demands the distinction between levels of knowledge, between registers of thought. Crossing the political and the ontological is not an operation that one must confirm without submitting it to critique. The ontological and the political are not untangled in order to undo the commitment to think and act the world (*penser* et *agir le monde*), but to give it the density of lucid thought. As such, and this is where lucidity can be useful, it suddenly appears impossible to disqualify the contemporary feminist movement by the vulgar accusation that it falls into the folding-into itself of identity (*repli identitaire*). By opposing identity and difference, under the gaze of equality, it is no longer possible to confuse identity and difference, to substitute one for the other, to superimpose them, in the place where the different would supposedly reclaim its identity. No, the different demands to be recognized in its similarity, which means deployment and not withdrawal (*repli*). It was sufficient simply to not confuse identity with the self and identity with the other. Some will hear this remark resonate elsewhere than in the space of the difference of the sexes. For it is quite simply a question of the concrete universal.

3.

This obligatory encounter between the ontological and the political bears the mark of the contemporary and determines the context of my research, epistomology and method, of the difference of the sexes. If, with the democratic era, the political order acquired an autonomy regarding the reference to nature, then the birth of a political feminism after the French Revolution and 1830 took on the aspect of historical engagement.

The historicity of the difference of the sexes is there first and foremost: in the fact that thanks to the question of equality, men and women enter into history not as sexually marked (*sexué*) beings (that has always been the case) but as beings likely to be conscious of that which the sexes make of history. This is why the recent history of women owed to itself to go from the sexual history of representations to the representation of the history of the sexes.

The bet that I am making, with the hypothesis or the thesis of historicity, is this: with the emergence of a history in which beings are free subjects, beings of reason, actors, citizens, in which women can be so just as men (you know that this was not nor is it yet as obvious as all that), the difference of the sexes is no longer in the order of fact nor of norm, and does not refer back to a nature in reality and in rule, as I said at the beginning. The conscious production of history foils the binary schema of the fact of nature constructed or deconstructed by social fact.

But added to this, obviously, is the whole of a world henceforth exclusively caught up in historicity. That we are historical beings, the slow death of metaphysics has taught us since the nineteenth century. A loss of transcendence and the conquest of immanence are the keys of contemporary philosophy. That sexually marked (*sexué*) beings did not appear in their historicity, until Nietzsche perhaps, is a remarkable phenomenon. Or rather, what I call a mishap.

If difference is historical, as I titled an article, it could be, to echo Marxist language, a determining factor. The sexes make history (*font histoire*), just as materialism is caught up in history, to the point that history itself is transformed by this affirmation. Production and reproduction become the materialist foundation of the historical dynamic. This is contemporary modernity: it is not nature that determines men and women, but their relation, a relation in which production and reproduction are wrapped up together. Substituting the relation to nature eludes neither sex (*le sexe*) nor sexuality; it designates history as a space of intelligibility and a production of intelligibility, and thus of the relation between men and women. It is also that of historicity.

Whether one begins with Nietzsche or Marx makes little difference. One must go to the end of their intuition about historicity, and include the difference of the sexes. The former thinker began to include women in a temporality; the second integrated reproduction into social relations. But these intuitions remained timid with regard to the mishap in which women were left behind. The critiques of generic man, of the subject of power, of domineering reason, showed the extent to which women remained outside of history, or rather showed that they had another history than the grand, official history. And while history in its ideological and materialistic laws, and historicity in its vertigo of man without God, occupied the thoughts of men, the emerging human sciences, including psychoanalysis, were inventing the synchronic, not diachronic, laws of the relation of the sexes. Psychoanalysis and anthropology believed in invariables – even if this is less true today, even if the invariables themselves henceforth have a history as well.

The historicity of the difference of the sexes places in doubt the atemporal representation of duality and of the relation between the sexes. Here, it is no longer a question of measuring the contemporary moment, which is imperatively a moment in history, and to force the question of the sexes to belong to it. What is at stake is a scientific decision as well as a political engagement. The scientific decision is the effect of the refusal – indicated many times already – of the false opposition between biological fact and social norm, the natural sex and socially constructed gender, singular sexuality and supposed roles, etc. Historicity obliges one to abandon these cleavages which are, as one could demonstrate, above all modern.

What is at stake is political engagement: the word is strong perhaps, but it designates this modern character of thought about difference and the life of the sexes, this character of equality which invites us to redefine over and over women and their relationships – intimate or public, civil or civic, familial or social, amorous or professional – from the point of view of identity or similarity as well as from the point of view of difference and the alterity of men. Equality, and its accomplice liberty, have insinuated themselves everywhere. This is what makes history. The subject is henceforth caught up in the object. The history of women is only of interest if it produces history in its turn.

4.

The rupture of the 1800s summarizes a large part of my work, and announces, I hope, work to come. Two parallel movements guide my interest in this rupture which is emblematic, even if it is not unique in the modern era. On one hand, the incredible democratic dialectic which put into play the exclusion of women without preventing their inclusion. On the other hand, this movement of the defeat of metaphysics in which the difference of the sexes appears as an important operator up to now. "Exclusionary" (*exclusive*) democracy was the subtitle of *Muse of Reason*. Acknowledging that *exclusive* is untranslateable in English because this adjective emphasizes the privilege of a selective choice more than exclusion and rejection, I understood why I clung to this subtitle: precisely for its double meaning, in which exclusion manifests itself through simple mechanical rejection than by a supposedly invisible absence. As *exclusif* does not mean excluding (*excluant*), inclusion is and always has been possible, even implied. This dynamic between unequal and equal is henceforth called discrimination.

Democracy is exclusionary (*exclusive*) with regard to women, but not only so. If this adjective is retained, it is for a second reason: because thus appears a formula proper to the history under examination, that of France in the period after the French Revolution. We talk often of singularity, of the exception of France, of its democracy and its republic. For my part, I claim that French history is less exceptional than exemplary, a situation that is precisely paradigmatic of an exclusionary democracy. Because the situation of France is exemplary, the cause of its delay with regard to other nations also has to do with this level of exemplarity; not so much the delay in civil or professional equality, for example, but the delay in the equality of power. That is to say, the delay in political power, but also in intellectual power; in a word, it is a question of symbolic power. Women have little acces to this symbolic power in France, including the institution of the university, where research on the difference of the sexes is not recognized, but only tolerated at times, and then with condescension.

Beside this political movement a parallel philosophical history takes shape, of which we can discern certain elements. First of all, there is what I call "the lucidity of philosophers," the fact that they know that the foregrounding of human alterity and of social and political equality would necessarily modify something. But what? This is what we now, after two centuries, will try to understand.

The difference of the sexes has always served as a means and a space of exchange in thought, in a fashion that we will call occasional, even if it is recurrent. For two centuries, one might add, it is an operator of political construction as well as of metaphysical deconstruction. At bottom, instead of its being a secondary issue, it may well be a crucial issue in contemporary thought.

This is my last bet, and what is missing from the work presented today. I said that ontology and politics cross and uncross to speak the difference of the sexes. Inversely, or reading against the grain, the difference of the sexes, since the beginning of the 19th century, is unbelievably present in philosophical, ontological, and political space. Yet this has not yet been shown.

I would like to demonstrate this in a future work. This work would have a dual objective: to indicate the importance of the difference of the sexes in contemporary thought and to open up a new representation of this importance. Having become a philosopheme like any other, the difference of the sexes would be, finally, a banal object of thought.

In one hundred years, she, woman, will be a poet, said Virginia Woolf, convinced that poetry rather than the novel would be witness to a position in writing at once linked to and separated from the position of sex. Let us extrapolate that in a few more decades we'll be there: at that moment in which the difference of the sexes will be the object of a serene critical interrogation. This, I hope, is my testimony and my contribution to (hi)story.

Translated by Kristine J. Butler

Note

1   In English in the original text. (Trans.)

Women's Democratic Personality: an essay of Feminology

Antoinette Fouque

To review the situation and my policy regarding the Women's Liberation Movement (I prefer this term to "feminism"), a movement in which I have been trying for 30 years to act as a woman of thought and to think as a woman of action,[1] I have chosen to address here only what has been and still is, today, at the core of the debates in France concerning women and what could be phrased in the following way, without really simplifying: are there two sexes, or just two genders? In fact, at the very moment when universalistic feminists are celebrating the 50th anniversary of Simone de Beauvoir's *The Second Sex*, chanting once again, half a century after she did, "one is not born a woman, one becomes a woman," the French Senate is rejecting, in the name of Universalism, a bill on parity in politics.[2] Supported and strengthened by an indifferentialist feminism, the "French exception"[3] has struck again.

In 1968, at the start of the Women's Liberation Movement, I was already asserting and have never stopped asserting ever since that "one is born a girl or a boy, one becomes a woman or a man." There are two sexes. The human species is heterosexed. It is its chance. It is not the difference of sexes that causes discriminations against women, but the failure to recognize it, its repression. Contempt for what we might lack – that small difference – is in tact masking denial and envy of our procreative capacities, with their enormous consequences. Dissymetry between sexes, which is rooted in women's specific "procreative function" (*fonction génésique*), cannot be reduced to abstract equality. And what is more universal than this function?

The scandalous political underrepresentation of women, in a country that vaunts having invented human rights and their universality, seems a mystery as long as one does not try to think of such a situation as a product of French-style misogyny, which is in a way engraved as much in the Tables of the Law of the Republic as in a perversion based on a denial of reality: I know that there are two sexes, but let us act as if we needed only one. Indeed denying that there are men and women has permitted the abuse resulting from the logic of equality, turned into a quasi-dogma, the inegalitarian consequences of which are still, even today, so visible. The passion for the sovereign One – God, Almighty Father, Only Son, Emperor or Phallus – that inspires Absolute Monarchy, has been metamorphosed by philosophers of the Age of Enlightenment into a universal Republic, a one and indivisible Republic: just so many avatars of the One that do not want to know anything about at least two or more, from which modern democratic spirit should emerge.

The men and women supporting egalitarian universalism, by denying to the point of paranoia, the most elementary principle, of reality – there are two sexes – are reducing humanity to a neutral, and therefore masculine, pseudo mixed mankind, monosexed hence homosexed, narcissistic, divided, sterile, literally egoistic. There is only me, without an other, only one God, only one libido and it is phallic. More difficult to identify than the conservative misogyny that sends women back to enslaved maternity and femininity, is progressive modern misogyny, which throws away the baby with the bathwater and difference with discrimination. For more than 30 years, I have never stopped pointing out that the perverse effects of this logic of the Same take women from invisibility, unpower, inexistence, to their pure and simple disappearance: a symbolic "gynocide" that redoubles the real gynocide.[4] Yet, this logic is still put forward today by many indifferentialist feminists and I have been and am still violently fought against in France for having wanted to move out of the enclosure of monosexed sterile Universalism and to work out a beyond-feminism (a "post-feminism," not an anti-feminism) in thought and act. Universalism,[5] that is totalitarian, forecloses the real and produces its particular dissidences: communitarism, differentialism, naturalism, etc... To assert that there are two sexes – always keeping in mind that nothing human is natural –, is to remove the foreclosure of "femaleness" and therefore to provide the means to liberate oneself from all these reductionist "isms."

Why should biological determinacies continue to be a prison for women? Shouldn't it be just the opposite, from the moment that one has control over one's fertility? The principle of reality cannot ignore those determinacies and a just Society would not exploit them. To recognize a determinacy does in no way abolish freedom and human responsibility. Women's freedom, their responsibility is to assert with courage their specific ability and not to deny the fact that they are women. Equality and difference must go hand in hand: one cannot be sacrificed for the other. Sacrificing equality for difference takes us back to the reactionary positions of traditional societies, and sacrificing the difference of sexes – and along with it, the richness of life that it brings – for equality, sterilizes women and impoverishes humanity as a whole.

Procreators of the living-speaking-thinking, "anthropoculturist" of the species, women are the very source of human wealth. But in no country is this work of renewing generations and the labor force, which is vital for the economy, taken into account in the evaluation of wealth, and women who do not exercise a professional activity are counted among the "inactive" population. Excluded from any social, economic, professional, political or cultural inscription, ignored and foreclosed, the "procreative function" – a production – remains the ultimate slavery, the ultimate expenditure of a work force, without remuneration or recognition. It constitutes, on the other hand, a genuine penalization of women in their professional and political life. Lastly, and perhaps above all, by not wanting to consider procreation as a creation, an act that is highly symbolic as well as real, one does not allow oneself to reach the stage of genitality, its unfurling to be understood as a metaphor and not as a reduction to the organic.

Having been conceived... conceiving. The intimate, physical, psychic experience, of gestation, as a specific place and time of welcome for the other, of spiritual as well as carnal hospitality, the geni(t)al experience of pregnancy henceforth active, conscious, chosen, has been inhabiting, inhabits, as the motif in the carpet, my Movements of thought. As much from an ontogenetic as a phylogenetic viewpoint. from the control of one's fertility to the right to procreation, from a strategy of the intimate to an economy of the gift, from demographic equilibrium to the genius of the species, gestation (and beyond, maternity and paternity) imposes itself as the paradigm of ethics, the programming, and the promise of an anthropopolitical revolution, the matrix of a "human contract." Forsaking the passion for the One to go toward the knowledge of two, is to remove the repression of the real that universalist and culturalist egalitarianism forecloses. Thinking this place of memory, this moment of the coming future – the epistemological field that I call *feminology* –, in no way inverts phallocentrism into gynecocentrism. Because gestation, like poetry, as an experience anchored in the real, in its imaginary and symbolic effects, is a process of decentering the subject. There, "I is another" (female or male). A model of hospitality to the foreign body, of thinking of the other, of love for one's neighbor, it endows women with the genius of the living, on the real level, with a democratic and xenophilious personality, on the imaginary level and with an ethical dimension, on the symbolic level.

In politics, parity, an idea that has been worked on in Europe for 10 years can remove the double bind: that of indifferentialism or discrimination-regression. Parity is the recognition that as the *demos*, the people, is constituted of two sexes, the *cratos*, the government, must be so as well. Be this the occasion for some men (or women) to reaffirm their passion for the One or to limit themselves to quantitative parity, it is only a stage. "Qualitative parity" introduces us to another logic: that of two, and even of 2 to the second power – in order to represent men and women, to elect men and women who elaborate heterosexed policy. Far from clashing head on with the universalist foundation of our values, parity, in its generative logic, gives it its genuine democratic dimension. From carnal sharing to a balanced political coupling, that is where the fecund universalism of humanity can be inscribed. The "par" in parity (partner, pair, couple) is also found in *parturiente* (woman in labor). Thus Pier della Francesca interpreted with genius the modernity of Catholicism: the "Madonna del parto," is both the pregenital idealization of incest (Mary pregnant by the Father-God) and the sublimation of procreation (she donates her Son to Him; Mary the virgin-woman-mother tolerates the natural graft, welcomes the nonself as a neighbor).

To have the "procreative function," a vital necessity for the human species, acknowledged to access political responsibilities the right and duty of every woman citizen, to symbolize the "female libido," specific to each woman, is at the same time to be born, and to know, remember, thank and think (in German, as in English, the person who thanks thinks, danken/denken). Thus, through a new "human contract" that is sexual and democratic, between men and women, not only "will love and truth replace hate and lies" (Vaclav Havel), but egocentrism and envy will be replaced by generosity and gratitude.

Notes

1. In fact, it is because I have devoted all my time to thinking and acting rather than to writing that my thought is so little or poorly known in the US.

2. In an "uncultural" alliance with left-wing, liberal feminists, right-wing reactionary conservatives in Senate have just defeated a bill aiming at inscribing in the Constitution the need for "women's and men's equal access to mandates and offices."

3. France which ranks second in the world regarding human development, falls 71st, regarding women's representation in Parliament. It rose, in 1997, from the last to the next to last rank of the E.U countries with less than 8% of women elected for both Chambers. Twice, in 1982 and very recently on January 14, 1999, the *Conseil Constitutionnel*, in charge of attending to the conformity of laws with the Constitution has refused to confirm laws introducing affirmative action in favor of women in politics, in the name of the "indivisibility" of electorate.

4. In France, a woman is killed everyday simply because she is a woman.

5. "Universal" is derived from "Universum" in Latin is a translation from "to holon" in Greek which means "totality".

Le regard de l'animal

Serge Bourjea

"Pourquoi écrit-on?" A cette question vieille comme la littérature,
et à laquelle il ne fut naturellement jamais répondu, je répondrai
paradoxalement ici par une idée simple, tout juste une hypothèse, un
désir peut-être. On écrit pour *interroger, ébranler, estomper* (ces trois
termes en gradation, empreintes d'un passage, d'un *pas* à franchir)
cette frontière improbable, hautement artificielle qui, depuis l'aube
de la civilisation, sépare l'homme de l'animal. Écrire serait écrire
l'animal qui nous demeure, le laisser se réinscrire en nous, tenter en
ce que nous sommes, d'en repérer la trace… Ou, pour le dire autrement, ce serait marcher sur ses *brisées*.

Mais j'irai aussitôt plus loin. Écrire me paraît relever d'*un certain regard* posé sur les choses, et qui est essentiellement un "regard
de l'animal". Non pas regard de puissance (cartésien, testien) que je
puis porter ou que je puis prêter à l'animal que, donc, *je ne suis pas*;
mais regard de, *depuis* l'animal sur moi posé, et qui me constitue
pour ce que je suis, mais en quelque sorte *sans moi*. Que je sois vu de
l'animal, une vue pour lui – pour cet "autre" radical, d'une autre espèce – ne fait aucun doute. Ce chat, mon chien, assurément *me*
regardent; sont susceptibles – et parfois intensément – de le faire.
Mais que voient-ils de *moi*? Quel moi suis-je en "eux", sinon pour

eux? J'ignore de quoi je suis signe dans ce lieu là où je *suis* le regard de l'animal. Là où je me dispose à le *suivre*.[1]

Or ce regard là – qui me voit *sans moi*, pour ce que je suis sans qu'il me soit jamais possible de constituer cette vue en savoir de ce que je suis – je crois le croiser très constamment dans une certaine littérature contemporaine, singulièrement écrite… par des femmes. On me dira que j'ai mauvaise vue (ou une vue *mauvaise*, ce qui n'est pas pareil). Ou que j'ai le mauvais oeil si j'insiste à dire, par exemple, que tout un pan de cette littérature là : de, *depuis* la [femme], me semble explorer vertigineusement et remettre en question ce que j'appellerais évidemment un *no woman's land*, cette "zone" incertaine d'elle-même qui coupe, écarte, sépare radicalement – et depuis l'origine de la civilisation – l'homme de l'animal.

Comme si la [femme] – je l'accroche ainsi dans mon propos, et pour ainsi dire je l'y réserve – figurait en ses écritures un "autre homme", qui ne se définirait plus dans une étrangeté radicale par rapport à l'animalité. Comme si cette figure de [femme] à l'oeil animal, était de quelque façon constitutive d'une certaine écriture contemporaine.

Puisque c'est un homme qui l'écrit ainsi,[2] tout ceci doit paraître immédiatement suspect à plus d'une… Je me contenterai, prudemment donc, dans ce qui suit sinon dans ce que *je suis*, d'illustrer mon propos par un simple regard jeté, posé plutôt, sur deux narrations que je placerai en regard ou sous les regards l'une de l'autre.

Il s'agira, d'une part, d'un texte de Clarice Lispector : *A Paixão segundo G.H.* (*La passion selon G.H.*),[3] dans cette relation indécise qu'il présente d'"elle", la [femme], et d'une animalité proprement préhistorique. Et, en miroir, d'un conte inédit d'Hélène Cixous : *Aube partagée*. Ce conte récrit, sans le vouloir sinon sans le savoir, un même face à face, mais en le dédoublant encore : celui d'"elle" – Hélène – et de la (sa) chatte "Thea"; celui de l'une et de l'autre face à "la chose", vivante et morte, *au vu* de cette *autre* qu'elles [ne] sont [pas] toutes deux.

Je rappelle schématiquement l'argument de Clarice.

"Elle", bourgeoise brésilienne, désoeuvrée, un après-midi de dimanche et de solitude en été : même l'employée de maison a reçu son congé. Qui est "elle"? Précisément ce que la font les autres ou, mieux encore, ce que la "voient" les autres, ce qui se donne à voir aux yeux d'autrui de ce qu'elle est ou croit être devenue. A la lettre, elle n'est plus que ses initiales, "G. H." (le "Genre Humain"?), un nom à peine que les habitudes ont gravé sur une peau d'animal mort : le cuir de ses bagages, dont on devinent qu'ils sont, comme elle, en souffrance.

[38] Je me vois telle que les autres me voient... [...] Finalement, j'étais devenue mon nom. Il suffit de voir mes initiales, G.H., gravées dans le cuir des valises : et l'on m'a toute entière... [...] Cette femme, G.H. dans le cuir des valises, c'était moi. [48]

"Elle", G.H., vient d'en terminer avec un amour sans passion, ce genre d'amour qui laisse bons amis les deux amants (ce qui est tout dire de sa nature) et décide, à la lettre, de revisiter sa demeure, d'y mettre de l'ordre, de mettre en "*elle*" bon ordre, en commençant par ce lieu là où le désordre physique et moral ne peut que régner par définition : *O quarto da empregada*, la chambre de la bonne. Petit détour anthropologique : la chambre de bonne dans les appartements brésiliens est un lieu singulier, celui de l'Autre dans le Même, le lieu où une sorte de double ou de dédoublement de soi peut exister, le plus souvent hors d'atteinte de mes regards. Matérialisation ménagère de l'inconscient, cette chambre impénétrable voit la bonne vivre en toute liberté, imaginairement livrée à ses instincts de femme. Sa porte se trouve naturellement en toute extrémité d'un couloir sombre, face à la sortie de service (vis à vis de *l'autre* sortie, dérobée, obscure, de la maison).

"Elle" entame ainsi une plongée paradoxale en elle-même, qui va la conduire jusqu'à l'animal en sa demeure, jusqu'à ce point extrême d'un parcours qui la verra confrontée, puis *identifiée* à cet être primitif que, donc, elle redevient, sans le vouloir ou ne sachant plus en elle ce désir de l'animal. Je me contente de nommer les étapes de cette descente en soi-même, en soulignant que c'est bien par la vue, par le regard porté et éventuellement rendu, que s'accomplissent à la fois le destin de G.H. (sa "passion") et l'écriture de ce roman qui, selon le regard, procède. S'accomplit ici sous nos yeux ce qu'il convient de nommer le déclin d'un *cogito*, à la scansion partout retrouvée : je suis ce que je vois; je suis ce que j'écris que je vois; je suis donc, à la lettre, ce que je *suis*.

Première étape : l'entrevue. Ce qui est vu ou constitue une première vue au sein des ténèbres attendues, au plus caché de soi, est paradoxalement la lumière elle-même. La mystérieuse porte à peine entrouverte, "elle" se voit confrontée à la demeure d'un soleil immobile, qui force un instant les yeux à se fermer. Il y a là certitude d'un ordre absolu de l'existence; sentiment de la perfection d'un vide parfaitement éclairé qui s'impose au regard et efface en lui tout marquage, jusqu'à celui, mémorial, des vieux journaux. Il y a seulement là "un quadrilatère de lumière blanche", page blanche retrouvée qui n'appelle encore aucune inscription.

[57] Je me dirigeai vers le couloir obscur qui prolonge la cuisine
[...] deux portes indistinctes dans l'obscurité se font face : la porte
de service et celle de la chambre de la bonne. Les "bas fonds" de
ma demeure. J'ouvris la porte qui cachait un amoncellement de
journaux et des ténèbres de crasse et de vieilleries. Mais la porte
ouverte, je dus cligner des yeux sous le choc douloureux de la
réverbération. C'est qu'au lieu de la pénombre confuse à laquelle
je m'attendais, je me heurtais à un quadrilatère de lumière
blanche : pour me protéger j'avais été obligée de cligner des
yeux. [...] J'étais stupéfaite de trouver une chambre absolument
propre [...] Je n'imaginais pas que cette bonne aurait, sans rien
me dire, arrangé sa chambre à son goût, lui retirant avec une
audace de propriétaire sa fonction de débarras... [57]

Cette pénétration conduit ainsi, d'un seul coup, vers une sorte
d'orient désert, vers un désert sec en soi, spontanément nommé "le
désert de Libye" (dans le conte d'Hélène Cixous, on verra que celui
de l'Egypte ancienne est tout aussi brutalement retrouvé). Désert
duquel toute vie semble retirée, si ce n'est celle – essentielle, indélé-
bile – dont témoignent encore les "traces", les empreintes laissées
d'un passage, d'une existence intense sur le *lit*. Cette chambre est en
fait le lieu où la vie se garde et regarde, "me" regarde, et me voit ou
me perce pour ce que je suis. Ce gros oeil, dans lequel "elle" pénètre,
permet en effet d'opposer, tout en les effaçant – les faisant se recou-
vrir les unes les autres, les rendant imperceptibles – les traces de la
vivante qui s'est absentée (la bonne), et celle d'une sorte de morte
pourtant bien présente ("G.H."). J'insisterai à dire que, pour
Clarice, cette scène est proprement une *scène d'écriture* qui, par effacement ou recouvrement successifs des traces, donne à voir non
l'inscription d'un portrait précis mais, à l'inverse, la *désinscription* du
personnage ("G.H.") et, parallèlement, le procès de quelque devenir-animal en lequel elle se retrouve, "elle", la [femme] de ce roman,
l'animal, l'écriture. On notera que les initiales gravées dans le cuir
des valises sont devenues illisibles, lettres mortes sous la poussière
qui les ensevelit, et que la "citation de soi" qu'"elle" est peu à peu
devenue, perd brutalement toute référence extérieure.

[62] Je contemplais la nudité du minaret : sur le lit dont les draps
avaient été enlevés, le matelas gisait, poussiéreux, avec ses
grandes taches déteintes de sueur et de sang délayés. [...] Dans
un coin trois vieilles valises sont empilées contre le mur selon une
symétrie si parfaite que leur présence m'avait échappé tant elles
respectaient le vide de la pièce. Sur ces valises et sur la trace

presque morte d'un GH, la poussière accumulée tranquillement et déjà sédimentée.

[...] [La chambre] était une violation de mes guillemets, des guillemets qui faisaient de moi une citation de moi-même. [...] Là rien n'était fait par moi...[63]

Mais cette expérience d'une dépossession de soi, va se dédoubler encore comme en un miroir. Il y a donc moi et l'autre de moi (la maîtresse et son double); il y a les ténèbres et la clarté, le paradoxe de cette chambre mystérieuse et close, qui est pourtant la demeure du soleil ("la chambre – dit délicieusement le texte – ne fermait jamais sa paupière"); il va y avoir à présent, plus avant dans le texte, alors que s'en accentue la plongée, un autre face à face qui précédera lui-même une fusion propitiatoire : celui de moi et de l'autre radical du moi, la bête depuis 350 millions d'années immonde : le cafard. A "*barata*".

D'un côté il y a "elle", mais rendue à ses instincts, à sa primitivité de bête, ses nerfs à vif, toute attention, guettant l'événement, l'apparition de quelque proie qui ne saurait tarder. C'est alors le désir de tuer, hors de tout interdit et de toute considération morale, de tuer sans haine mais en toute "jouissance", qui *la* domine, bête sans pudeur, animal magnifique. En elle, le devenir animal procède ainsi :

[74] Je guettais, j'étais toute aux aguets [...] toute une puissance latente palpitait en moi. [...] Cette vigilance était ma propre vie [...] vigilance à vivre, inextricablement liée à mon corps, processus même de la vie en moi. [...] Comme un aveugle ausculte sa propre attention, je me sentais pour la première fois habitée par un instinct. Et je frémis d'une jouissance extrême comme si enfin mon attention s'appliquait à la grandeur d'un instinct qui était mauvais, total et infiniment doux – comme l'eau d'une source [...]

Je m'enivrais pour la première fois d'une haine limpide comme l'eau d'une source, je m'enivrais du désir légitime ou non, de tuer. [...] Quinze siècles durant je n'avais pas lutté... Comme si pour la première fois j'étais à l'échelle de la Nature [...] sans aucune pudeur, je me sentais devenir l'inconnue que j'étais...[76]

Face à "elle", de sa taille tout juste, sorte de cercueil debout, de double inanimé de ce qu'est devenue "G.H.", se tient une armoire de bois sec qui ne s'entrouvre que sur son propre évidement. Armoire béante qui l'attire comme une bouche, comme un orifice pour une autre naissance, vers laquelle elle engage son visage. Parturition inversée, cette entrée dans la ténèbre, au sein de la lumière, est retrouvaille avec l'animalité, la primitivité de toute créature. Le regard ici s'épuise pour un instant sans durée, marqué d'un double aveuglement : perdue dans ses pensées, "elle" cesse de regarder quoi que ce soit; et l'obscurité l'empêche tout d'abord de rien distinguer au sein de l'armoire. Seule la comparaison avec la "poule" – que l'on retrouvera étrangement chez Hélène Cixous – note cette intimité chaude, duveteuse, nidale, à quoi la vie l'a reconduite.

> [67] Je parcourus l'armoire des yeux. [...] Je passais les doigts sur les inégàlités du matelas [...] J'ouvris un peu la porte étroite et le noir du dedans s'échappa comme une haleine [...] Dans l'entrebâillement, je passai ce que je pus de mon visage. Et comme si l'obscurité de l'intérieur m'épiait, nous restâmes un instant à nous guetter sans nous voir. Je ne voyais rien, je ne pouvais que respirer l'odeur sèche et chaude comme celle d'une poule vivante...[68]

Je résume ce qui suit et qui nous tient haletant : *entre* elle et son autre, dans l'antre de l'autre, dans l'embrasure de la porte entrebâillée, surgit l'animal qu'elle devient, la bête millénaire qui l'attendait ou qu'elle attendait, de toute éternité. Mais une bête qui va s'humaniser dans le temps qu'"elle", au contraire, s'abêtit, se dissipe et s'absorbe en elle. Voici que le cafard immonde prend visage, puis l'orne d'un regard sous des cils démesurés; voici que l'animal "sous mes yeux" me devient séduisant, entre avec moi dans une relation étrange qui est bien celle d'une "amour" (le texte le dit ainsi) ou plus précisément d'une "passion", si la notion, échappant à toute idée de sentiment, dit quelque chose de la violence de l'instinct.

> [78] Mais c'est alors que je vis le visage du cafard. Il était de face, à la hauteur de mon visage et de mes yeux [...] un visage sans épaisseur. Les antennes sortaient comme des moustaches de chaque côté de la bouche. La bouche marron était bien dessinée... Ses yeux noirs à facettes regardaient... c'était un cafard vieux comme un poisson fossilisé... Il était roussâtre. Et tout couvert de cils... Je le regardai, avec sa bouche et ses yeux : on aurait cru une mulâtresse à l'agonie. Mais les yeux étaient noirs et radieux. Des yeux d'amoureuse... Œil frangé, sombre, vif, épousseté. Chaque oeil reproduisait le cafard tout entier...[81]

Salamandre, Chimère ou Griffon, tout autant que poisson mais fossilisé, alliant le minéral au vivant, effaçant la frontière des règnes, la bête se connaît comme un être aussi ancien qu'une légende. Sa bouche pourtant, finement dessinée, au contour d'une précision inimaginable, est bien réelle, sensuelle ; et ses yeux, surtout, fascinent, qui sous leurs cils font signe.

Le *geste* alors se produit, qui n'est nullement celui d'une castration, du retranchement de cet intrus, de cet inconnu qui soudain *fait face*, mais au contraire celui de la fusion, de la réduction de la distance, de la différence entre homme et femme, femme et animalité, vie et minéralité. Le cafard cesse d'appartenir au règne animal, mais il n'est pas pour autant homme ou femme. Il est figure folle de l'androgyne, et il est aussi, sans contradiction, un être minéral, posé là comme une pierre depuis la nuit des temps.

Voici le geste : "elle" ferme brusquement la porte un instant entr'ouverte, dans un mouvement impulsif où la haine et le désir se conjoignent, ce geste étant à la fois celui d'un crime perpétré, et celui d'une caresse. Et la matière même de la vie, explosion séminale, s'exprime dans l'entre des deux corps...

Il n'y a plus désormais l'humain / l'animal, le dehors / le dedans, le conscient / l'inconscient (et toute interprétation psychanalytique du passage s'en trouve du même coup invalidée). Il n'y a plus la réalité et la fiction, le personnage d'un roman et l'expérience de l'écrivain qu'il permettrait de traduire... Rien ici, à la lettre, *ne veut plus rien dire* dans l'ordre de la métaphysique, à l'échelle des règnes séparés de la Création. Il y a seulement l'antre béant où les deux se rejoignent, quel que soit l'un et quel que soit l'autre, où l'un s'indistingue de l'autre. Je dirai – pour couper court – qu'il n'y a plus que *la page blanche*, mais une page rendue à sa fertilité vivante, contrairement à celle, stérile, de Mallarmé : chair joyeuse, promise à la jouissance, opposée à la chair ineffablement triste. Car l'entrevue n'est pas terminée dans l'instant où se referme la porte du placard, et c'est *le cafard que donc elle est*, c'est l'identification amoureuse avec la bête qui lui fait face, qui délivre l'entière leçon : ce *vis à vis* d'"elle" et de l'animal retrouvé, permet en effet de découvrir "l'identité profonde", non point de "G. H." seulement, mais de la vie elle-même en ce qu'elle a de plus vivant :

[78] Je regardais, incrédule. [...] je n'avais pas poussé la porte avec assez de force. J'avais bien attrapé le cafard. Mais je l'avais laissé en vie. En vie et me regardant[...] [81]Ce que j'ai vu c'était la vie me regardant [...] matière brute et plasma sec [...] J'avais regardé le cafard vivant et en lui j'avais découvert l'identité de ma

> vie la plus profonde... Je passais de son côté, me solidarisais
> avec lui [...]
>
> [82] Et soudain je gémis tout haut. C'est que, comme du pus, jail-
> lissait à la surface, la plus véritable consistance et je sentais, avec
> épouvante et dégoût, *que mon 'je / est' venait d'une source
> antérieure à l'humain*[4] [...]
>
> [87] C'est alors que, lentement, comme d'un tube, lentement se
> mit à sortir la matière du cafard qui avait été écrasé. La matière
> du cafard qui était son dedans, la matière épaisse, blanchâtre,
> lente, se répandait à l'extérieur comme sortant d'un tube de den-
> tifrice. Sous mes yeux dégoûtés et séduits [...] la matière blanche
> jaillissait lentement sur son dos, comme un fardeau. Le fardeau
> de son propre corps [87]

Je ne sais si l'on peut interpréter ceci comme une expérience
mystique, épiphanique à proprement parler. Il y faudrait une révélation, le sentiment soudain d'une transcendance, d'un passage, d'un
pas possible vers un au-delà. Or, si expérience il y a, il s'agit de celle
d'une régression vers le primitif en moi, en chacun, en "elle"; régression ou repli vers ce qui est nommé ailleurs la "goutte de vie",
"goutte virulente", "goutte de matière", ou encore "la goutte acide" –
celle d'un "métal sur la langue", celle d'une "plante verte écrasée". Expérience qui permet de définir en moi un autre moi que celui dont
m'assure ma pensée, mais qui est un "moi protozoaire, protéine pure",
ainsi que l'indique pour finir le texte. Non point un moi individué,
promis dès lors à la "connaissance", mais *un devenir du moi* : son
procès dans l'ineffable, hors de l'atteinte des mots, à l'abri de l'inces-
sante différence. Un Moi de l'entrevue, de l'entre-deux vues, dans le
concours des visions qui invalident et brouillent les points de vues.

> [85] Le cafard est séduction pure. Cils, cils qui sans cesse cillent
> et appellent. [93] Je suis : ce que j'ai vu, ma civilisation avait dis-
> parue... j'avais rejoint la vie ancienne et profonde du cafard...,
> rejoint la terre et le soleil dans le désert profond de Libye... je suis
> seulement en train d'aimer le cafard...[94] Certainement ce qui
> m'avait jusque-là protégée de la vie "sentimentisée" dont je vi-
> vais, c'est que le meilleur en nous c'est l'inhumain, c'est la chose,
> la partie chose des gens. [96]

Passion et devenir-animal, presque minéral ou moléculaire,
selon cette "elle" éternelle, que ne sauraient plus longtemps identi-
fier les initiales effacées de "G.H", dans le cuir des valises...

Dans le conte d'Hélène Cixous "Aube partagée", tout est également affaire d'images en miroir, opposant mais identifiant vertigineusement la femme à l'animal, en l'occurrence ici "elle" et son double, "la chatte"; puis les deux ensemble à ce qui figure un *autre* radical : "la chose". Je prendrai pour point de départ de ma lecture une phrase qui la résume entièrement, une de ces phrases de Cixous à quoi on peut être attaché, je le suis; et sans doute devrais-je dire aussitôt que *je la suis*, cette phrase là, jusqu'au lieu où elle nous conduit :

> ... fantôme la vision c'est comme si je te voyais, je le vois encore, nous le voyons. [...] Thea s'affaisse sur le lit de papier, les pattes ouvertes déroulées en ailes, possédée par le spectre douloureux.

Qu'est-ce qu'un "lit" lorsqu'il est de papier, et qui est "elle", Thea, lorsqu'elle s'affaisse ainsi et pour ainsi le dire tombe sur la page, s'y fixe pour l'éternité sous mes yeux? Qui est "elle", avec ses "ailes" déliées, et comment dès lors l'écrivez-vous? Thea est la chatte d'Hélène Cixous, tout le monde sait cela, mais ici elle est bien la déesse, elle est bien l'écriture.

Tout le conte d'Hélène est basé sur l'idée d'un "partage", d'une part, d'une partition ou, pour le dire autrement, d'un *départ*. Moire primitive retrouvée, se divisant, se démultipliant dans les Parques, mais se donnant encore comme source, comme origine de tout ce qui, d'elle, s'engendrera, sera susceptible de le faire. Il s'agit bien ici du récit d'une *parturition* qui nous conduit vers un autre accouchement, vers des retrouvailles avec ce que, sans doute, nous n'avons jamais cessé d'être.

Le temps et le lieu sont partis. Dans l'"aube partagée" (c'est le titre du conte), à 6 heures du matin, en ce crépuscule du matin qui est à la fois le point de départ du jour et le terme de la nuit, quelque "chose" d'innommable est entrevue, comme suspendue dans l'espace et le temps. Arrêtée dans sa chute ou stoppée en plein essor, on ne le saura pas exactement, cette chose est "là", sur le "balcon", en ce lieu indécis, interlope, qui *la* place entre intériorité et extériorité. Et sur ce balcon la voici suspendue "entre le 11è et 12è barreau", "entre les mailles du grillage", sans qu'il soit en rien assuré si elle est au dehors ou en deçà du garde-fou. "Chose" elle-même est ce lieu qui n'en est pas un, ce temps qui est celui de l'écart. "Entre", sa vision, sa trace à peine perceptible, incertaine.

Qu'est-elle en effet cette vue, cette chose entrevue? Les qualifications vont se fracturer, se dédoubler, se diffracter, s'engendrant et s'effaçant successivement les unes les autres. Il s'agit au départ de *presque rien* sinon "une grande feuille noire morte accrochée au grillage du balcon debout". Feuille dont on peut dire seulement qu'"elle est là", et successivement nommable en tant que "la chose", la "chose immuable", "l'inertie noire", "la fixité, la solidité"; et bientôt "l'étrangeté de l'autre côté", "la morte / le mort", ou enfin "l'apparition"... "Elle", la chose, est-ce inanimé, vivant, ou mort? D'un ordre minéral, végétal, ou animal? D'aucun ordre sans doute ou de celui d'une impensable *viemort*, d'un interrègne reconduisant incessamment de l'une à l'autre des hypothèses, les retenant et les annulant toutes, tour à tour. De cette chose placée là sous nos yeux, on peut dire seulement que le sujet s'y reprend sans cesse, ou demande à être redéfini en fonction de ce qu'"elle" est:

> Maintenant j'étais *prise* dans la vision de la chose immobile *prise* dans mon grillage...

Qui est "prise", à la lettre? La chose, ou moi? Et qu'est-ce encore qu'un "moi" dans la vision de l'autre, si cet autre est immobile à jamais et cependant "quelque chose de nécessaire à la vie"?

On le voit bien, il en va dans la narration d'une question de *point de vue*, de la possibilité ou de l'impossibilité d'être "prise" ou une prise, à la place de l'autre. "Je n'arrivais pas à me voir faire disparaître la chose" dit la protagoniste du récit, de l'autre côté de la porte-fenêtre qui fonctionne comme un miroir sans tain. Or le problème est moins d'échapper à cette confrontation terrible avec cette "chose" là (avec l'inconnu de soi, avec la "mort", ce qui se donne pour tel en ce qu'"elle" est), que d'éviter un autre face à face problématique, qui dédoublerait et inverserait le premier : celui de "la chose" avec Thea, avec l'animale. "Il fallait que j'évacue le mort ou la morte avant que la chatte n'ait eu le temps de l'apercevoir". C'est qu'il y a là *scène* (je vois ce que je ne devrais pas voir, ce qui est l'interdit de toute vue); mais également une sorte *d'autre scène* primitive, ou son envers en miroir (appelons-la scène ultime, peut-être) : *la vue / de la vue de la chose*, c'est-à-dire la vue du rapport terrible de la [femme] et de la [mort]. On "accrochera" à nouveau ces notions, pour les retrancher ou les priver de tout écho trop existentiel, de leurs références anthropologiques assurées. [Femme] est ce qui ne suppose pas nécessairement une masculinité comme son envers (ou son endroit). [Mort] ce qui ne s'indique pas seulement d'une cessation de la vie.

La structure de cette double scène, du reste, est ici très subtile, puisque si une première triangulation y est tracée sans conteste (il y a "elle" / son double animal "Thea" / et "la chose"), ce n'est qu'en opposition et confrontation avec une autre triangulation, biblique plus encore que freudienne celle-là. Quelque chose comme : sainte Anne, la Sainte Vierge et Jésus, l'*infans* tel que le mouton le regarde, tel que l'animal en témoigne et pour ainsi dire le suppose, dans le tableau célèbre de Léonard de Vinci...[5] Il y a en effet la "mère", celle qui s'indique, à la lettre, comme une "sage femme", la mère des parturitions, des partages : celle qui, aussi bien et si l'on peut ainsi l'écrire, *accoucherait de la mort* ("elle me dira, montre moi et elle le fera, la sage-femme, avec son absence étrange d'inquiétude et de phobie"). Il y a "elle", la narratrice, de qui s'engendre le récit, de qui naît la parole. Et il y a sa fille, "qui dort", en toute innocence et ignorance, dans cette hypothèse para freudienne que c'est, je cite, "la mère qui doit lutter avec la mort".

Mais voilà que l'animal *tranche*, vient proprement couper en trois : "voilà que Thea est là postée sur la table en sphinx qui ne sait pas si j'ai le mot de l'énigme".

Je résume et condense à présent l'argument. Il y a donc un double face à face qui compose la structure ternaire de la scène : moi et la chose; Thea et la chose; elle, moi et la chose. Mais il y a aussi la lignée des femmes ou de la féminité qui se développe depuis la fille, presque encore une enfant, à la mère et à la mère de sa mère, jusqu'à nommer le "Sphinx", l'animal-dieu, au buste de femme et aux ailes d'oiseaux, le *monstre* énigmatique (et "monstre" est ce qui soudain se montre, se donne à voir infailliblement). "C'est le moment de communion" dit le texte, celui de l'entre-deux et de l'entretien, multipliés.

Or, c'est une double fusion qui va s'opérer, un peu comme dans le texte de Clarice Lispector, conduisant à présent en "terre égyptienne", au désert d'origine où nous sommes rendus, dans une sorte de régression vers l'animalité, qui est aussi une remontée vers les sources de la civilisation. D'une part, c'est l'impérieuse nécessité d'un contact étroit, intime avec "la chose" qui s'impose : si les objets de l'écart, de la différence, ont été envisagés pour en assurer la maîtrise (tour à tour "gants en caoutchouc", "gants de cuir", "bâton" ou "bambou", papier "journal" surtout), l'ouverture brusque de la porte fenêtre et la présence simultanée de l'enfant et de la chatte, les rendent soudain inutiles ou dérisoires. D'autre part, on ne sait plus à vrai dire qui est l'animal et qui est la déesse, de la chatte ou de sa maîtresse, puisque toutes deux, devant cette énigme de "la feuille noire" (devant le monstre), se trouvent brusquement *livrées* à leurs "instincts". "La même bise nous souffle le même affolement à la figure", dit le texte, et c'est l'instant où l'"inertie noire" crucifiée au balcon, reprend miraculeusement vie, ressuscite, et retourne à la lumière où elle s'engloutit. Le récit mérite ici que l'on y regarde de près, que l'on s'attarde au détail de sa facture, dans un geste analogue à celui de la [femme] et de la chatte recueillies devant la "bête", flairant la "mort(e)". On y retrouve la "poule", brève incarnation par ses "ailes" de la "chose", et l'on ne saurait passer trop vite sur l'homophonie de l'aile et de l'elle, sur le trait qui les rassemble et les distingue à la fois:

> Un instinct me prend me jette sur l'oiseau, preste j'attrape *les ailes* comme d'une poule, [...] je cours à la fenêtre, l'instinct me mène, me guide, nous voici au balcon, l'instinct, *les ailes*, la morte s'élance d'un vol puissant et gagne l'autre bout de la ville d'un trait.

Mais c'est la proximité de ces "elles" et de l'instinct qui, pour ainsi le dire, saute aux yeux dans la phrase précipitée, prodigieuse, qui en témoigne. Comme si toucher à l'"elle", l'accrocher ainsi par ces parts du corps, c'était rendre à l'instinct sa force et sa capacité à lutter contre la mort. Saisie par instinct, comme le ferait d'un oiseau un chat ou une chatte, la "chose" revit, se réinscrit dans l'espace et le temps, reprend miraculeusement son vol. Encore faut-il souligner que nous ne sommes pas pour autant au terme du mouvement, et que le récit ne saurait trouver ici sa clôture. L'instinct est retrouvé, sans doute, mais il reste douloureusement lié à de "l'humain", à ce qui se nomme en lui, précisément, une "cochonnerie". Cette souillure ultime (il serait donc des animaux "sales", promis à *la souille*) démarque sans doute l'instinct de toute morale et des Tables de la Loi, mais elle ne permet pas pour autant de retrouver l'intégrité de la force vitale, la pureté ou la primitivité de l'animal. Moïse au Sinaï ne s'est vu imposer aucun interdit divin, et le "Tu ne tueras point" n'a rien d'un Commandement : à la lettre, il était déjà inscrit, écrit dès l'origine, à même le corps humain, et très précisément dans ses "moelles" (comment résister à la nécessité instinctive de réécrire ce terme élémentaire, de l'ébranler un peu, et de le faire jouer sur lui même pour le prononcer, dans ma lecture à voix basse : "moi – elles"?)

> C'est l'instinct ! Ce maudit instinct humain, cette cochonnerie, cette phobie, ah quelle lâcheté mauvaise est tapie dans mes moelles [*moi- elles*] et maintenant je comprends que Moïse n'a rien reçu de Dieu là-haut. C'était dans ses moelles cet interdit humain... Tu ne tueras pas chez moi. Cette crainte, cette souillure. Non, rien de moral. C'était dans mes moelles [*moi-elles*] et avant que je sache...

On comprend qu'un dernier pas restait à franchir qui consiste à rendre son *innocence* à l'instinct humain, pour faire d'"elle" ce qu'elle n'aurait jamais dû cessé d'être entre nous : la qualification même de la vie, féline. Laver l'instinct de ses dernières souillures, non pas le "purifier" à vrai dire (ce terme, trop terni par la morale), mais lui restituer son intégrité, quelque chose comme son immaculée conception : c'est là vers quoi tend en effet l'alliance finale, la communion primitive, d'"elle" et de Thea; de la [femme] et de l'animal.

J'insisterai tout juste à dire que l'échange alors peut s'accomplir pleinement, dans la mesure où l'une désormais *est* l'autre. Se retrouve ici le "je /est" de Clarice, si le verbe être à la troisième personne du singulier, désaccordé du sujet "je", dit quelque chose en moi de ce qui me reste étranger, l'inconnu de moi-même que pourtant je suis, mon animalité. Si le "je est un autre" qui se déclare et se décline dans le conte d'Hélène Cixous, suppose donc que l'animal me regarde et me voit pour ce que "je / est":

> Ah mon dieu mon dieu qu'ai-je fait !? J'ai trahi ma semblable, ma fiancée, ma petite épouse au coeur illimité, ah mon dieu si cet oiseau revient je le lui donnerai, je le jure, oui, il vaut mieux que je le jure c'est plus sûr, oui, s'il revenait, moi aussi je jouerais avec son petit corps tiède, je lui donnerais de secs durs petits coups de patte et je l'égorgerais avec gaieté.

L'une étant l'autre, la race en elles peut *procéder*. Les voici, processionnaires, tendues vers le point vide de la disparition, en une sorte de culte ou de vénération *à rebours*, barbare, primitive, de ce qui ne se sera donc pas manifesté : c'est à nouveau le "je suis" qu'il me faudrait commenter alors, pour dire l'ambiguïté d'une suite de soi, d'une poursuite, d'une *chasse*, de ce que donc je suis:

> …le visage empreint de la patience de notre race […] pénitente *je suis* Thea sur le balcon […] L'oiseau, elle l'incarne, petite statue commémorative.

Quelle est cette commémoration et où en prendre connaissance? Dans le livre, sans doute, recueil des traces où rien n'aura eu lieu que l'empreinte, l'empreindre plutôt, d'une écriture qui *est* précisément cet événement là, à jamais attendu et pour toujours perdu:

> Voici le moment où il faut refermer le livre trop profond. Voici l'heure de l'enterrement […] je pense qu'il est de mon devoir de clore le récit…

Je le pense aussi. Qu'un livre refermé, rendu illisible, est l'écriture même et que cette écriture, pour l'essentiel, est [femme].

Quelles leçons tirer de cette double lecture "en regard", du texte de Clarice et de celui d'Hélène ?

Je dirais tout d'abord, même si cela est l'évidence, que les deux textes de Lispector et de Cixous n'auront cessé de se dire l'un l'autre, de se lire l'un par l'autre, comme en un miroir. Rencontre heureuse – vérifiée en bien d'autres circonstances, pour d'autres oeuvres – dans laquelle on ne sait plus au juste où est l'original et quel en est l'écho, si la notion même d'originalité fait sens, garde pour "elles" une quelconque signification.

Mais il y faut ajouter, au risque de la perversion, que ce jeu d'écho et de frontière, que l'oscillation qui s'indique en permanence entre l'une et l'autre des deux positions, désigne assurément *l'entre des deux* comme le lieu même, ambigu, de l'écriture. Où le texte, s'il y a *texte*, s'écrit-il au juste ? Quel en est le lieu et quand y a-t-il lieu ? En *quoi* ? Est-ce dans les profondeurs de l'oeuvre fixée, figée à jamais par la mort de son auteur, et que l'on n'en finit plus de sonder, de solliciter pour ce qu'elle *devient* sous le regard du lisant ? Est-ce au contraire dans l'inventivité troublante, tourbillonnante, du récit en train de s'écrire et qui, tâtonnant, se forme en *vis à vis* (en contre marque) de ce à partir de quoi il s'écrit ? On tranchera pour répondre : ni ici ni là, mais *à la surface*, sur cette zone intangible du miroir où rien n'a lieu "vraiment", sinon la possibilité quelque peu magique de renvoyer incessamment l'un à l'autre, ce qui appartient à l'extériorité la plus actuelle, et ce qui est à reprendre à la profondeur la plus éternelle. Les deux textes confrontés, le roman et le conte, le disent à leur manière. Dans l'univers de Clarice, il n'y a pas le côté de "G.H." et, distinct, celui du cafard, mais précisément "la matière blanche" qui entre eux s'exprime, assurant leur union, donnant substance à leur commune identité. C'est de cette pâte ductile, fertile (de façon plaisante comparée à celle d'un "tube dentifrice")[6] que s'*informe* la vie, qu'"elle" est à nouveau vivante, c'est-à-dire visible et non plus seulement lisible. Dans le récit de Cixous, c'est plus précisément encore *la vitre*, assurant la liaison d'"elle" et de "la chose" dans le temps où elle les maintient à distance, qui permet le regard et rend possible la vision. Lorsque s'ouvrira la porte fenêtre, lorsque l'être franchira le seuil de balcon (c'est-à-dire se tiendra au lieu même de l'échange), l'affolement et le vertige de la réversibilité seront à l'oeuvre ; le mort reviendra à la vie, et "elles" (quelle qu'en soit l'identité, mère – femme – fille – chose ou animalité) échangeront infiniment leurs rôles, deviendront tour à tour, et paradoxalement ensemble, ce qu'elles sont et ne sont pas.

Comment le dire, pour moi, homme, et les regardant, les lisant toutes deux dans la fascination? Les chats ne sont pas mon fort. Par éducation je serais plutôt chien, et par profession je suis plus à l'aise (je crois l'être) dans l'écriture consacrée des hommes. Valéry, pourquoi pas? il le dit aussi et si bien (je le convoque toujours dès qu'il s'agit des livres)... On trouve dans *Mélange* une formule étrange et heureuse que j'aimerais installer "là", dans l'entre des deux, comme écran de leurs regards, au lieu où elles se disent, tout en permettant de la lire, "elle", l'écriture. Se demandant ce qu'il est en tant qu'il est (un) vivant; s'interrogeant sur ce qui l'assure de son existence au cœur de l'espèce à laquelle il appartient; se détournant ainsi du *cogito* cartésien et de la substance comme de la pensée, "il" (Valéry) retrouve le regard de l'animal comme sa seule garantie d'exister. C'est vu par la bête, depuis la "bêtise", c'est-à-dire au sein d'un univers pleinement intelligent mais à jamais impénétrable (innommable), que je puis m'assurer de ce que je suis. La comparaison impose le sens : face à moi-même, vis à vis de ce que je suis, je suis vu ou une vue *comme* pour l'animal ("un chien"). Et ce que le chien voit de moi, *si je le suis*, est comparable à ce que je verrais d'un livre tissu d'une écriture inconnue, à jamais incompréhensible et cependant obvie. Parole non pas profonde, mais précisément *de surface* :

> Avec soi seul on est ce que l'on est : un fait local, et l'on peut se voir soi-même (ou représenter) *comme un chien regarde un livre.*
> [Paul Valéry, *Œuvres* 1, 332]

Il ne m'est pas indifférent que, dans le texte valéryen et sous la rubrique "Narcisse", s'inscrive alors l'essentiel à mes yeux. Qu'un "miroir nous fait sortir de notre visage".

Notes

1. Le verbe "suivre", à la première personne du singulier du présent de l'indicatif, a ceci de commode en Français qu'il introduit une précieuse ambiguïté avec le verbe "être". C'est cette ambiguïté que nous avons choisi d'installer au cœur de notre réflexion, dans la proposition maintes fois retrouvée : "je *suis* ce que je *suis*".

2. Ce texte a été donné une première fois sous forme de conférence à l'Université de Amherst au Massachusetts, en avril 1998, dans le cadre d'une table ronde sur l'écriture des femmes. J'étais alors le seul homme à cette tribune, je dois l'observer, et devant une salle presque exclusivement féminine. Inquiétudes et plaisirs du visage de l'"autre"...

3. Toutes nos références seront données à partir de Clarice Lispector, *La passion selon G.H.*, traduction de Claude Farny, Editions des Femmes, Paris, 1998. Dans la mesure où nous avons procédé à un "montage" des citations, nous donnons la pagination, entre crochets, en en-tête et à la fin de chaque fragment.

4. Le texte de Clarice Lispector, comme bien souvent, est ici très délicat à traduire. Comment rendre l'expression portugaise "meu *eu / é* " qui, à la lettre, constitue une faute de grammaire? Claude Farny a choisi de traduire par "je-être", ce que nous préférons

garder dans sa forme littérale : "mon je / est", remplaçant le tiré par une barre de fraction, qui note la rupture plus que l'alliance entre le pronom et le verbe.

5.   Hélène Cixous fait allusion à une "Apparition". Au tableau célèbre de Gustave Moreau qui porte ce titre, nous préférons celui de Léonard, pour éclairer la structure du conte. Renvoyant à l'analyse par Freud de la figure d'Anna "metterza" (bien la troisième), comme figure-mère de la toile, nous ne retiendrons pas pour autant l'hypothèse du "milan" qui se dessinerait entre les personnage. Que l'agneau, une brebis, regarde l'enfant Jésus, lui-même regardé par les mères, est plus que suffisant à rendre la complexité du jeu des regards qui s'exercent ici comme là.

6.   L'image de la pâte dentifrice surprend. Au-delà de sa couleur immaculée, elle s'impose sans doute par la dynamique de son expulsion hors du tube. Mais on peut penser également à sa fonction d'écran, de polissage des dents, qui en font une matière intermédiaire entre la profondeur de la gorge et l'extériorité où retentit la parole.

Aube partagée

Hélène Cixous

Nous cherchons en vain l'apaisement.

La maison est pleine de traces, elle nous détient dans sa mémoire à douleurs, il y en a sur le tapis de l'entrée, sur les sols, dans les coins du séjour, dans la cuisine jusque sous l'évier, cela s'arrête là, puis ça repart vers le balcon, et là, c'est accroché pour l'éternité, entre les 11° et les 12° barreaux, les pattes minuscules et puissantes accrochées dans les petits carrés du grillage. En vain nous y retournons. Tout est là encore, l'odeur forte comme un nom inoubliable, fantôme la vision c'est comme si je te voyais, je le vois encore, nous le voyons. Toute la maison est maintenant un mausolée. Thea a trouvé la résignation mais non l'apaisement. La résignation est un épuisement du coeur. A force de se frotter le coeur sur les barreaux, elle atteint enfin l'épuisement de l'espérance. Alors, dans le pitoyable confort de la fatigue elle s'affaisse sur le lit de papier, le corps très plat, les pattes grandes ouvertes déroulées en ailes, possédée par le spectre douloureux.

Tout a commencé à l'aube. Elle était grise et âpre à six heures. C'est en me penchant contre la fenêtre du matin que je l'ai vue : une grande feuille noire morte accrochée au grillage du balcon debout, la tête ronde inerte, le bec rentré, le corps effacé, au deuxième regard j'ai senti la force de cette inertie noire plus lourde épaisse que celle d'une feuille, et alors j'ai vu : accroché là par de fines pinces invisibles dans le lacis, une sorte d'oiseau mort collé debout entre les espaces. Ah non, je ne voulais pas l'avoir vu. Et maintenant que faire? Maintenant j'étais prise dans la vision de la chose immobile prise dans mon grillage. Horrifiée. Un dialogue sombre et fou a commencé entre moi vers la chose et sa menace étrange. Car elle m'avait jetée instantanément dans l'insoluble. Quel accident inimaginable aura précipité la présence qui morte ne lâchait plus le grillage comme si mourant elle avait refusé dans un dernier mouvement de tomber dans le vide. Et elle avait d'un ressort accroché son corps entre le ciel et la terre et la mort et l'écrasement. D'où m'est tombée l'apparition ? Qui l'aura foudroyée ? Un autre oiseau ? Un éclair ? Et elle s'est arrêtée, et pour rien, au milieu de la chute. Pour mon tourment. Sur mon balcon. Car maintenant j'avais cette chose sombre et lourde grande comme ma main accrochée à ma poitrine comme une broche macabre. Et je pensais à Thea. Le problème était le suivant : il fallait que j'évacue le mort ou la morte avant que la chatte n'ait eu la chance de l'apercevoir. Sinon la chatte voudrait naturellement en faire la connaissance et par suite…, mais comme l'oiseau était agrippé à l'extérieur du grillage, Thea voudra passer pardessus et cela ne doit pas être. Derrière la fenêtre je n'arrivais pas à me voir faire disparaître la chose, elle aura les pattes durcies et je vais devoir lutter avec la mort. Mes mains sont devenues sèches et froides jusqu'à l'épaule j'ai dit non.

Alors j'ai pensé je vais demander à ma fille qui dort, mais c'est inutile, car je le sais c'est la mère qui doit lutter avec la mort. Et je ne pouvais pas je ne peux pas. Alors j'ai essayé de m'obliger à penser. Mais les mains ne voulaient pas. Il y avait le mystère du refus horrifié dans la peau de mes doigts, je ne peux pas toucher le mort ou la morte, l'impossible c'est ce toucher, le tact de la mort. Me voilà avec l'impossible installé dans mes mains, accroché par d'invisibles petites pattes noires. Alors j'ai pensé je vais demander à ma mère, à 9 heures je vais lui téléphoner et comme je le sais, elle me dira montre moi et elle le fera, la sage-femme, avec son absence étrange d'inquiétude et de phobie. Mais après, moi j'aurai la honte et je la garderai pour toujours devant la mort et ce sera grave jusqu'à la fin, j'aurai perdu quelque chose de nécessaire à la vie, et pourrai-je encore affirmer que je suis ta mère ?

J'ai aussi pensé à mon aimé puisqu'il viendra cet après-midi mais je n'ai pas osé lui causer cette peine, car je le crois mon aimé souffre des mêmes peines fantômales que moi quoiqu'il soit un homme alors que je suis une femme, devant la mort nos mains sèchent de même. Et aussi je ne voudrais pas lui faire peur avec ma peur. Cependant une heure vient de passer et voilà que Thea est là, postée sur la table en sphinx qui ne sait pas si j'ai le mot de l'énigme et je ne peux plus échapper aux aiguilles. Maintenant je dois répondre. Il n'y a pas de chemin derrière moi.

Alors je pense aux gants, les gants en caoutchouc qui sont dans la salle de bains, je vais les chercher, je fouille mais ils ont disparu car je n'avais pas besoin d'eux. Mais je pense aux gants de cuir.

Maintenant c'est le moment de faire venir ma fille. Au lieu de réveiller ma fille avec le sourire allumé tous les matins depuis tant d'années, – je n'ai pas pu m'empêcher – et je lui ai jeté la phrase vite comme une chose qui me brûle : j'ai dit : j'ai un problème, et elle a poussé un petit cri d'alarme. Et je lui ai dit c'est un oiseau mort. C'est ainsi que j'ai remis à ma fille que j'aime comme moi-même le petit fardeau de la douleur. Maintenant c'est toi qui souffres. Mais je peux me redresser et aller au combat.

A l'égard de la morte ou du mort j'éprouve être violemment attaquée. Tout me vise : la fixité, la solidité, la bête a dû passer la nuit à me guetter rien ne l'aura fait lâcher ni la tempête, et la mort lui donne une force monstrueuse elle nous tient tête, elle qui ne connaît plus le temps ni la fatigue. Ce qu'elle m'inflige est l'étrangeté de l'autre côté. On ne peut rien contre un mort n'est-ce pas. Qu'est-ce qui est plus fort? Alors je pense au bâton quel soulagement. Je vais chercher le bambou. Ce ne sera pas moi, ce sera la chose de bois qui va s'appuyer sur la petite poitrine noire et féroce et peser peser jusqu'à ce que la chose casse et tombe. Je passe dans la salle de séjour, les mains gantées, le bâton dressé et maintenant sans trembler j'ouvre grand les portes-fenêtres, et j'y vais et je passe fermement devant ma fille qui tremble pour moi.

C'est alors que la chatte bondit. Et que vis-je? La bête n'est pas de l'autre côté du grillage, elle est de ce côté-ci. Agrippée, raide, épaisse, elle rend le bâton vain. Je la prendrai donc avec les gants. Mais Thea gravement en fait son affaire. Ah je ne peux pas séparer ces deux-là sans méchanceté. La chatte hume, s'étonne doucement. Moi aussi je ne sais pas pourquoi la présence du spectre me paraît encore plus *unheimlich* à l'intérieur qu'à l'extérieur. Ensuite. Les choses vont maintenant à la vitesse de Thea. Elle prend la chose dans sa bouche, les ailes s'ouvrent, tout cela sans effort, et elle vient la poser sur le tapis. La mort est maintenant dans la maison. Elle repose sur le ventre les bras légèrement entrouverts la tête à peine dessinée, les yeux sans éclat ont la taille d'un grain de poivre. L'incertitude, l'étonnement, le deuil, entrent en Thea. Trois fois elle fait le tour du corps. Elle ne sait pas. Est-ce mort ou vivant, 1a chose ne répond pas. Alors Thea se lamente doucement. Je ne t'aurai donc pas rencontrée vivante? Ah mon ami encore une rencontre manquée, doucement elle se frotte à mes genoux et toutes les deux nous menons un léger deuil incertain, car maintenant que la bête est allongée et non dressée terrible aux barreaux, elle suscite chagrin et compassion. Nous deux goûtons le goût de la pitié. Quoique Thea méfiante envoie un sec coup de patte sur le corps. Pour voir. L'oiseau mort. Les deux ailes se dressent et retombent. C'est pire. S'il y a encore un souffle un reste un souvenir réflexe. Thea incertaine. Recommence l'expérience. Pas de réponse. Je suis allée chercher des journaux. Parce qu'on ne va pas passer du temps avec un cadavre. C'est mauvais pour les vivants. Mais je ne veux pas brusquer Thea je la laisse humer et tourner en gémissant tendrement. Elle pleure celui qu'elle n'a jamais connu. C'est un moment de communion.

Il ne convient pas de longtemps demeurer vivant avec un mort. Voici le moment où il faut refermer le livre trop profond. Voici l'heure de l'enterrement. Nous allons l'enterrer dans la poubelle dit muette ma pensée, et il y a un accent de vengeance dans sa violence. Mais délicatement j'étends un journal sur le petit corps car il fut vivant. Attends, dit la chatte, encore un au revoir. Et elle soulève le journal sans violence. Alors c'est le moment pour l'oiseau de passer au néant. Dis-je. Mais je n'ose pas précéder ma chatte. Car je reconnais le droit des animaux entre eux.

Lorsqu'enfin je pense qu'il est de mon devoir de clore le récit, d'un geste rapide effrayé j'attrape la chose. Alors elle s'élève de quelques centimètres, puis rampant parcourt la salle. Moi, je suis laissée dans l'inattendu. Thea court. C'est le miracle. Maintenant lui est accordé l'inespéré, le combat. Que va-t-il se passer? Va-t-elle tuer l'oiseau dans le séjour, dans la cuisine, la salle de bains, le sang sur mon lit l'essuyer sur le tapis sur les carreaux. Heureusement que ma fille m'est témoin et moitié car autrement le diable m'eut emportée.

Mais elle est là, pliée, la même bise nous souffle le même affolement à la figure.

Qu'y a-t-il dans ton coeur? La soumission à l'horreur : on nous a tirées du lit de bonne heure pour que nous assistions à un petit assassinat. Ton horreur me donne la force qui me ferait défaut si j'étais seule.

Un instinct me prend me jette sur l'oiseau, preste j'attrape les ailes comme d'une poule, on ne doit pas mourir chez moi, où vais-je la jeter, je cours à la fenêtre, l'instinct me mène, me guide, nous voici au balcon, l'instinct, les ailes, la morte s'élance d'un vol puissant et gagne l'autre bout de la ville d'un trait. Ce n'est pas ce que je voulais.

Dans la maison c'est la tragédie, Thea mon âme mon amour court par toute la terre égyptienne recueillant les traces, tous les petits morceaux d'odeur et d'événement repasse cent fois partout où elle a été, où il fut, rassemble tout mais il manque l'essentiel, le principal, le morceau magique sans lequel jamais la vie ne reviendra au dieu disséminé, il manque l'oiseau, elle crie, elle laboure son fin visage de ses griffes, elle laboure mon coeur coupable, en vain elle essaie toutes les magies animales poussant des prières aiguës dans le coin de la cuisine, suppliant le tapis, courant en sanglotant aux barreaux, levant des yeux de suppliante sur le grillage déserté, espérant sans espérance, scrutant le fond du ciel qui ne la trompe pas, le monde entier lui a volé son amour et personne ne le lui rend. En vain elle crie et moi aussi je pousse de grands cris secrets. Ma fille ma soeur mon amour quelle douleur me cause la douleur que je t'ai causée !

Et tout ça pourquoi?

C'est l'instinct ! Ce maudit instinct humain, cette cochonnerie, cette phobie, ah quelle lâcheté mauvaise est tapie dans mes moelles et maintenant je comprends que Moïse n'a rien reçu de Dieu làhaut. C'était dans ses moelles cet interdit humain.

Tu ne tueras pas chez moi. Cette crainte de la souillure. Non, rien de moral. C'était dans mes moelles et avant que je sache, j'ai jeté cette chose qui bougeait dans le ciel, parce que je ne voulais pas de sang sur mon lit. Quelle impureté mon dieu qui va me pardonner?

Abattues, exténuées, fuies par les fidélités à soi-même qui sont les jambes abandonnées de notre âme, ma fille et moi nous nous appuyons lourdement à la table du petit déjeuner et nous ne mangeons pas.

Le chagrin de la chatte est celui d'une mère qui ne trouve plus son bébé dans la maison, il nous rend folles, toutes les mères orphelines sortent de notre chair en poussant des cris vers le ciel moqueur c'est celui d'un amant dont on a dérobé l'organe du coeur pendant son sommeil, on ne peut ni vouloir vivre ni vouloir mourir parce qu'il faut le retrouver.

Heureusement que nous sommes ensemble pensons ensemble, nous aimerions bien manger les petits pains chauds du matin mais notre corps rempli du vide tragique ne peut pas avaler une bouchée de nourriture, heureusement que nous sommes toutes les trois ensemble. Et c'est ma faute. Et je l'avais dans la moelle. Et toi aussi.

Cette journée n'en finit pas. Douce et malade d'espoir, toutes les heures Thea se lève et va triste faire le tour de l'Egypte, car il est grand et courageux de ne pas renoncer au miracle auquel l'on a renoncé. Sans espoir elle parcourt les campagnes et les jardins et sans un mot elle va se recoucher en forme d'oiseau sur son lit desséché.

Et je pleure.

Ah mon dieu mon dieu qu'ai-je fait !? J'ai trahi ma semblable, ma fiancée, ma petite épouse au coeur illimité, ah mon dieu si cet oiseau revient je le lui donnerai, je le jure, oui, il vaut mieux que je le jure c'est plus sûr, oui, s'il revenait, moi aussi je jouerais avec son petit corps tiède, je lui donnerais de secs durs petits coups de patte et je l'égorgerais avec gaieté.

D'ailleurs, ne nous avait-il pas trompées? Vivant faire le mort?

Thea attend sur le balcon assise devant le grillage, le visage empreint de la patience de notre race, nous qui sommes nées pour attendre les retours, même si nous savons : ce ne sont pas les morts qui ne reviennent pas ce sont les vivants.

Elle vient me chercher pour que je lui ouvre la porte-fenêtre de l'église. J'ouvre, moi qui ne crois pas, j'ouvre à celle qui croit, car je suis à genoux devant la foi.

Elle va vers le treillis. Ce qui est venu une fois peut venir une deuxième fois. Toute ma foi qui n'est pas en moi, est en elle. Sainte petite maîtresse d'humilité.

Pénitente je suis Thea sur le balcon, la tête penchée, encore un péché humain.

C'est le soir.

Maintenant je suis très fatiguée, il y a eu beaucoup de larmes sous les arches des heures. Je voudrais écrire cette chose terrible qui s'est passée ce matin entre nous, ce naufrage de ma tête avec des esquilles d'épaves qui s'entrechoquent dans ma tête, mais je vois que presque tout ce que nous avons vécu a été remporté par le temps. Ce qui est arrivé est reparti, j'ai tout oublié.

Jeudi 23 mai 1996. Le matin à six heures, Thea va frapper, elle va sur le balcon, ramassée la tête dans les épaules, la queue roulée sous le ventre, appartenant à la race des feuilles immobiles, semblable au premier coup d'oeil à une main debout agrippée à une inaudible prière. La solitude d'une main seule sans son autre main est poignante. Elle revient à l'endroit de l'oiseau. Attendant son autre main? Non, ce n'est pas cela. Lorsque ma fille s'en va, elle la chatte n'est pas jetée dans le désarroi infini, elle sait à escient de chatte que ma fille reviendra. Je comprends maintenant si bien, elle revient à la place de celui qui ne revient pas, c'est ce qui lui donne son apparence de feuille noire frémissant de son roux. L'oiseau elle l'incarne, petite statue commémorative.

Les prostituées philosophes

Leslie Kaplan

Zoé était debout dans une rame de métro entre Vaneau et Sèvres-Babylone quand elle vit un garçon de son âge assis la tête dans les mains. Il était en train de parler tout seul. Zoé s'approcha, depuis quelque temps elle faisait une étude sur les gens qui parlent tout seuls dans la rue, elle voulait établir une statistique, ce qu'ils disaient, les thèmes. Mais jusqu'à présent elle n'avait jamais entendu ce que marmonnait le garçon, il répétait à voix basse, Je le tuerai, je le tuerai. Quand le métro arriva dans la station il releva la tête et fixa Zoé. A ce moment-là, sans qu'elle puisse se l'expliquer, Zoé eut la certitude qu'il parlait de son père.

Le garçon descendit, Zoé le suivit avec l'intention de l'aborder. Quand ils furent dehors, elle se planta devant lui et lui demanda, Pourquoi? Le garçon n'eut pas l'air étonné.

Il répondit, Parce qu'il veut ma mort. Il ajouta, Et ça ne te regarde pas.

Zoé le trouvait beau. Elle sourit, et dit, Je m'appelle Zoé. Le garçon haussa les épaules et dit qu'il s'appelait Thomas.

Voilà le début.

Comment est-ce que je le connais, ce début? C'est Zoé qui me l'a raconté. Je suis une amie de sa mère, une amie d'enfance, et j'aime Zoé comme la fille que je n'ai pas eue. Elle passe, elle me tient au courant, et moi, je l'écoute, je lui parle, je l'emmène au cinéma, je lui donne des livres. Je l'aime. Je l'imagine, je pense à elle. J'adore penser à elle, à sa vie, à toutes ses vies possibles.

Zoé a quinze ans, un an de moins que Thomas. Elle est fine, maligne, parfois très emmerdante. Pour qui, emmerdante? pour ses parents, sans doute, pour ses professeurs. Elle discute tout, cette fille. Mais peu importe. C'est Zoé qui nous emmène dans cette histoire.

Elle et Thomas se sont promenés, Thomas a parlé sans arrêt toute l'après-midi. Zoé ne disait rien ou presque, ce qui pour elle était inhabituel. Ils ont remonté la rue de Rennes. Zoé était effarée de ce que lui disait Thomas. Elle écoutait et regardait autour d'elle, les magasins, vaisselle étalée sur le trottoir, instruments de musique, tentures et tissus, elle essayait de voir le plus possible, avec au bout la Tour, la garder dans l'oeil tout en regardant les vitrines. Zoé essayait toujours de faire ce jeu, elle pensait qu'il lui apprenait la perspective. D'autant plus qu'il lui semblait que Thomas, lui, ne voyait rien. Elle avait une chanson dans la tête, elle l'avait entendue la veille, Every Night and every Morn / Some to misery are born. Chaque Soir et chaque Matin / A la tristesse naissent certains. Every Morn and every Night / Some are born to sweet delight. Chaque Matin et chaque Soir / Certains naissent au doux espoir. Some are born to sweet delight / Some are born to endless Night. Certains naissent au doux espoir / Certains à l'infini Noir. Elle avait envie de la chanter à Thomas mais elle se disait en même temps que ce serait déplacé, et la chanson restait collée dans sa tête. Ils s'arrêtèrent devant un magasin de vaisselle. Thomas voulut entrer, mais sortit aussitôt. "Ça me donne envie de tout casser."

- Mais qu'est-ce qu'il fait dans la vie, ton père? demanda Zoé.

Thomas gonfla les joues, ensuite les dégonfla plusieurs fois. Ne dit rien. Ensuite:

- Je ne sais pas. C'est un entrepreneur. Un self made man. Il a des entreprises. Je n'en sais rien.

Il n'y a pas longtemps, ajouta Thomas, j'ai lu un roman, Thomas ne dit pas le titre, il avait peur de frimer, le héros se rappelle une scène qui s'est passée quand il était enfant. Il voyait des paysans en train de battre à mort un vieux cheval. Il était avec son père, il lui demandait d'intervenir, son père refusait et se détournait.

Après quoi, dit Thomas, le héros tue deux bonnes femmes.

- Comment, demanda Zoé qui n'avait pas lu le livre, il est un enfant quand même?

- Non, non, dit Thomas, c'est après, il est grand.

Zoé réfléchissait. Elle était mortellement inquiète et très heureuse en même temps.

Elle prit la main de Thomas, Allez, on court. Ils coururent jusqu'à la place du 18-Juin, arrivèrent complètement ivres, et s'affalèrent à une terrasse.

Le garçon apparut tout de suite. C'était un jeune, l'air voyou. Vous désirez?

- On désire, Ils furent pris d'un fou rire à trois. Zoé lui demanda, Et vous, votre père, il est comment?

Le garçon prit un air pincé, et rejeta ses cheveux en arrière.

- Une horreur, ma chère, une horreur.

- Ah bon, dit Zoé. Elle se sentait dessoûlée. Elle ajouta, Moi j'aime bien mon père.

- J'ai rien envie, dit Thomas.

Zoé commanda des oranges pressées. Le garçon demanda, Pourquoi vous parlez des pères?

- Pourquoi pas, dit Zoé. Thomas se renfrognait.

Tout d'un coup du juke-box on entendit une voix large, forte, on aurait dit qu'elle était juste à côté, Joshué livrait la bataille de Jéricho et sa trompette faisait tomber les murs. Zoé et Thomas écoutaient, ravis.

- Si les murs commencent à tomber, dit le garçon. Il avait l'air mécontent. Il s'en alla.

L'air était bleu et tendre, on était au printemps et Zoé décida qu'ils continueraient jusqu'à Denfert pour marcher entre les marronniers du boulevard Arago. A ce moment-là elle remarqua deux femmes assises à la table à côté, belles et grosses. L'une était penchée vers l'autre et lui demandait, Alors tu l'aimes toujours, ton type?

Zoé détourna la tête.

Quand ils payèrent le garçon leur dit, Au revoir, d'un air appuyé et ajouta, Je m'appelle Pierre. Ils dirent Au revoir poliment, ajoutant, Zoé, Thomas. Zoé prit exprès la rue du Départ. Maintenant Thomas était très joyeux, il trouvait Zoé drôle. Elle avait un T-shirt agressif, jaune, avec Hello marqué dessus, et des couettes. Qu'elle dénoua, petit geste. Thomas apprécia, s'attendrit et trouva flatteur pour lui le geste de Zoé. Planait un mélange agréable, questions, suppositions, une bonne humeur.

Zoé et Thomas dans la ville. Belle ville, grande, étalée, active et sérieuse. Parfois sérieuse. Zoé regarde. Thomas regarde aussi.

Deux hommes en bleu de travail. L'un est très, très grand, l'autre est beaucoup plus petit, un peu malingre même. Il est en train de parler de ce qu'il lit. L'image reste, ce type petit, penché sur son livre, ses lèvres formant les mots, et la phrase qui vient toujours dans ces cas-là, Il a eu des difficultés à l'école, prononcée avec un intérêt faux.

Les arbres du boulevard Arago, les deux rangées de marronniers. L'odeur du vert.

Un monsieur noir habillé comme dans les années trente, redingote, col dur, il porte un paquet marron très long et souple, intrigant.

Un petit garçon passe, il lit un livre en marchant. Son équilibre. Il avance comme s'il était guidé par les mots du livre, les pieds posés sur un mot, un mot, un mot. Cela plaît beaucoup à Thomas et à Zoé.

Une femme en jogging fluo, avec de grandes boucles d'oreille bleues. D'un commun accord silencieux, Zoé et Thomas ne font aucun commentaire.

Deux Suédois, on dirait des acteurs de Bergman, ils découvrent qu'ils ont tous les deux vu une rétrospective récente, Thomas parce qu'il voit tout, il essaie, Zoé parce que je l'avais emmenée. Mais, fait remarquer Thomas, peut-être ils parlent danois.

Une mère et une fille. Ressemblance étonnante, et en même temps, un saut. La mère est un peu vieille, un pull, des bas épais. La fille porte un blouson de cuir clouté et des jeans noirs, elle a un visage trop maigre, marqué. Mais les cheveux abondants, bouclés, les traits, sont les mêmes. Elles se tiennent par le bras. La fille parle d'un ami qui a des difficultés, prison.

Zoé et Thomas marchent un long moment, s'assoient sur des bancs, repartent. Puis ils prennent le métro ensemble pour rentrer.

Dans le métro. Ils sont assis en grande discussion, tout d'un coup on se penche vers eux, Contrôle des billets. C'est un grand type enveloppé dans une cape, il a un chapeau noir avec des bords très larges. Il est effrayant. Il rit et demande une pièce. Furieux ils refusent. Le type les regarde d'un air menaçant, ensuite il rit de nouveau et s'en va.

Ils ont repris leur discussion quand ils entendent un accordéon, pas une musique, juste l'ouverture et la fermeture de l'instrument, et ce qui est bizarre, c'est que le son est tout près du sol. Ils regardent dans l'allée, c'est un enfant minuscule, trois ans au plus, avec un béret d'homme, qui passe dans les rangs. Zoé essaie de le prendre dans ses bras, l'enfant s'enfuit. Ils sortent. Zoé est arrivée, Thomas doit continuer, il habite près du Trocadéro. Bien sûr ils ont pris rendez-vous pour se revoir.

Mais qu'est-ce que Thomas a raconté à Zoé?

- L'année dernière, a raconté Thomas, ma mère a demandé un poste à l'étranger, mon père m'a pris avec lui. J'étais content. J'aime bien ma mère, mais toujours elle, ses amies, ses histoires… J'étais content d'être avec mon père. Et voilà, il me dit, Je t'installe à côté de chez moi, tu as ton appartement, j'ai le mien, c'est mieux. Moi au début je trouvais ça très bien, il avait tout prévu, tout. Une dame passait, le frigidaire était toujours plein. Je pouvais appeler mon père quand je voulais, je ne le voyais pas toujours mais je pouvais l'appeler.

Et puis j'ai commencé à avoir peur. C'est drôle parce qu'en fait j'ai jamais peur de rien, je me balade partout, j'ai jamais peur. Mais quand je rentrais tout seul, j'avais peur. Peur de quoi ? Je ne sais pas. Peur. Je pouvais l'appeler, mon père, mais je ne voulais pas. Non, je ne voulais pas. J'avais l'impression qu'il se serait moqué de moi. J'étais fatigué, tu ne peux pas savoir ce que j'étais fatigué. Et j'avais mal à la tête, mais mal. Alors un jour, comme ça, j'ai cassé la télé. Je l'ai mise au milieu du salon, j'ai pris un marteau. Ç'aurait pu être dangereux, remarque. Elle marchait, j'ai tapé dedans. C'était rien, un présentateur idiot, je ne sais plus, mais c'était pas pour ça, je crois pas. Je m'en foutais. N'importe quoi, j'aurais cassé. Et après j'ai compris que je casserais tout. J'ai eu cette idée que j'allais tout casser, tout l'appartement, tout. Et chaque jour je casse quelque chose. Un verre, une assiette, le bras d'un fauteuil. Un pied. Il y a des fauteuils avec des pieds, des doigts de pied, tu vois ? J'ai calculé, j'ai quatre semaines. La dame qui vient faire le ménage a pris ses vacances, elle revient à la fin du mois. Si je ne casse pas, je reste là à ne rien faire, et il y a la peur qui revient, qui s'installe.

Une fois je l'ai vue.

- Tu as vu quoi ? avait demandé Zoé, mais elle devinait.

- La peur, dit Thomas, il n'avait même pas l'air de lui répondre, il donnait l'impression de parler de nouveau tout seul. Je suis rentré un soir, j'avais traîné, je tourne la clef dans la serrure et déjà je sais qu'il y a quelqu'un. J'entre. Et je la vois. Elle était assise au bar, sur un tabouret, c'était une femme très belle, un peu star, décolletée. Au début j'ai pensé qu'elle ressemblait à ma mère, après je me suis dit, non, et je cherchais, je cherchais, et tout d'un coup je me suis senti mal, je savais à qui elle ressemblait. A moi, elle me ressemblait à moi. Elle était assise là au bar, les jambes nues, ce décolleté. J'ai cru que je devenais fou. Elle souriait, elle souriait, toute sa figure était mangée par ce sourire, jusqu'au menton, jusqu'aux oreilles, et elle s'est mise à me faire signe, l'index replié, comme ça, c'était dégoûtant, et elle m'appelait, Thomas, Thomas, ma petite tomate.

Quand je suis avec mon père, il commande toujours des jus de tomate, c'est une de ses habitudes, Avec ou sans vodka, Thomas ?

- Et alors, demanda Zoé.

Thomas ne disait plus rien.

Rien, dit Thomas. J'ai cassé le tabouret. Il ajouta au bout d'un moment, Après elle est partie.

- Mais tu avais encore peur ? insista Zoé.

Thomas ne répondit pas. Il ne parlait plus.

*****

The Philosophic Prostitutes

Zoe was standing in a subway train somewhere between Vaneau and Sèvres-Babylon when she saw a boy of her age holding his head in his hands. He was speaking to himself. Zoe came closer. For a while now she had been studying people who spoke to themselves in the street. She wanted statistics, what they were saying, the principal themes. But until then she had never heard what the boy was mumbling, he was repeating in a low voice, I'll kill him, I'll kill him. When the subway came into the station, he raised his head and stared at Zoe. At that very moment, without knowing how to explain it, Zoe was certain that he had been speaking about his father.

The boy got off, Zoe followed intending to come up to him. When they were both outside, she stood in front of him and asked, Why? The boy didn't seem surprised.

He answered, Because he wants me dead. He added, And that's none of your business.

Zoe found him good-looking. She smiled and said, My name's Zoe. The boy shrugged his shoulders and said his name was Thomas.

That was the beginning.

How do I know it was the beginning? Zoe told me. I'm a friend of her mother's, a childhood friend and I love Zoe like the daughter I never had. She comes by, she fills me in, and I, I listen to her, I talk to her, I take her out to the movies. I give her books. I love her. I dream about her, I think about her. I love to think about her, about her life. About all of her lives.

Zoe is fifteen years old, a year younger than Thomas. She's clever, mischievous, sometimes she's a real pain. For whom is she a pain? for her parents, no doubt, for her teachers. This girl argues about everything. But no matter. It's now Zoe who leads us into this story.

She and Thomas went off for a walk, Thomas didn't stop talking for the whole afternoon. Zoe said nothing or almost, which, in her case, was not customary. They walked up rue de Rennes. Zoe was taken aback by Thomas's story. She listened and looked around, the stores, dishes piled up on the sidewalk, musical instruments, wall-paper, cloth, she tried to see as much as possible, and kept the Montparnasse Tower in sight in eye distance, all the while looking at store windows. Zoe always tried to play this game, she thought it taught her perspective. All the more that it seemed to her that Thomas looked at nothing. She had a song in her head, she had heard it the night before, Every Night and Every Morn/Some to misery are born. Chaque Soir et chaque Matin/A la tristesse naissent certains.

Every Morn and every Night/Some are born to sweet delight. Chaque Matin et chaque Soir/Certains naissent au doux espoir. Some are born to sweet delight/Some are born to endless Night. Certains naissent au doux espoir/Certains à l'infini Noir. She wanted to sing it to Thomas but at the same time she thought it wasn't the right moment, and the song stuck in her head. They stopped in front of a store selling dishes. Thomas wanted to go in, but left immediately. "I feel like smashing everything."

But what does your father do in life? asked Zoe.

Thomas puffed up his cheeks and then slowly let the air out many times over. Said nothing. Then:

I don't know. He's an entrepreneur. A self-made man. He owns businesses. I don't know anything about them.

Not too long ago, added Thomas, I read a novel, Thomas doesn't give away the title, he doesn't like to bluff, the hero remembers a scene which had occurred when he was a child. He saw peasants beating an old horse to death. He was with his father, he asked him to intervene, his father refused and turned away.

After that, Thomas says, the hero kills two dames.

- How, asked Zoe who hadn't read the book, isn't he a child?

- No, no, Thomas says, it's afterwards, he's a man.

Zoe thought about it. She was deathly afraid and happy at the same time.

She took Thomas's hand, Let's go, let's run. They ran up to the Place du 18-Juin, got there totally drunk and collapsed at a terrace café.

The waiter appeared immediately. Young, looked like a hood. What'll you have?

- We'll have, we'll have. The three of them burst out laughing. Zoe asked him, And you, your father? how is he?

The waiter raised his eyebrows, threw his hair back.

- A horror, my dear, a horror.

- Oh, said Zoe. She felt sober again, She added, As for me, I'm fond of my father.

- I don't want anything, said Thomas.

Zoe ordered two orange juices. The waiter asked, Why are you talking about fathers?

- Why not, said Zoe. Thomas scowled.

All of a sudden out of the juke box one could hear a rich and powerful voice, One would have said it was close by, Joshua fit the battle of Jericho and the walls came tumbling down. Zoe and Thomas listened, captivated.

- If the walls come tumbling down, the waiter said. He looked angry. He left.

The air was bluish and sweet, it was springtime and Zoe decided they would keep on going until Denfert and then walk under the chestnut trees on boulevard Arago. At that moment, she noticed two women sitting at the next table, beautiful and heavyset. One leaned over to the other and asked, So are you still in love with that guy?

Zoe turned away.

When they paid, the waiter said, Au revoir, stressing his words and added, My name's Pierre. They said Au revoir politely, adding, Zoe, Thomas. Zoe specifically chose the rue du Départ. Now Thomas was very happy, he thought Zoe was funny. She wore a striking yellow T-shirt with Hello on it, and pony tails, Which she let loose, a little gesture. Thomas liked that, warmed up, and found Zoe's gesture flattering. Hovering, a pleasant *mélange*, questions, suppositions, good humor.

Zoe and Thomas in the city. Beautiful city, large, spread out, active, serious. Sometimes serious. Zoe looks. Thomas does too.

Two men wearing overalls. One is very very tall, the other one is much smaller, rather puny. He's talking about what he's reading. The image remains, this little guy hunched over his book, words forming on his lips, and the sentence which always follows in such cases, He had difficulties in school, spoken with a false air of conviction.

The trees on boulevard Arago, the two rows of chestnut trees. The smell of green.

A black gentleman dressed as in the thirties, riding jacket, starched collar, he's carrying a very long and supple brown package, intriguing.

A little boy passes by, he's reading a book as he walks. His equilibrium. He walks ahead as if the words in the book were leading him, his feet on a word, a word, a word. This greatly pleases Thomas and Zoe.

A woman in a fluorescent jogger's outfit, wearing large blue earrings. In common and silent agreement, Zoe and Thomas decide not to say anything.

Two Swedes, one would say they were Bergman actors, they discover they had just seen a recent retrospective, Thomas because he sees everything, he tries, Zoe because I had taken her to see it. But, Thomas observes, maybe they are speaking Danish.

A mother and a girl. Striking resemblance, and at the same time, a wide spread. The mother's on in age, a sweater, thick stockings. The girl wears a studded leather jacket and black jeans, her face is too thin, worn. But they have the same full head of hair, curled, the same features. They hold each other by the arm. The girl talks about a friend in difficulty, prison.

Zoe and Thomas walk a long while, sit on benches, continue. then both take the *métro* to go home.

In the *métro*. They're sitting down, deep in conversation, all of a sudden someone leans over them, Tickets please. It's a tall guy wrapped in a cape, he wears a very large black brimmed hat. He's frightening. He laughs and asks for change. Furious, they refuse. The guy looks at them menacingly, then he laughs again, goes away.

They start talking again, when they hear an accordeon, no music, just the opening and the closing of the instrument, and what's strange, is that the sound is very close to the ground. They look down the aisle, it's a tiny child, maximum three years old, with a man's beret, and he's passing through the crowd. Zoe tries to pick him up in her arms, the child runs away. They get out. Zoe has arrived, Thomas stayed on, he lives near Trocadéro. Of course they've arranged to see each other again.

But what did Thomas tell Zoe?

- Last year, Thomas said, my mother requested an assignment abroad, my father took me in. I was happy. I like my mother, but it's always herself, her friends, her stories... I was happy to be with my father. And he says to me, I'll put you up nearby, you'll have your own apartment, I've got my mine, that's better. In the beginning I found that very good, he had taken care of everything. A cleaning woman came by, the fridge was always full. I could call my father whenever I wanted, I didn't see him all the time, but I could call him.

And then I began to be afraid. That's funny because, in fact, I'm never afraid of anything, I walk around everywhere, I'm never afraid. But when I came home all alone, I was afraid. Afraid of what? I don't know. Afraid. I could call my father, but I didn't want to. No, I didn't want to. I felt that he would tease me. I was tired, you can't imagine how tired I was. And I had headaches, real headaches. Then, one day, just like that, I smashed the television set. I placed it in the middle of the living room, I took a hammer. When I think of it, it might have been dangerous. The set was on, I hit it. Nothing important, an idiotic speaker, I don't know anymore, but that wasn't the reason, I don't think so. I didn't give a damn. Whatever was on, I would have broken it. And then I realized that I would smash everything, the whole apartment, everything. And everyday I break something. A glass, a plate, the arm on the chair. A foot. There're chairs with feet, toes, you know? I checked it out, I've got four weeks. The cleaning woman is on vacation, she's coming back at the end of the month. If I don't smash things, I stay there with nothing to do, and then fear comes back, and moves in.

Once I saw it.

- What did you see, Zoe had asked, but she had guessed.

- Fear, said Thomas, he didn't even seem to answer her, once more he gave the impression of speaking to himself. One night I came home, I had just wandered around, I turned the key in the lock and I already knew there was someone. And I see her. She's sitting at the bar, on a stool, she was a very beautiful woman, a little like a star, wearing a *décolleté* . In the beginning I thought she looked like my mother, then I said no, and I started looking, looking, and all of a sudden I felt ill, I knew whom she looked like. She looked like me, like me. She sat there at the bar, bare legs, a *décolleté*. I thought I was going crazy. She was smiling, smiling, all of her face eaten away by that smile, right down to her chin, to her ears, and she started making signs in my direction, her index finger curled, like that, it was disgusting, and she called out to me, Thomas, Thomas, my little tomato.

When I'm with my father he's always ordering tomato juice, it's one of his habits, With or without vodka, Thomas?

- And then, asked Zoe.

Thomas no longer spoke.

- Nothing, Thomas said. I broke the stool. He added after a moment, Then she left.

- But you were still afraid, Zoe repeated.

Thomas didn't answer. He no longer spoke.

Translated by Serge Gavronsky

Regard sur un regard : exception française ou exception américaine

Michèle Sarde

« Sans doute ne naît-on pas Française, on le devient. » C'est par cette paraphrase de Simone de Beauvoir, énoncée sur le mode du doute, que s'ouvrait le volume que j'ai consacré à mes compatriotes : *Regard sur les Françaises*. Publié en 1981, il avait été conçu et rédigé à la fin des années soixante-dix, décennie qui correspondait dans mon histoire personnelle avec mon installation aux États-Unis, et dans l'histoire collective avec l'émergence des mouvements de femmes en Amérique, comme en France dans la mouvance postsoixanthuitarde.

Le point de départ en était évidemment déjà mon expérience de Française de la vie en Amérique. Vue d'ailleurs, la francité m'apparaissait avec des contours plus précis. Je découvrais des évidences auxquelles la mondialisation progressive nous a habitués depuis. Je prenais conscience que j'avais vécu dans un monde tendant à amalgamer à la représentation de l'universel des singularités nationales. Je comprenais que la "patrie des droits de l'homme" où j'avais grandi confondait elle aussi ce qui était limité à l'hexagone et ce qui avait cours dans d'autres cantons de la planète.

La sortie de l'idéologie était un autre détonateur. Dans le discours théorique des féministes de l'époque qui s'achevait, les femmes composaient, par leur aliénation et leur nécessaire libération, une catégorie universelle qui pesait de son poids sur l'autre moitié de l'humanité. Dans ce contexte, l'appartenance nationale n'avait pas de raison d'être. C'est depuis, entre autres avec les vagues de procès liés au harcèlement sexuel, que les Français et les Françaises ont pu observer *in vivo* que les femmes pas plus que les hommes ne se comportaient de la même façon de chaque côté de l'Atlantique. Dans le début des années quatre-vingt, cette vérité n'avait pas encore cours.

Cherchant à distinguer ce qui séparait radicalement l'approche des femmes dans les deux cultures, je me suis trouvée confrontée à un paradoxe qui tenait au fait que les femmes avaient été adulées et apparemment bien traitées en France puisque beaucoup d'entre elles s'en enorgueillissaient mais que d'autre part elles avaient, dans une certaine mesure avec leur consentement, été écartées de la sphère publique et du pouvoir politique. Le titre original de mon livre fut d'abord : "Les Françaises, mal aimées", puis "Les Françaises trop aimées?", titre inacceptable pour l'éditeur, qui m'expliqua d'abord qu'une interrogation n'était pas de mise dans un titre et qu'enfin celui-là n'était vraiment pas accrocheur. Je résistai avec timidité et l'éditeur eut gain de cause : le livre s'appellerait immodestement : "Regard sur les Françaises" afin de souligner qu'il s'agissait d'une sorte de point de vue de Sirius non exempt d'une inévitable subjectivité.

À la réflexion, il m'apparaît que ce changement de titre est à l'origine du malentendu qui fit peut-être le succès relatif du livre – lequel bénéficia de son passage par *Apostrophes*. Certes il insistait sur la singularité du discours français, plus tard transformé en "exception française", et devenu la tarte à la crème d'une certaine presse franco-française. Mais il tentait aussi d'en estimer le coût.

Il est vrai qu'associée avec la mixité et une morale sexuelle tolérante, "l'exception française", pièce maîtresse de l'art de vivre français, permettait entre hommes et femmes jeunes des rapports harmonieux réglés par une étiquette de la séduction auxquels les hommes et les femmes de notre génération et des précédentes n'auraient pas plus renoncé qu'à celle de la table.

Néanmoins le coût pour les femmes dans leur ensemble était élevé. "La femme mariée est une esclave qu'il faut savoir mettre sur un trône", écrivait Balzac dans *La physiologie du mariage*, ignorant peut-être à quel point il reflétait la société française au delà même de son époque. À l'analyse, le discours adulateur à l'égard d'une certaine catégorie de femmes ne réussissait pas à masquer le mépris dans lequel était tenue l'espèce toute entière. Un discours masculin collectif voué à l'adoration des femmes et de leur beauté se tarissait dès lors qu'elles cessaient d'être belles et de se taire. Les Françaises avaient été piégées par un excès d'honneur. L'exception française, dont tout le monde et particulièrement les femmes étaient si fiers, avait retardé la conquête du droit de vote ou l'égalité en matière politique.

J'écrivis que la société française avait trop longtemps aimé les femmes à l'horizontale pour pouvoir les respecter debout, qu'elle les avaient trop désirées silencieuses ou confinées au bavardage pour vouloir écouter ce qu'elles avaient à dire. Que trop souvent les intellectuelles, prises en otage d'une culture où leur statut les masculinisait, avaient pratiqué une certaine collaboration de sexe. Je ne fus pas entendue. Et à l'image de celles dont je dénonçais le désir de vouloir préserver les privilèges anciens avec les droits nouveaux, je me contentai d'être approuvée sans exiger d'être lue.

Plus tard, il y eut de nouvelles démonstrations de ce mépris dans lequel on tenait les femmes qui osaient s'exprimer et s'affirmer. Il y eut le bref mandat d'Edith Cresson, l'expulsion infamante des Juppettes, le manifeste sur la parité qui osait dire que le roi était nu et que la république traitait trop souvent les femmes en domestiques facilement remerciées.

Aux États-Unis, la confusion de la sphère publique et de la sphère privée plaçait les femmes en situation de pouvoir dans la résolution officielle et juridique des conflits de l'intimité. Une stagiaire de la Maison-Blanche était en situation d'ébranler la présidence et de faire destituer un président. Ce n'est certes pas le pouvoir que désirent les femmes. Mais il n'est pas impossible que les mésaventures des Paula Jones et des Monica Lewinsky n'aient frayé le passage à une élection d'Hillary Clinton (ou d'Elisabeth Dole) à la présidence.

L' "affaire" néanmoins signale que les rôles traditionnels de la comédie machiste – glorification de la virilité, avilissement de la sexualité féminine, ridiculisation du cocufiage – en vigueur dans la plupart des autres cultures sont ici brouillés : le séducteur/séduit, fût-il président, fait figure de coupable, la séductrice/séduite de victime, et c'est la femme trompée qui capitalise non seulement en dignité[1] mais en crédibilité politique. Puritanisme à l'envers ou exception américaine ? Quelles que soient de l'autre côté les sympathies qu'on peut avoir pour la tolérance à la française, les obsèques de Mitterand n'offrent qu'un symbole conforme à une tradition ancienne où les reines cohabitaient avec les favorites et où l'on anoblissait les batards des rois. Conformisme à l'envers ou exception française ?

Quelle que soit la réponse, il faut admettre que l'acceptation par les Américaines de certaines formes de discriminations positives à travers *affirmative action* ou de la censure imposée par le *politically correct* – décrié à partir de ses excès – ont permis certain progrès des femmes dans les sphères où elles étaient minoritaires. Après avoir atteint certains de ses objectifs, cette politique est certes remise en question. Mais les Américaines ne lui ont guère reproché de lui devoir quelques avancées irréversibles. Il y a là une originalité que personne ne songea à taxer ouvertement d' "exception américaine", bien que ce soit le seul pays au monde qui ait poussé aussi loin le juridisme en matière de discrimination sexuelle. Les Françaises ont peut-être tort de se refuser à comprendre que le terme de "minority", associé à celui des femmes ne mesure pas leur nombre mais leur peu d'importance et qu'il s'agit avant tout de dépasser, et non de nier, l'injustice qu'il y a pour une majorité de personnes à être réduite à une minorité de pouvoirs.

Qu'en est-il aujourd'hui de la fameuse exception française dans un pays où les forces de conservation, avec la complicité de nombreuses femmes éclairées, se mobilisent pour empêcher que la langue suive l'évolution des moeurs et féminise les statuts et les professions enfin conquises par les femmes...?, dans un pays dont le Sénat tente de bloquer une modification de la constitution qui pourrait enfin, après plus de cinquante ans d'exercice des droits politiques, permettre aux Françaises d'accéder à une forme de parité et ne plus faire honteusement figure de parentes pauvres des élues européennes? En quoi peut-on toujours parler d'exception française à moins qu'il ne s'agisse d'exception négative? Dans ce domaine comme dans beaucoup d'autres, l'égalitarisme français finit par étouffer et dénaturer le beau principe d'égalité.

L'acharnement avec lequel on s'applique en France à se démarquer des modèles américains qu'on connaît mal, quelle que soit leur valeur ou leur efficacité, finit par avoir des effets pervers. La volonté, souvent affichée chez les Françaises de se démarquer de leurs consoeurs américaines par leur culte de la différence, et leur conception de l'universel, héritée d'une révolution, qui en pratique nia les droits des femmes, m'entraîneraient à suggérer que l'exception se trouve plutôt du côté américain de l'Atlantique que de l'autre.[2] Qu'on les approuve ou non, il faut admettre que là où les Américaines diffèrent des Françaises – pour le meilleur ou pour le pire –, elles diffèrent souvent aussi du reste de la planète.

En tout état de cause, les partis-pris anti-américains, fréquents dans les médias et la classe politique française, entraînent une méconnaissance si flagrante des cousins et des cousines d'Amérique auprès du grand public français,[3] que nous avons essayé, Catherine Hermary-Vieille, autre écrivaine française vivant en Amérique, et moi, de leur transmettre la modeste expérience que des décennies de vie aux États-Unis nous avaient permise d'accumuler. C'est à l'intention de ce public que *Le salon de conversation* a été conçu. Cette pure fiction ne parle pas que des femmes mais elle parle aussi des femmes.

Isabelle de Courtivron a bien voulu en publier dans ces pages un extrait. Il s'agit d'une discussion dans la classe de français (appelée "Salon de conversation") de l'Alliance française de Houston entre deux professeurs françaises (Corinne et Fabienne) et leurs neuf étudiants et étudiantes, dont l'une Jacqueline, est une veuve de GI, qui a quitté sa France natale dans les années quarante.

Notes

1. Ce qui fut aussi le cas de Danièle Mitterand.
2. L'exception dans les formes et les stratégies car pour ce qui est de l'avancée des femmes dans la sphère politique, il n'y a pas grande différence entre les deux sociétés.
3. À l'inverse, on pourrait en dire autant des médias américains.

Le salon de conversation

Catherine Hermary-Vieille, Michèle Sarde

" – Je dois dire que j'ai du mal à comprendre les femmes françaises, dit Karen. Bien entendu, je ne parle pas de celles qui sont présentes ici et qui connaissent autre chose. J'ai voyagé plusieurs fois en France et rencontré professionnellement des Françaises. Je les trouve, voyons… un peu perverses, cherchant à faire feu de tout bois : plaire aux hommes et se tailler une place dans leur profession. Elles sont capables de signer un contrat avec une grosse entreprise et l'instant d'après, jouent à la coquette et à la femme soumise. Elles veulent le beurre et l'argent du beurre. Nous, les femmes américaines, nous savons bien que c'est impossible. Nous refusons ces simagrées d'un autre temps. Aujourd'hui il est avéré que le pouvoir de l'oreiller est un pouvoir indirect qui s'est souvent retourné contre celles qui l'ont pratiqué. Ce que nous voulons, c'est le vrai pouvoir, celui que les hommes ont usurpé pendant des millénaires.

– Et pourtant, s'exclama Daphne, nos magazines féminins regorgent de conseils pour séduire les hommes : comment être plus belle, plus femme, plus intéressante. Avec mes trois enfants qui bouffaient mes journées, ces lectures me donnaient le cafard.

– Les femmes américaines blanches rêvent de plaire mais se refusent à interpréter les messages de séduction, nota Cleonice. Peut-être n'aiment-elles pas suffisamment les hommes. Ce n'est pas le cas des Africaines-Américaines.

– Elles l'ont bien manifesté en acquittant O.J. Simpson, au cours du premier procès. On l'a déjà dit dans ce salon. C'est en majorité des femmes noires qui composaient le jury !, intervint Brandon.

Les femmes noires sont tout aussi conscientes que les Blanches de l'inégalité entre hommes et femmes dans nos sociétés, dit Cleonice. Anita Hill l'a démontré il y a quelques années lorsqu'elle a accusé Clarence Thomas, qui était candidat à la Cour suprême, de harcèlement sexuel. Par son courage, elle est devenue un modèle pour toutes les femmes. Et Clarence Thomas tout comme Anita Hill était noir.

– Je ne sais pas s'il s'agit de courage, dit Fabienne. J'étais un peu jeune à l'époque mais j'ai trouvé qu'elle était cruelle pour cet homme, qui finalement n'avait rien fait d'autre que de lui raconter des histoires lestes, dix ans auparavant. Franchement il y avait prescription. En plus leur affrontement a paraît-il été médiatisé sur toutes les chaînes de télé vingt-quatre heures sur vingt-quatre ! C'est un véritable viol de la vie privée.

– Le viol se situe à un autre niveau, corrigea Pamela avec indignation. Nous avons déjà eu cette conversation avec Fabienne. Vous les Françaises, vous n'avez pas du tout la même conception que nous de votre corps et du viol. Vous acceptez d'un homme des choses inacceptables. À la limite vous les provoquez.

– J'ai vu en France des filles ou des femmes habillées d'une façon vraiment provocante, dit Karen, qui esquiva le regard ironique de Brandon. Elles paraissaient presque fières des regards masculins qui les déshabillaient.

– Il n'y a rien que de très normal à vouloir provoquer le désir, ne put s'empêcher de dire Corinne. Cela fait partie depuis la nuit des temps des jeux de séduction entre hommes et femmes.

– Moi, quand je suis arrivée aux États-Unis, j'étais une très jeune femme, expliqua Jacqueline. Et une honnête femme, comme on disait à mon époque, amoureuse de son mari. Mais je dois dire que ça me manquait de n'être jamais plus regardée par un homme. Ni dans la rue, ni dans les fêtes. Nulle part. Un jour j'ai confié à Stanley que, je ne savais pas si c'était parce que j'étais mariée ou si j'avais en traversant l'Atlantique perdu toute espèce de charme, mais j'avais l'impression d'être devenue Carmélite.

– Et… il l'a bien pris ? demanda Fabienne avec intérêt.

– Pas vraiment ! Il a piqué une colère ! Il fallait bien une première scène de ménage ! Mais il y en a eu d'autres, rassurez-vous !

– Bien que nous ne soyons pas de la même génération, j'ai ressenti exactement la même chose, confia Fabienne. Les seuls garçons qui me regardent sont les Noirs… je veux dire les Africains-

Américains. Et en général les non Américains. Et bien je dois dire que ça me manque un peu aussi."

Daphne était éberluée par l'insolence de Fabienne. Un tel raisonnement lui paraissait relever de l'immoralité et du laxisme. Elle s'était toujours demandé comment le libertinage et l'adultère qui composaient la trame des romans et des films français pouvaient être compatibles avec la vieille tradition catholique. Fabienne était un produit typique de sa culture. Quant à Jacqueline, elle était si vieille qu'on ne pouvait même pas lui en vouloir. Mais ces réactions de la part de Françaises que Karen trouvait plutôt sympathiques, surtout Corinne, la perturbaient.

"Pour moi, commença Pamela, c'est juste le contraire. Quand j'ai débarqué à Lyon, je n'en pouvais plus de ces mains baladeuses, de ces regards insistants, de ces attouchements dans le métro. J'en avais parlé à Madame Collinet qui m'avait assurée que je n'avais pas à me plaindre, et que si cela ne me plaisait pas, je n'avais qu'à envoyer une paire de claques au dragueur, ou une bonne plaisanterie bien humiliante pour lui. Comme si je pouvais faire cela en français ! J'en suis incapable dans ma propre langue. Une fois, un ami des Collinet m'avait demandé si j'accepterais de poser nue pour lui. J'ai été si médusée que je suis devenue écarlate. Je n'ai rien pu répondre et quand j'ai protesté auprès de Madame Collinet, elle m'a répondu que c'était un compliment que m'avait fait ce grand artiste et que je réagissais comme une petite prude conventionnelle !

– Le résultat, c'est que les Français ne respectent pas les femmes quand elles se mêlent de faire de la politique ou même des affaires à haut niveau, dit Karen. J'étais en France lorsqu'Edith Cresson était Premier Ministre. Personne ne la prenait au sérieux, pas même elle-même.

– Elle a scandalisé tout le monde, jeta David, lorsqu'elle a répondu que la Bourse, elle n'en avait rien à cirer. Mais votre grand de Gaulle n'avait pas dit autre chose quand il a affirmé que la politique ne se faisait pas... au panier.

– Vous voulez probablement dire à la corbeille, rectifia Corinne. Tout de même, David, vous ne pouvez pas sérieusement affirmer que c'est la même chose.

- Tout de même, Professeur Lesage, vous autres femmes en France, vous n'avez pas beaucoup de solidarité les unes envers les autres, reconnaissez-le.

- Nous n'avons pas de solidarité mécanique. Moi j'admire les femmes qui le méritent. J'admire les grandes résistantes, j'admire Simone Weil – la philosophe –, j'admire Colette ou George Sand. Pour leurs talents propres, pas parce qu'elles sont des femmes.

– Moi j'admire toutes les femmes qui essaient de faire quelque chose, dit Pamela. Edith Cresson comme Simone Veil ou les ministres que vous appeliez indignement les Juppettes et qui se sont fait "larguer" – comme dit Fabienne – par Juppé, comme Edith Cresson s'est fait larguer par Mitterrand. J'admire Madame Thatcher. J'admire Janet Reno, notre ministre de la Justice et aussi Madeleine Albright, notre nouveau Secrétaire d'État, qui a obtenu le plus haut poste jamais occupé par une femme aux États-Unis. Mais en cela les Françaises ont peut-être un peu de retard par rapport aux Américaines qui ont eu un mouvement féministe très puissant dans les années soixante-dix.

– Je suis désolée de vous démentir, Pamela, dit Corinne, mais le pourcentage des femmes dans la vie politique est à peu près le même aux États-Unis et en France. Ni en France, ni aux États-Unis elles ne sont représentées en nombre suffisant à la Chambre des Députés ou au Sénat. Et ne parlons pas des ministres et secrétaires d'État. Ce sont les pays du Nord de l'Europe qui obtiennent le meilleur score dans ce palmarès des conquêtes des femmes, loin devant nos deux pays. Quant aux mouvements féministes, ils sont très anciens en France. Déjà Olympe de Gouges à l'époque de la Révolution rédigeait la Déclaration de la Femme et de la Citoyenne.

– Oui, mais elle s'est fait couper la tête par ses copains révolutionnaire. Elle avait eu beau dire que si les femmes avaient le droit à monter à l'échafaud, elles avaient aussi le droit de monter à la tribune, plaisanta Fabienne, elle a eu droit à l'échafaud mais pas à la tribune.

– J'avais fait une enquête pour mon journal sur le sujet du féminisme dans les deux pays, dit Cleonice. Derrière tous ces comportements, il y a deux modèles différents. Les Françaises sont universalistes. Au delà des différences et d'une féminité qu'elles revendiquent, elles se considèrent avant tout comme appartenant à l'espèce humaine. Les Américaines elles considèrent que l'universel est une imposture dès lors qu'il y a inégalité de droits. C'est pourquoi elles ne voient pas d'inconvénient à se ranger dans la catégorie de *minority*, comme les Noirs, les Indiens ou les homosexuels. Le terme de minorité implique qu'elles ne jouissent pas des droits de la majorité. Et la "majorité", ce sont les hommes blancs.

– Les femmes ne s'intéressent pas à l'art de gouverner, jugea Jacqueline. Et elles ont raison. La politique, c'est trop sale. Les femmes ne devraient pas se souiller dans ces tripatouillages. Et puis elles refusent d'être sous les spots d'une lumière parfois trop crue. Faire de la politique, c'est se livrer soi, sa famille, son passé aux critiques possibles. Or les femmes ont un amour des secrets qui indique leur faiblesse.

– Je proteste, intervint Brandon. Vouloir préserver sa vie privée n'est pas une preuve de lâcheté mais de force. Les hommes politiques seraient prêts à se damner pour obtenir et garder le pouvoir. J'admire les femmes de refuser ce marché là.

– Mais vous avez eu aussi Simone de Beauvoir avant notre Betty Friedan. Je me souviens que ma femme dans les années soixante lisait Betty Friedan avec passion et refusait de repriser mes chaussettes, dit Ed avec son accent irrésistible. J'ai toujours éprouvé une violente antipathie pour cette Friedan

– Le MLF en France dans les années soixante-dix a été aussi important que le *Women's Lib* américain, précisa Corinne. Mais il y avait une légère différence dans la philosophie. Les Françaises insistaient sur la nécessité de reconnaître les diversités entre hommes et femmes. Egaux. Oui. Mais dans la différence. Les Françaises pour la plupart entendaient et entendent toujours être valorisées justement pour leur différence. Les Américaines, elles, voulaient avant tout devenir les égales des hommes avec les mêmes droits et les mêmes devoirs. Il est resté quelque chose de ces deux conceptions dans les cultures d'origine. En France, on s'est battu au XIXe siècle pour que les femmes ne descendent plus à la mine ou échappent au travail de nuit. Aux États-Unis, on se bat pour que les femmes fassent tous les travaux, de jour et de nuit.

– Je ne suis pas féministe, dit Daphne. Mais la conception américaine me paraît plus juste. Qu'est-ce que j'ai gagné à consacrer ma vie à Richard et à mes enfants? J'aurais mille fois préféré la carrière de Karen, qui s'est battue comme un homme. Aujourd'hui elle n'a besoin de personne et ne court pas après une pension alimentaire.”

"A Glance at a Glance: French Exception or American Exception?"

"No doubt one isn't born French, one becomes French." The volume that I devoted to my female compatriots – *Looking at French Women [Regard sur les Françaises]* – begins with this paraphrase (a statement in the dubitative mood) from Simone de Beauvoir. Published in 1981, the book was conceived and edited in the late 70s, a decade that corresponds in my personal history to my moving to the United States, and, in collective history, to the emergence of women's movements in America and France in the wake of '68.

The starting point for the book was obviously my own experience, as a French woman, of life in America. As I perceived "Frenchness" from outside France, its outlines became more precise to me. I was discovering obvious things to which gradual globalization has since accustomed us. I was becoming aware that I had lived in a world that tended to conflate the representation of the universal with national quirks. I understood that the "country of the rights of man" in which I had grown up had lumped together what was limited to France and what was happening in other regions of the planet.

The emergence of ideologies was yet another detonator. In the theoretical feminist discourse of an era that was drawing to a close, women made up, by their alienation and their necessary liberation, a universal category that was weighing on the other half of humanity. In this context, there could be no justification for national belonging. Since then, with, among other things, the wave of trials linked to sexual harassment, French men and women have been able to observe *in vivo* that neither men nor women behave in the same way on opposite sides of the Atlantic. Yet in the early 80s, this was not common knowledge.

As I was attempting to discover what it was that so radically differentiated the approaches of women in the two cultures, I found myself confronted with a paradox that stemmed from the fact that women had been adulated and apparently well treated in France (and many of them were proud of this), while at the same time they had been brushed aside – and to a certain extent, with their consent – from the public sphere and from political power. The original title of my book was "French Women, Badly Loved"; then it became "French Women, Too Loved?" The latter title was unacceptable to my publisher, who explained to me that, in the first of place, a question was not appropriate for a title, and in the second, this particular title had nothing catchy about it. I resisted timidly, and the publisher won his case: the book would be immodestly titled *Regard sur les Françaises*. "Looking at French Women," in order to emphasize that it was meant to be a kind of "view from above" nonetheless not immune to the inevitable subjectivity.

Upon reflection, it seems to me that this change in title has been the cause of a misunderstanding that was partly responsible for the relative success of the book – which benefited from its appearance on [the French literary TV show] "Apostrophes." Yes, the book emphasized the uniqueness of French discourse – a uniqueness that later became known the "French exception," and became the topic of choice for a certain Very French press. At the same time, however, it attempted to calculate the cost of this phenomenon.

Still, combined with co-education and tolerant sexual morals, this "French exception" – the centerpiece of the French "art de vivre" – allowed for harmonious relations between men and women, relations governed by a code of behavior for seduction which men and women of our generation and the previous ones were no more ready to abandon than they were ready to forsake their table manners.

Nevertheless, the cost for women in general was high. "The married woman is a slave whom we must know how to enthrone," wrote Balzac in *La physiologie du mariage*, unaware perhaps to what extent he was reflecting French society even beyond his own era. On closer analysis, this discourse that glorified a certain category of women could not mask the scorn in which all women were held. A collective male discourse dedicated to the adoration of women and their beauty dried up as soon as women stopped being beautiful and ceased to remain silent. French women had been trapped by an excess of honor. The French exception, of which everyone, and women in particular, was so proud, had delayed women's right to vote and their political equality.

I wrote that French society had loved women lying down for so long that it couldn't respect them standing up; that it so desired women to be silent or confined to mere chatting that it was unable to listen to what they had to say; and that too often women intellectuals, held hostage by a culture in which their status "masculinized" them, had practiced a kind of sexual collaboration. No one listened to me. And just like those women in whom I criticized the desire to preserve the old privileges while acquiring new rights, I contented myself with being approved without demanding to be read.

Later, there were other manifestations of the scorn in which women who dared to express or affirm themselves were held. There was Edith Cressons' brief mandate as Prime Minister, the ignominious expulsion of the Jupettes (women followers of the former Prime Minister Alain Juppé), the manifesto on equal representation [*la parité*] that dared to say that the emperor had no clothes and that the Republic too often treated women as easily-thanked servants.

In the United States, the conflation of the public and private spheres placed women in a position of power in the official and legal resolution of conflicts of intimacy. An intern at the White House was in a position to shake up the presidency and to have a President impeached. This is obviously not the kind of power women want. But it is not entirely impossible that the misadventures of the Paula Jones and the Monica Lewinskys have paved the way for the election of Hillary Clinton (or Elizabeth Dole) to the presidency.

The "affair" nonetheless signals that the traditional roles in the machistic play – the glorification of virility, the debasement of female sexuality, the ridiculing of cuckolds – that occur in the majority of other cultures have been turned inside out here: the seducer/seduced man, President or not, plays the part of the guilty one, the seductress/seduced woman the part of the victim, and it is the betrayed wife who capitalizes not only on dignity[1] but also on political credibility. Puritanism turned inside-out or American exception? Whatever the sympathies one might have on the other side for toleration *à la française*, Mitterand's funeral merely offers a symbol that conforms to an old tradition where queens lived together with the king's favorites and where king's bastards were made noblemen. Conformism turned inside-out or the French exception?

Whatever the answer to these questions, it is obvious that American women's acceptance of certain forms of reverse discrimination because of Affirmative Action and the censorship imposed by political correctness – criticized for its excesses – allowed them to make progress in areas where they had previously been in the minority. Once these policies had attained some of their objectives, they of course became open to dispute. But American women have never minded owing some irreversible advances to them. This phenomenon is original, unique, and no one has dreamed of openly denouncing it as an "American exception," even though America is still the only country to have pushed laws regarding sexual discrimination to such a degree. French women may very well be mistaken when they refuse to accept that the combination of the terms "minority" and "women" does not refer to their number, but to the lack of importance granted them, and that it is a matter, above all, of *going beyond* rather than *denying* the injustice involved in reducing a majority of people to holding minority of power.

So what about the famous "French exception" today, in a country where conservative forces, with the complicity of many enlightened women, are mobilizing to prevent language from following the evolution of mores and feminizing words for professions to which women at long last have access? In a country where the Senate is attempting to block a change in the constitution that would finally allow French women, after more than fifty years of exercising political rights, to have access to a kind of parity, and to no longer be the poor cousins of female European elected officials? How can we speak about the "French exception" other than negatively? In this domain, as in many others, French egalitarianism winds up by stifling and perverting the noble principle of equality.

The relentlessness with which the French strive to break away from American models that are poorly understood, whatever their value or efficiency, ends up having perverse effects. French women's often very-pronounced desire to break free from their American counterparts by using their cult of difference and their conception of the universal (inherited from a Revolution that in fact denied women's rights), leads me to suggest that the exception is to be found American side of the Atlantic rather than on the French.[2] Whether we approve of them or not, it must be acknowledged that American women are different from French women – for better or for worse – in the same way that they are different from the rest of the planet.

In any case, the anti-American biases that are so frequently found in the media and in the French political class, lead to the French public's flagrant misunderstanding of its American cousins, male and female.[3] Catherine Hermary-Vieille, another French writer living in America, and I have therefore tried to transmit to this public the modest experience that decades of life in the United States have allowed us to accumulate. It is for this public that the *Salon de conversation* was conceived. This purely fictional account doesn't *only* speak about women; it *also* speaks about women.

An excerpt from the *Salon de conversation* appears below. It is a discussion in a French class of the Alliance française in Houston, between two French professors (Corinne and Fabienne) and their nine students, men and women, one of whom, Jacqueline, the widow of a GI left her native France for America in the 40s.

Notes

1. This was also the case for Danièle Mitterrand.
2. The exception is in forms and strategies, for as far as women's advancement in the political sphere is concerned, there is not much difference between the two societies.
3. Conversely, we could say the same thing of the American media..

Le Salon de Conversation

"I must say that I find it difficult to understand French women, said Karen. Of course, I don't mean the women here, who have other experiences. I have traveled many times in France and have met French women professionally. I find them... how can I put it? ... slightly perverse, trying to turn everything to account: to please men and at the same time grab a foothold in their profession. They are able to sign a contract with a huge company and, the next minute, play the flirt, the deferential woman. They want to have their cake and eat it too. We American women know that that's impossible. We reject those affectations from the past. Today it has become obvious that sex appeal – what the French call "le pouvoir de l'oreiller," or "pillow power," – is not straightforward and has often turned against those who exercised it. What we want is real power, the power that men have usurped for millennia.

– And yet, exclaimed Daphne, our women's magazines are full of advice about how to seduce men: how to be more beautiful, more womanly, more interesting. When my three children were devouring all my time, reading this stuff was depressing.

– White American women dream of pleasing men but refuse to interpret the messages of seduction, remarked Cleonie. Maybe they just don't like men enough. This isn't so for African-American women.

– They proved it by acquitting O.J. Simpson in the first trial. We already said as much in this discussion group. The jury was made up of a majority of Black women, said Brandon.

"Black women are just as conscious as white women of the inequality between men and women in our societies," said Cleonice. Anita Hill proved this to be so a few years ago when she accused Clarence Thomas of sexual harassment. She became a model for all women because of her courage. And both she and Thomas were black."

– I don't know if it was really courage, said Fabienne. I was quite young at the time but I thought she was cruel to a man who, in reality, had done nothing more than tell her some dirty stories ten years earlier. Really, it seems to me at the statute of limitations had run out. On top of it, apparently their confrontation was broadcast on every TV station twenty-four hours a day ! Now that's a veritable rape of privacy.

– The rape occurred at another level, Pamela stated indignantly. I already had this conversation with Fabienne. You French women do not have the same idea of your body and of rape. You accept the unacceptable from men. I would even go as far as to say you provoke it.

– In France I've seen girls or women dressed truly provocatively, said Karen, avoiding Brandon's ironic glance. They seem almost proud of the male gaze that's undressing them.

"There's nothing unusual in wanting to provoke desire," Corinne couldn't help interjecting. "It's been part of the game of seduction between men and women since the beginning of time."

– When I came to the States, I was very young, Jacqueline explained. And an honest woman, as they say, in love with her husband. But I must say that I really missed not being looked at by men any more. Not in the street, not at parties. Not anywhere. One day I confessed this to Stanley, saying that I didn't know if it was because I was married or if I had, in crossing the Atlantic, lost any and all charm that I had had, but I had the impression that I had become a nun.

– And ... how did he take it? asked Fabienne.

– Not too well ! He got really angry ! Our first lover's quarrel. But don't worry, there were plenty afterwards !

– Even though we are from different generations, I felt exactly the same thing, Fabienne confided. The only boys who look at me are Black, I mean African-Americans. And, in general, non Americans. And I must say that I miss it a little bit too."

Daphne was flabbergasted by Fabienne's insolence. Such reasoning seemed to have something immoral, "loose" about it. She had always wondered how the libertinism and adultery that were the very fabric of French films and novels could be compatible with the Catholic tradition. Fabienne was a typical product of her culture. As for Jacqueline, she was so old that you couldn't even be annoyed at her. But the reactions of these French women, whom Karen liked – especially Corinne – were disturbing to her.

"For me, Pamela began, it's just the opposite. When I first came to Lyon, I couldn't stand all those wandering hands, insistent stares, and the men brushing against me on the subway. I mentioned this to Mme Collinet who assured me that I had no reason to complain, and that if I didn't like it, I just had to give a couple of good slaps to the guy who was hitting on me, or crack a joke that would humiliate him. As if I could do that in French ! I can't even do it in my own language. Once, a friend of the Collinet's asked me if I would pose naked for him. I was so astounded that I blushed bright red. I couldn't even answer, and when I went to Mme Collinet to protest, she told me that the great artist had paid me a compliment and that I was reacting like a conventional little prude !

– The result of all this is that the French don't respect women when they get involved in high-level politics or even business. I was in France when Edith Cresson was Prime Minister. No one took her seriously, she didn't even take herself seriously.

– She scandalized everyone, said David, when she stated that she wasn't in the least bit interested in the stock market. But your great de Gaulle said the same thing when he affirmed that politics couldn't be carried out... in the basket.

– You probably mean in the wastebasket, Corinne corrected him. Still, David, you can't seriously claim that it's the same thing.

– In any case, Professor Lesage, you have to admit that women in France don't have a great deal of solidarity with one another.

– We don't have an automatic, mechanical solidarity. Personally, I admire women who deserve to be admired. I admire the great members of the Resistance, I admire the philosopher Simone Weil, and I admire Colette and George Sand. For their own talents, not because they are women.

– Well I admire all women who attempt to accomplish something, said Pamela. Edith Cresson and Simone Veil, or the women Ministers whom you unfairly call "Jupettes," [followers of Juppé, but literally "little skirts"], and who were dropped by Juppé, just as Edith Cresson was dropped by Mitterand. I admire Margaret Thatcher. I admire Janet Reno, our Attorney General and Madeline Albright, our new Secretary of State, who has the highest position ever occupied by a woman in the United States. But in this regard French women might be a little behind in comparison to American women, who had a very powerful feminist movement in the 60s.

– I'm sorry to have to contradict you, Pamela, said Corinne, but the percentage of women in politics is about the same in the US and in France. Neither in France nor in the US are they sufficiently represented in the House or in the Senate. And let's not even talk about ministers and secretaries of State. It is the Northern European countries who have fared the best, far ahead of our two countries. As far as feminist movements are concerned, they go very far back in France. Already Olympe de Gouges, at the time of our Revolution, drew up the Declaration of Woman and Women Citizens.

– Yes, but she had her head cut off by her Revolutionary friends. Even though she claimed that if women had the right to appear on the scaffold, they also had the right to appear in the tribunal, joked Fabienne, she made it to the scaffold, but never to the tribunal.

– I did a poll for my magazine on the subject of feminism in our two countries, said Cleonice. Behind all these behaviors, there are two different models. French women are universalists. Beyond the differences, beyond a femininity that they insist on, they consider themselves first and foremost as belonging to the human race. American women on the other hand believe that the universal is an impostor when equal rights don't exist. This is why they have no trouble placing themselves in a category such as 'minority,' as the Blacks, Indians, and homosexuals have done. The term minority implies that they do not participate in the rights of the majority. And the 'majority' is White men.

– Women are not interested in the art of governing, Jacqueline said. And they are right. Politics are too dirty. Women shouldn't soil themselves in these meddlesome affairs. And then, they refuse to be in the too-bright glare of the spotlight. To participate in politics is to offer yourself, your family, and your past to possible criticism, and women have a love of secrets that reveals their weakness.

– I protest," Brandon interjected. To want to preserve one's private life is not proof of cowardice but rather of strength. Male politicians would give anything to get and keep this power. I admire women for rejecting that deal.

– But you also had Simone de Beauvoir before we had Betty Friedan. I remember that my wife was passionately reading Betty Friedan in the 60s and refused to dam my socks, said Ed in his irresistible accent. I always despised that Friedan.

– The MLF [Women's Liberation Movement] in France in the 60s was just as important as the American Women's Lib, said Corinne. But there was a slight difference in their philosophies. French women insisted on the necessity of recognizing the differences between men and women. Equal, yes. But in their difference. French women for the most part expected and still expect to be appreciated precisely for their difference. American women on the other hand wanted above all to become equal to men, with the same rights and responsibilities. Something has remained of these two different ways of conceiving things in the original cultures. In France, they fought in the 19th century so that women would no longer have to go down into the mines, or so they wouldn't have to work nights. In the United Sates, they are fighting so that women can do all kinds of work, day and night.

– I am not a feminist, said Daphne. But the American version seems fairer to me. What did I gain by devoting my life to Richard and to my children? I would have much preferred a career like Karen's – who fought like a man. Today she needs no one and doesn't have to chase after alimony."

Translated by Alyson Waters

Special thanks to the following contributors and publishers for permission to reprint.

— Hélène Cixous for the rights to publish "Aube."
— *Les prostituées philosophes* by Leslie Kaplan was published by P.O.L. in 1997.
— Michèle Sarde, for the rights to publish *Le salon de conversation*, by Catherine Hermary-Vieille and Michèle Sarde, JC Lattès,1997.
— Cover photograph from *Agrippine et l'ancêtre* by Claire Brétécher, licensed by Hyphen S.A, Paris, France, 2000.

The editors thank Philip Khoury, Dean of Humanities, Arts and Social Sciences at MIT for providing funding for the translations.

We are grateful to Geneviève Sellier for generously giving of her time and expertise to the preparation of this issue.

Generous support for the editorial and artistic preparation of SITES is provided by
The University of Connecticut
Robert Smith, Vice-Provost
Ross McKinnon, Dean
David Herzberger, Chair, Dept. of Modern and Classical Languages

Sylviane Agacinski is a philosopher. She teaches at l'Ecole des Hautes Etudes en Sciences Sociales. She has published *Aparté, conceptions et morts de Sören Kierkegaard* (Flammarion, 1977), *Volume, philosophies et politiques de l'architecture* (Galilée, 1992), *Critique de l'égocentrisme, l'évènement de l'autre* (Galilée, 1996), and *Politique des sexes* (Seuil, 1998). *Le passeur du temps* is forthcoming with Seuil.

Sylvie Blum-Reid is Assistant Professor of French and Film at the University of Florida (Gainesville). She has written on nostalgia and photography in contemporary French novels. She is currently working on a manuscript about Vietnam in literature and cinema.

Serge Bourjea is Professor of French Literature at the Université de Montpellier. A specialist of Paul Valéry, he is director of the "Centres d'études valéryennes" and the associated journal, "Le bulletin des études valéryennes". He has contributed to major international and French literary journals, and has published many articles on modern and contemporary poetry.

Claire Brétécher is the author of the well-known comic strip *Les Frustrés*. She worked for *Tintin, Spirou, Pilote*, and co-founded the review *L'Echo des Savanes* with Gotlib and Mandryka in 1972. Her album *Agrippine et l'ancêtre* was awarded the Prix Alph-Art Humour at the Festival de la BD in Angoulème in January 1999. Her comic strips have appeared in *Le Nouvel Observateur* for many years now.

Kristine Butler, Assistant Professor of French at the University of Minnesota, Morris, has published on Caribbean women's literature, on film directors Chantal Ackerman, Pedro Almodóvar and Jean-Luc Godard. Her dissertation, titled "Hearing Voices: Audition and Artistic Identity in French Text and Film," discusses the ways in which the phenomenon of listening becomes a metaphor for problems of artistic perception in novels and films from the late 19th and early 20th centuries.

Odile Cazenave is Visiting Associate Professor of Francophone literature at Wellesley College and an Adjunct Associate Professor at the University of Tennessee. The author of *Femmes rebelles: naissance d'un nouveau roman africain au féminin* (L'Harmattan, Paris 1996; in translation with Lynne Rienner publishers, summer 1999), she has published several articles on women writers, on questions of identity and interracial relationships as well as on the writing of the body. Her most recent work is on the new generation of African writers in Paris, for which she was awarded a fellowship at the Bunting Institute of Radcliffe College (98').

Roger Célestin is Associate Professor of French and comparative literature at the University of Connecticut, and co-Chair of French Studies. He has written on Montaigne, Flaubert, Tournier, travel literature, and detective fiction. He is the author of *From Cannibals to Radicals. Figures and Limits of Exoticism* (University Press of Minnesota, 1996).

Hélène Cixous was born in 1937 in Oran, Algeria. Since 1974, she has been directing the Centre de recherche d'études féminines at the University of Paris VIII. She has published numerous books, novels, essays and plays. Some of her most recent titles include: *Beethoven à jamais* (Des femmes, 1993), *Photos de racines* with Mireille Calle-Grüber (Des femmes, 1994), *La ville parjure ou le réveil des Erynies* (Théâtre du soleil, 1994), *La fiancée juive* (Des femmes, Antoinette Fouque, 1995), *Or, les lettres de mon père* (Des femmes, Antoinette Fouque, 1997), *Voiles* with Jacques Derrida (Galilée, 1998).

Whitney Chadwick is Professor of Art at San Francisco State University. Among her books are *Myth in Surrealist Painting* (1980); *Women Artists and the Surrealist Movement* (1985); and, co-edited with Isabelle de Courtivron, *Significant Others: Creativity and Intimate Partnership* (1992).

Dawn M. Cornelio is a Ph.D. candidate in French Studies at the University of Connecticut. She has presented papers on Régis Debray and mediology as well as Charles Perrault's *Griselidis*. Combining her interests in translation and twentieth century prose and poetry, she is presently completing her dissertation on Jean-Michel Maulpoix's *Une histoire de bleu*.

Madeleine Cottenet-Hage is Professor of French at the University of Maryland. She has published on Francophone women writers, film, and cultural topics. She has a special interest in surrealism and short fiction.

Isabelle de Courtivron is Professor of French Studies at MIT. She has written books on Violette Leduc and Clara Malraux, and is the co-editor of *New French Feminisms* and of *Significant Others: Creativity and Intimate Partnership*. She is currently working on bilingual/bicultural writers.

Eliane DalMolin is Associate Professor of French and co-Chair of French Studies at the University of Connecticut. She has published articles on Aloysius Bertrand, Théodore de Banville, Charles Baudelaire, Paul Valéry, Yves Bonnefoy, and François Truffaut. Her book *Cutting the Body* is forthcoming with University Press of Michigan.

Assia Djebar is Distinguished Professor of French and Director of the Center for French and Francophone Studies at Louisiana State University. She is the author of numerous books, including *Femmes d'Alger dans leur appartement* (Des femmes, 1980, in translation *Women of Algiers in their apartment*, U.P. of Virginia, 1992), *L'amour, la fantasia* (J.C. Lattès, 1985, in translation *Fantasia, an Algerian Cavalcade*, Quartet, 1985), *Vaste est la prison* (Albin Michel, 1995) for which she was awarded the Prix Maurice-Maeterlinck in 1995, and *Ces voix qui m'assiègent* (Albin Michel, 1999). She also received the Prix de la Critique Internationale in Venice for her film, *La nouba des femmes du mont Chenoua*, 1979, the International Literary Neustadt Prize (1996, USA), the Prix Marguerite Yourcenar for her collection of short stories *Oran, langue morte* (1997) and the Prix international de Palmi (1998, Italy).

Eric Fassin, teaches Sociology at the Ecole Normale Supérieure in Paris, after several years at Brandeis U. and NYU. He works on the politics of gender and sexuality, as well as race and ethnicity, in a comparative French-American light - including transatlantic intellectual politics.

Antoinette Fouque is a militant, theoretician, editor, psychoanalyst, research director and European deputy. She has been one of the major international figures of the Women's Movement for more than 30 years. She is the author of many essays including *Women in Movements, Yesterday, Today and Tomorrow*, (Des femmes-USA, 1992) and *Il y a deux sexes* (Gallimard, 1995).

Geneviève Fraisse is a philosopher and a former "déléguée interministèrielle aux droits de la Femme," during Lionel Jospin's administration. Among her books are *La raison des femmes* (1992), *Muse de la raison, démocratie et exclusion des femmes en France* (1989), and *La différence des sexes* (1996). She co-edited *L'histoire des femmes en Occident*, Tome IV, le 19e siècle, with Michèle Perrot.

Heidi Genoist is currently a Ph.D student in Romance Languages and Literatures (French) at Harvard University. Originally from New Mexico, she did her undergraduate and MA work at UNM in Albuquerque. She has also lived and studied in Liège, Belgium and Nanterre, France. Her current research centers around contemporary Francophone women's poetry.

Anne Gillain teaches film at Wellesley College. She has published books on François Truffaut, *Le cinéma selon François Truffaut* (Flammarion, 1988); *François Truffaut: le secret perdu* (Hatier, 1991), *Les 400 coups* (Nathan, 1991) and, more recently, a monograph on *Manhattan* by Woody Allen (Nathan, 1996). She is working on a book on cinema and psychoanalysis.

Benoîte Groult is a writer and an essayist. Her fiction includes *Les vaisseaux du cœur* (1988) and *Journal à quatre mains* in collaboration with her sister Flora Groult. She is well known for her feminist essays which include *Ainsi soit-elle*

(1975) and *Le féminisme au masculin*. From 1984 to 1986, she presided the "Commission pour la féminisation des noms de métier."

Leslie Kaplan is an American-born novelist and poet who writes in French. Among her books are *Les prostituées philosophes* (P.O.L. 1997), *Les mines de sel* (P.O.L. 1993), *Le silence du diable* (P.O.L. 1989) and *L'excès-l'usine* (P.O.L. 1982).

Richard Lewis currently teaches photography at Salem State College in Massachussetts. He is the recent winner of the Kodak/Hasselblad Educator's Award.

Florence Marsal is a Ph.D student in French Studies at the University of Connecticut. She has presented papers on the pedagogy of foreign languages and on Vladimir Nabokov's *Lolita*. She specializes in French medieval and 20th century literature.

Christiane Perrin Makward (MA, U. of Dakar, Ph.D, Sorbonne), Professor of French and Women's Studies at Penn State, has published translations of, and articles on Francophone and contemporary French women writers. Her books include the autobiography of Corinna Bille, an essay on Mayotte Capicia and a *Dictionnaire littéraire des femmes de langue française* with Madeleine Cottenet-Hage et al.

Tom Pozen is finishing his dissertation entitled *Optimism and Critical Practice* in French literature. He is currently a Lecturer of French in the Department of Foreign Languages and Literatures at the Massachussets Institute of Technology.

Michèle Respaut received her Ph.D. from Brown University. She works and publishes on 19th and 20th century literature, language learning, women's writing as well as literature and medicine. She was awarded the Pinanski Prize for Excellence in Teaching. Michele was Faculty Director of the Alumnae Summer Symposium, "The Healing Arts: Medicine in Historical, Cultural and Political Perspective." Several of her articles in this field are forthcoming. Michèle is at work on a book entitled *Mourning Children/Children in Mourning*.

Brigitte Rollet is senior Lecturer in French at the University of Portsmouth (UK). She is the author of *Coline Serreau* (MUP, 1998) and of various articles on French cinema. She is currently writing a book for Cassel on women filmmakers in France.

Michèle Sarde is a Professor of French Studies at Georgetown University and a writer. She has published essays (*Regard sur les Françaises*, Stock 1981), biographies (*Colette, Libre et entravée; vous Marguerite Yourcenar*) and novels (*Histoire d'Eurydice* *pendant la remontée*, Seuil, 1991). *Le livre de l'amitié* (in collaboration with Arnaud Blin) is her most recent publication.

Audrey Sartiaux is a Ph.D student at the University of Connecticut. She has published papers on *Les liaisons dangereuses* and the film adaptation by Stephen Frears *Dangerous Liaisons*, on Assia Djebar's *L'amour, la fantasia*, and *La princesse de Clèves*. She has also presented a paper on "The Position of Women in Muslim Countries." Her interests are in the fields of Cinema, Women, and 20th century literature.

Mary Schwartz is currently a Ph.D student in Romance Languages and Literatures (French) at Harvard University. She has received her BA in French from Mount Holyoke College. She is currently working on Marie Krysinska, a turn-of-the-century poet and novelist.

Geneviève Sellier, agrégée, is professor of Film Studies at the University of Caen and works on the history of French cinema and on Gender Studies. Her books include: *Jean Grémillon, le cinéma est à vous* (Paris, Méridiens-Klincksieck, 1989), *Les enfants du paradis, analyse critique* (Paris, Nathan, 1992), in collaboration with Noël Burch, *La drôle de guerre des sexes du cinéma français* (1930-1956), (Paris, Nathan, 1996).

Mariette Sineau has a Doctorate in Political Science. She is a research director at the Centre National de la Recherche Scientifique, and works at the Centre d'Étude de la Vie Politique Française de la Fondation Nationale des Sciences Politiques, in Paris. She works on women in politics and more specifically on French women's voting habits. Her most recent publication is *Qui doit garder le jeune enfant? Modes d'accueil et travail des mères dans l'Europe en crise*, Paris: Librairie Générale de Droit et de Jurisprudence, 1998, in collaboration with Jane Jenson.

Susan Rubin Suleiman is C. Douglas Dillon Professor of the Civilization of France and Professor of Comparative Literature at Harvard University, and currently Chair of the Department of Romance Languages and Literatures. Her recent books include *Risking Who One is: Encounters with Contemporary Art and Literature, Budapest Diary: In Search of the Motherbook*, and the edited volume *Exile and Creativity: Signposts, Traverlers, Outsiders, Backward Glances.*

Women

IN FRENCH STUDIES

Women in French Studies, the annual journal of **Women in French**, an allied organization of the Modern Languages Association, publishes articles in both English and French on any aspect of women in French-speaking literatures or cultures. WIF members, men and women who work in these areas, may submit articles for consideration to Adele King, Department of Modern Languages and Classics, Ball State University, Muncie, IN 47306. *Women in French Studies* also sponsors an annual prize for the best essay submitted by a graduate student. Essays should be sent to Katherine Stephenson, Department of Foreign Languages, University of North Carolina, Charlotte, NC 28223-0001.

The annual subscription is $12 for the US and Canada and $24 for overseas (payable in US dollars, postage included). Checks or money orders, made out to *Women in French* should be sent to Adrianna Paliyenko, Department of French, Colby College, Waterville, ME 04901-8846.

For membership forms, contact Yolande Helm, 21 Sunset Lane, The Plains, OH 45780. Membership is $25 ($37 Canadian) for full and associate professors (three-year membership, $70 US), $15 ($24 Canadian) for others (three-year membership, $40 US). Membership includes two newsletters and a copy of *Women in French Studies*.

Women in French Studies is indexed in the MLA Bibliography, and is a member of the Council of Editors of Learned Journals.

Submission of Articles

Articles may be submitted to either Roger Célestin or Eliane DalMolin, Editors, at the journal's office: *Sites*, University of Connecticut, Department of Modern and Classical Languages, 337 Mansfield Road, Box U-57, JHA 228, Storrs, CT 06269-1057, USA. Authors are asked to submit *two copies* of their articles to facilitate and speed the review process; they will be informed of the decision at the earliest possible date. Submissions to the journal will be evaluated by the editors and members of the editorial advisory board; outside specialists may be consulted as needed.

Submission of an article will be taken to imply that it has never been published previously in any form and has not simultaneously been offered to any other publication. It is a condition of acceptance of an article that the publisher acquires the copyright of the typescript. Therefore the article cannot be published elsewhere in the same form, in any language, without the publisher's consent.

Form and Length

All articles shall be typed on one side of the paper only, and doubled spaced with a wide (3 cm) margin on each side of the text. Pages of each copy must be sequentially numbered. Section heading should be entirely in capitals, on a separate piece of paper; titles should be in small letters, with main words capitalized. In either case, the text should start on the next line. The maximum preferred length is twenty double-spaced pages; there is no minimum length. Exceptionally long articles will be considered when of particular merit, and short notices are welcome especially for the questionnaire section.

Names, affiliations and complete mailing addresses for authors should appear on a separate title page. If affiliations for authors differ, list addresses separately beneath each author's name. Indicate for the typesetter which author will check proofs. Authors should also provide an abbreviation of the paper's title (no more than 35 characters) for use as a running head. Include acknowledgments under a separate head at the end of the paper but before the Works Cited list.

The publisher encourages authors to submit accepted manuscripts on computer disks. Word Perfect 3.1 (Apple) is the preferred software. Authors must enclose a printed copy of the manuscript (in duplicate) along with the disk. All disks should be marked with the name of the software package that was used and the file name.

Illustrations

Illustrations should be presented as "camera-ready copy," numbered with consecutive arabic numbers (Figure 1, Figure 2, etc.), have descriptive captions, and be mentioned in sequential order in the text. Keep illustrations separate from the text, but indicate clearly their approximate position within the text. Permission to reproduce illustrations and any other material which has been previously published must be obtained by the author and sent to the editors.

Preparation: Line drawings should be prepared in black (India) ink on white paper or tracing cloth, with all necessary lettering completed. Photographs must be in good original prints of maximum contrast. Color prints or transparencies should be submitted only if the color is necessary to the understanding of the discussion.

Captions: A list of captions relating to the illustrations, with relevant numbers (Figure 1, Figure 2, etc.), should be set out on a separate sheet of paper attached to the typescript. The permission statement provided by the copyright holder should be included at the end of each caption.

References

The full list of notes and "Works cited" should be collected at the end of the paper. Full bibliographical information should appear only in the list of "Works cited," not in the notes. In general, format should follow *MLA Style Sheet* guidelines, in alphabetical order, and set out in the manner described and illustrated below. Note that the initials of the first author (only) are placed after the name.

Proofs

If necessary, authors may receive page proofs (including illustrations) for correction, which must be returned to the printer within 48 hours of receipt. Please ensure that a full postal address is given on the first page of the manuscript so that proofs will arrive without delay. Authors' alterations in excess of 10% of the original composition cost will be charged to the authors.

Deadlines

Due to the thematic nature of each issue of *Sites*, deadlines are final since late articles cannot be saved for subsequent issues.